SOCIAL AND POLITICAL PERSPECTIVES ON ENERGY POLICY

Edited by
Karen M. Gentemann

PRAEGER

PRAEGER SPECIAL STUDIES • PRAEGER SCIENTIFIC

Library of Congress Cataloging in Publication Data
Main entry under title:

Social and political perspectives on energy policy.

   Bibliography: p.
   Includes index.
   1.   Energy policy--Social aspects--United States
--Addresses, essays, lectures.   I.   Gentemann,
Karen M.
HD9502.U52S613   333.79'0973   80-21963
ISBN 0-03-058636-4

Published in 1981 by Praeger Publishers
CBS Educational and Professional Publishing
A Division of CBS, Inc.
521 Fifth Avenue, New York, New York 10175 U.S.A.

© 1981 by Institute for Research in Social Science

123456789   145   987654321

Printed in the United States of America

PREFACE   2146351

What is the role of the social sciences in energy policy research? Can social scientists provide answers to critical questions
emerging in the energy arena? Which social science methodologies
apply to energy policy questions? What have the social sciences contributed to the resolution of energy problems? What are the future
roles of the social scientist in energy research and policy?

These questions were addressed at a series of workshops on
Energy and the Social Sciences sponsored by the Institute for Research
in Social Science at the University of North Carolina at Chapel Hill in
the fall of 1977. Researchers and faculty from local educational and
research institutions, state and local government officials, and local
citizens active in energy and environmental affairs met on five Satur-
days to interact with other researchers and government analysts who
prepared the chapters compiled in this volume. It is perhaps a comment on the state of the art of social science energy-related research
that this collection retains its relevance despite the time lag from the
workshops until now.

While several of the authors may not consider themselves social
scientists, the issues they raise are social science issues in terms of
the kinds of questions asked and research strategies employed. Indeed,
much of the literature on energy that addresses social science issues
has been written by those with nonsocial science labels—Barry Commoner and Amory Lovins, for example. The role of social science
research, therefore, should be understood to be broader than the academic labels attached to individuals. Indeed, the breadth of social
science research needed in the area of energy and energy policy would
be difficult to overestimate. To date, the primary focus of such research, according to Thomas J. Wilbanks, has been in economic
model-building, legislative-regulatory policy analysis, integrated
technology-issue assessment, and environmental impact assessment.
Further social science research is needed, however, to provide insight and information on desirable institutional configurations for developing alternative energy strategies, to anticipate the differential
impacts of energy systems on the population, and to ascertain regional variations in energy development and use. We need social science research to delineate the role of the private citizen in energy
policy development, to develop strategies for involving the public in
conservation behavior, to describe the political and institutional constraints associated with developing both local and national energy pol-

v

icies, and to assess the impact on health of various energy alternatives. Basic social science research is also needed in the development of theoretical frameworks within which to analyze the energy crisis.

This book addresses some of these critical issues. While it does not cover the scope of potential social science research, it does address a broad range of issues and includes theoretical topics as well as empirical analyses. Most chapters are concerned with the social and political environment in which energy policies are developed and implemented, areas which have received less attention than the economic aspects of energy policy. The book is arranged into three sections, the first addressing the question of the nature of the crisis; the second, the social and health impacts of various energy policies; and the third, the political and social context within which energy policies are formulated and adopted. Wilbanks introduces the topics with an overview of the role of the social sciences in energy research.

Wilbanks ascribes the need for social science research on energy policy to two fundamental social changes: a rise in pluralism and a societal reassessment of technology as an unqualified good. His insightful discussion of the historical relationship between energy policy development and the social sciences puts into perspective current research needs. He is critical of the tendency to identify social problems as political and therefore out of the realm of scientific analysis, and he outlines the potential scope of social science research on energy policy. Wilbanks is not unaware of the constraints on the role of social science research in the energy area, but, nevertheless, he predicts a growth in policy research for which social scientists will be held accountable.

The first section addresses one of the more troubling questions of the energy policy debate—the fundamental issue of whether the crisis is primarily a crisis of scarce resources or whether scarcity has only precipitated a larger crisis that questions the basic relationship between humankind and nature. The latter outlook also raises the issue of how societal decisions are made in a democratic system. David Orr addresses this more global concept of the energy crisis. He argues for a redefinition of terms to bring this concept into perspective. Orr contends that definitions structure the policy alternatives available to us, which makes it critical to distinguish between the energy crisis as a problem and as a dilemma. Thinking of the crisis as a set of problems leads us to define the solution in terms of technological fixes. Personal discomfort or danger is pictured as remote because technical solutions, the theory goes, will always be found to resolve our troubles, even if the troubles are created by the technology itself. Dilemmas, on the other hand, offer hard, uncomfortable choices rather than easy solutions. The choices become political and social, rather than technological.

Orr challenges the Rasmussen report, which likens the chance of an individual being exposed to a nuclear accident to the probability of being struck by a meteorite. He calls for greater attention to be paid to the risks involved in centralized energy development and suggests that, as a society, we must make a decision about our energy future rather than leaving it up to the "experts."

Roger Hansen, reflecting a similar view—that the development of technology controlled by the few leads to an environmental/energy dilemma—recommends that a more comprehensive perspective be brought to bear on the development and introduction of new technologies. He advocates the use of technology assessment, a broad-based assessment of the social implications of the introduction on expansion of a technology. Hansen describes the utility of technology assessments in arriving at policies that will have the least disruptive and most potentially useful impacts on society. Various methodological approaches to technology assessment are listed, and the procedural steps of such an assessment are described. The author, who is primarily interested in the usefulness of technology assessment as a tool in the identification and evaluation of policy options, analyzes its benefits while also warning of pitfalls. In so doing, Hansen provides a framework for assessing the context of energy policy development.

Crossnational comparisons, as demonstrated by Joel Darmstadter, provide further insight into the nature of the energy crisis. Darmstadter analyzes U. S. energy usage by examining the basis of the often quoted higher magnitude of U. S. per capita energy consumption relative to those of other Western countries. To do so, he goes beyond the aggregate statistics of intercountry comparisons and asks why differences exist between developed countries. Some explanations are provided by examining the role of transportation, industry, and household consumption patterns in higher U. S. energy usage. Freight transport, for example, contributes to a high U. S. energy/gross domestic product ratio even though the U. S. freight transport industry is more oriented toward energy-saving forms such as rail, pipeline, and water traffic than is Western Europe. The explanation for this difference lies in the size of the U. S. and the practice of long-distance hauling. No one segment of the society can be singled out to explain the high U. S. energy/output ratio, although four areas account for 60 percent of the differential: passenger transport, industry, residential space conditioning, and freight transport. Darmstadter urges the adoption of conservation strategies appropriate to the U. S. situation, and he suggests technical, price, and tax policies that take into account differences among countries.

In the second section of the book, attention is directed to the social and health effects of alternative energy plans and policies. John Hatch and Tony Whitehead, for instance, examine the impact of the energy crisis on the poor and cite differential health statistics and changes in labor patterns as examples of this impact. Alternative national energy policies are reviewed in terms of their ability to remedy these impacts. The authors describe "hard" versus "soft path" policies, conservation, restructured electric rate schedules, and various relief programs as well as how these policies differentially affect lower-income people. Hatch and Whitehead maintain that any of these policies taken alone will have some negative repercussions for poor people. They argue, instead, for holistic strategies built on elements of each. Further, they make a case for implementing holistic policies through community organization strategies. In particular, they cite the need for consumer participation in policy planning, locality development, and consumer education.

Marvin Olsen continues the social impact analysis by speculating on a future that has been assured by a conservation-minded public and by assessing the impact of conservation behavior on the economy, the educational system, transportation, housing, recreational activities, and politics. He projects a series of disruptive short-term impacts that will ultimately result in a return to humanistic goals and a simpler way of life. Olsen's scenarios envision an increase in planned communities in which people can shop, work, and play a short distance from their contiguous living quarters. He sees the emergence of new values, including greater status equality in the family as a result of shared household responsibility and a deemphasis on material consumption. To more precisely predict the social impact of conservation and other energy strategies, Olsen advocates the use of social indicators to introduce greater rigor into these types of analyses. He also urges grouding social impact research in quality-of-life considerations.

Carl Shy describes the effects of nuclear and fossil fuel energy systems on occupational and public health, concluding that fossil fuel development is far more hazardous to health than our national energy policies seem to recognize. In particular, he cites the documented evidence of the damages already inflicted on both workers and on the public by coal production and usage. Nuclear power, Shy argues, when used under normal operating conditions, presents less danger to the health of workers and of the public. Shy emphasizes that his analysis does not address the dangers associated with sabotage, with a meltdown, or with certain safety aspects of nuclear waste disposal, all of which, he says, are serious issues that may ultimately result in the decision not to use nuclear power. His analysis does, however, help focus attention on the demonstrable dangers of coal, a fuel that constitutes a major component of our national energy plan to become less dependent on foreign sources of oil.

In the third section, the social and political contexts of energy policies are analyzed. Elizabeth Martin, for instance, discusses the potential for developing a national conservation ethic based in part on altruistic motives. She critiques the assumption that Americans will conserve only due to self-interest and demonstrates the significance of altruism as a little understood behavioral incentive. Several hypotheses regarding the social and political determinants of altruistic conservation are tested. The conclusion is that some conservation behavior may be motivated by altruism. Moreover, Martin offers several policy alternatives that take altruistic conservation behavior into account and suggests that the extent to which policies are viewed as equitable and to which they enhance trust in national leaders, they will influence Americans to willingly make sacrifices in the national interest.

Edward Helminski believes that the potential social upheaval precipitated by the energy crisis can be avoided through a rational policy of development and conservation, and he describes the characteristics of such policies. He cites some past mistakes that have resulted in the "boom town" phenomenon and critically assesses the political factors and processes involved in formulating energy policies. Helminski sees the need for public participation in energy policies because the diverse and complex nature of the energy decision-making process will result, at best, in ineffective production policies if it is framed under a space program type of mentality. Helminski also analyzes the role of the federal and state governments as well as the private sector in energy production. He presents a set of guidelines for institutionalizing a participatory decision-making process to meet the needs of all of these various government agencies and citizens.

Anne Stubbs addresses the problems of energy management faced by government policymakers and discusses the unique role governments play as both energy users and regulators. She describes the research needs of government officials and suggests areas in which social science research might address both supply and demand management issues. Further, Stubbs presents a six-item research agenda for social scientists concerned with energy management policy in which she stresses the importance of empirical research in addition to model-building analyses. Research on energy flows, Stubbs says, must incorporate the institutional aspects of governments' capability for management. Modeling techniques must also make allowances for management efforts. Stubbs emphasizes the importance of disaggregating energy data bases from national to regional, state, and local levels, and she discusses the particular types of data needed—

technical, climate, household energy use, and social indicators of attitudinal and behavioral changes.

Not surprisingly, each author has a distinct perception of the important topic areas in social science energy research. We can and should expect a wide range of interests to be reflected in future energy research efforts. Some of the research needs are explored in this volume. Others that we might look for in the future will be empirical analyses in such areas as public participation in energy decision making, utility rate restructuring, and public safety in the nuclear debate. We will undoubtedly see research on the urban versus rural dilemma in production policies and siting decisions. Various models may be tested in analyzing the acceptance and spread of appropriate technology and other "soft path" techniques. Ethnographic methods may be employed to determine the willingness of communities to convert to solar and wind power as primary sources of energy. Numerous other topics will also become apparent as the energy crisis continues to develop as a social crisis, one that challenges our democratic system and raises ethical and moral questions.

My comments would be remiss if I failed to acknowledge the help of several people important to the development of this book. First, I wish to thank Susan E. Clarke, previously director of Research Programs at the Institute for Research in Social Science and now an assistant professor of Political Science at Northwestern University, for her good advice on the selection of topics and authors for the workshops for which these chapters were written. I am especially appreciative of Mary Ellen Marsden, a research associate at the Institute for Research in Social Science, for her invaluable suggestions and comments on the format of this book and for her editorial revisions. Those reviewers of the workshop papers, who shall remain nameless, provided expert opinion and advice for which I am most grateful. I also wish to acknowledge the superb typing assistance of Bonita Samuels, Vonda Whitley, and Lou Anne Robinson of the Institute for Research in Social Science; the graphic artistry of James Worrell; and the meticulous attention paid to the development of the index by Ruth Gambee; and finally, my thanks to Frank Munger, director of the Institute for Research in Social Science, for making the resources of the Institute available to me to bring this book to fruition.

Karen M. Gentemann

CONTENTS

Chapter

LIST OF TABLES

LIST OF FIGURES AND MAPS

INTRODUCTION

Our energy crisis is more a social crisis than a technological one. We do not lack technologies and resources to provide desired quantities of energy in familiar forms. We already have, or almost certainly can develop, technologies to fit a very wide variety of specifications for resource use, environmental protection, and human safety.

Yet the crisis is very real. Finite world oil and gas resources continue to be depleted, while the growing world energy appetite increases collective dependence on them. A U.S. energy import level that caused serious problems during the 1973/74 embargo has risen significantly and is likely to continue to rise. An essential transition to inexhaustible and renewable sources of energy has yet to be begun. Because of the importance of energy in the structure of economies, we face the possibility of major political and social upheavals if energy needs and expectations are not met. But very little seems to be happening to deal effectively with any of these situations, for reasons that are social, economic, and institutional.

Most fundamentally, our crisis is one of irresolution. We find it agonizingly difficult to form a broad consensus in American society about our objectives and how to reach them. We are undecided about institutional roles and relationships, uncertain about impacts and risks, and unclear about the connections among social, economic, environmental, and energy policy goals. Meanwhile, adversarial decision-making structures convert uncertainties into disagreements or, worse, into antagonisms, and prospects for action fade away time after time.

Given this predicament, which affects many other areas of science policy besides energy, it is paradoxical that so little of our energy research effort is directed at social and institutional questions. Too often, such questions are simply dismissed as "political," meaning not researchable, as contrasted with technical questions that are susceptible to scientific analysis. A consequence is that social and political perspectives on energy policy—which are inescapable—are affected very little, and then usually only indirectly, by the work of the research communities supposed to be the experts on such matters. If the research base is at all valid and useful, the chance that policy based on poorly informed perspectives will be wrong is increased.

Such a danger is not a foregone conclusion, but it is certainly serious enough to deserve specific attention. This book addresses the need in two ways: by providing important perspectives that are solidly grounded in social science (for example, Helminski on consensus building) and by providing evidence that a wide range of policy issues can benefit from competent social science research (for instance, Martin on conservation through altruism). Rather than covering the entire spectrum of the social sciences, the authors focus on a gap left by the pioneering 1974 survey of research needs and opportunities, Energy and the Social Sciences, which itself noted that "research in social science areas other than economics is underrepresented, basically through a lack of representativeness among participants" (Landsberg et al. 1974, p. 171). The present volume draws upon a literature that, at this point, is fragmented and sometimes "fugitive" in the sense that key references are unavailable in many libraries.

In introducing the book, I consider several broad issues in relating the social sciences to energy research and policy: the relationship between social/behavioral questions and the research and development (R&D) process, the scope of high priority social science R&D, and the institutional context for social science R&D. I conclude with a brief summary of the prospects for contributions by social science research to energy policy making.

SOCIAL SCIENCE RESEARCH AS ENERGY RESEARCH AND DEVELOPMENT

At a session on energy research policy at the 1978 meeting of the American Association for the Advancement of Science, an individual stood up during the discussion period and loudly said, "If it's based on physical measurements, it's science. If not, it's politics."

This attitude is deeply imbedded in the structures and traditions of science policy. Policy making is based on a kind of ad hoc mixture of the fruits of a (R&D) process and the ideas and viewpoints of a variety of people and groups that are part of a policy-making process. Although the two processes overlap, there are clear differences in the criteria for judging the importance of their respective outputs. In one, the putative emphasis is on verifiable evidence; in the other, it is on social and economic influence.

No one seriously questions the role of social scientists in the policy-making process. They have as much access to key parts of the system, such as the U. S. Congress, as other citizens, and their contributions often turn out to be influential because they are judged to be reasonable, useful, and insightful. Moreover, because it is part of their job, they sometimes understand the system itself better than the average citizen, and this helps them to get their views heard.

But the R&D process is another matter. It tends to operate in a world of laboratories and machines, of instruments and edifices. Here, social scientists are outsiders, occasionally needed as gap fillers or managers but seldom becoming an integral part of the mainstream of research, which is intended to produce useful, marketable physical devices or substances. This is particularly true for the social sciences other than economics, which is recognized to be an unavoidable dimension of marketability.

For government decisionmakers, however, this limitation of the scope of the R&D process is acceptable only to the extent that their needs are limited to physical devices or substances. In such policy fields as energy, transportation, and health, this is certainly an important part of the need, and it is usually the clear-cut objective of R&D in business and industry. But other needs remain.

These needs can be associated with the three general reasons for spending public money on research and development activities.

To develop options. Certain desirable options, such as ways to cure cancer, may be realized only through public support. For private firms, the R&D process is too risky or too expensive, and the financial rewards of the developer are likely to be less than for other possible targets of R&D. Examples in energy include nuclear power and oil shale retorting in their early stages, energy-efficient appliances, and a number of solar energy options.

To avoid bottlenecks. Some options that might be desirable in the future could turn out to be unfeasible if possible impediments are not anticipated. For instance, the government provides support for materials research so that if certain materials being used for energy technologies turn out to be inadequate, a technical capability will be on hand to solve the problems. Environmental research is another example of this concern.

To provide information. Public policymakers need information about options and their likely effects in order to reduce uncertainties about what policy decisions make sense. Public R&D support can be an effective way to get reliable information that would not otherwise be available to government decisionmakers, and it offers an attractive alternative to relying exclusively on information provided by external institutions, most (or all) of which have a vested interest in decisions that might be influenced by the data they submit. To a policymaker preoccupied with next week's recommendation or next year's budget proposals, this need is clearly the most pressing of the three (Kash et al. 1976).

In the field of energy and probably in other areas of science policy as well, all of these purposes of R&D—seen from the position of the public policymaker—embrace the territory of the social sciences as well as of the physical and life sciences. For the R&D needs previously noted, Table I. 1 shows some social science/energy illustrations. (These kinds of needs will be discussed in more detail later.) But an attitude persists that, although such items are indubitably important to policymakers, they are not really part of R&D.

TABLE I. 1

Social Science Aspects of Energy R&D

- Developing Options
  - Institutional alternatives
  - Market corrections
- Avoiding Bottlenecks
  - Models and data to answer future questions
  - Decision-making structures
- Providing Information
  - Social and economic impacts
  - Market penetration prospects
  - Energy-related preferences, attitudes, and social relationships

---

On closer examination, such an attitude is shown to be a product of the culture of technology and the history of institutions rather than of the intrinsic character of science. The social sciences, at least in some of their manifestations, use the same patterns of reasoning as the other sciences; their rules of procedure and methods of analysis are equivalent, and their concern with replicability and verification is as high. The major U. S. institutions for defining the scope of the sciences, such as the National Academy of Sciences and the National Science Foundation, include the social and behavioral sciences without reservation (see, for instance, National Academy of Sciences 1969). It is no longer possible for a well-informed person to argue that social issues are not scientifically researchable (although it is certainly possible—and certainly correct—to argue that scientific research on the issues is only one of several valuable lines of investigation).

Unquestionably, social science is very difficult science. In some ways, the so-called "soft sciences" are the hardest of all to do well, for a number of reasons. Social processes are especially complex, which tends to limit numerical precision. Frequently, social research cannot be experimental research, which tends to limit data generation and replicability (as is the case for research in public health, astronomy, and other fields of science). It sometimes involves variables whose values are very difficult to measure, and it is complicated by the fact that its realm is human society. Not only do social scientists face particular challenges in distinguishing between their roles as scientists and as citizens, but people who are not social scientists have an everyday familiarity with the processes being studied. (Every civil servant who is part of a family unit knows how families work; does he or she need a sociologist to do research on that?) But the difficulty of social science is not a satisfactory explanation for its peripheral position in the R&D picture; if anything, difficulty should be a cause for special emphasis.

A more legitimate question is what the "development" stage in the R&D process means for the social sciences. What are their "technologies"? Who are their "engineers"—the people who take the findings of science and make them useful for solving problems? There is some evidence that social science research usually affects policy only indirectly, by gradually influencing the "climate of informed opinion" (Weiss 1977). Is this because the social sciences are in fact different from the others or because the social science R&D process is simply immature?

Obviously, social science research can lead to the development and use of action instruments that achieve practical purposes. These instruments can take such forms as a parole system, a new form of welfare payments, or a form of psychotherapy (National Academy of Sciences 1969); more broadly, they include management systems, decision-making procedures, analytic models, regulations, and incentives. In principle, such "soft technologies" pass through stages of research, development, demonstration, and utilization. (An econometric forecasting model is a familiar example). They pass from the hands of basic and applied research scientists to the hands of professionals in fields such as planning, public administration, business administration, and social work, along with social scientists and others who accept action-oriented positions in business, government, consulting firms, and elsewhere. [1] Increasingly, the literatures and professional communities that specialize in "technology assessment" are including "soft technologies" within their scope of attention, and increasingly policymakers are faced with comparing "hard" and "soft" technology options for reaching the same objective.

In this sense, at least, social-science approaches to energy policy should be full partners in the energy R&D process, giving decision-makers considering "social fixes" the same kind of research substructure as when they consider "technological fixes," in Alvin Weinberg's (1966) words. A particular benefit might be that, in linking the stages of the R&D process more clearly and directly for the social sciences, some progress would be made toward resolving a nagging paradox in applied social-scientific work: research that appears more scientific is often less useful because it is so narrowly focused, while research that has a more realistic scope appears less scientific.

SOCIAL SCIENCE RESEARCH AND DEVELOPMENT TO MEET ENERGY NEEDS

In the 1970s, U. S. energy policy came to be dominated by economic, social, and institutional questions. As an extreme example, consider a narrow technology-oriented national energy plan that ignores international relations as an area of policymaking—the sort of situation in which the social sciences would seem to play the smallest role. In such planning, because of concerns about federal budget deficits and public attitudes toward tax increases, traditional energy policy instruments (federal budget allocations for technology R&D, taxes) have in many cases been displaced by such options as nontax incentives (such as pricing policies), regulations, and procedural changes. The conventional view that energy needs are met by doing things with energy supply alternatives has been broadened to consider characteristics of energy use as well. Nearly everyone agrees that our ways of managing energy technology development and making decisions about the location and use of new facilities need improvement. And we struggle with the persistent dilemma that our most attractive energy alternatives are associated with higher energy prices—as cause, consequence, or both—while the primary concern in American society is with the rising cost of living. The scope of the social science R&D needed to deal with such questions, plus the additional questions raised by energy planning that is less narrowly conceived, is so large that it is difficult to decide what the priorities should be.

The Need

The need for social science research on energy policy questions is so evident that documenting it seems to belabor the obvious. But the present role falls so short of the need, and the recognition of the need by many energy policymakers is so recent and still so limited, that some reminders may be useful (Wilbanks 1977).

For example, as part of a study of R&D needs and priorities for inexhaustible energy resource options, in April 1977 officials of the Energy Research and Development Administration (ERDA) asked advisory panel members (mostly physical scientists and engineers) to make judgments about the relative importance of criteria for evaluating alternative technologies. In the summary ranking of criteria (Table

TABLE I. 2

Criteria Rankings for Comparing Inexhaustible Resource Options

	Sociopolitical Panel	Technology Panel	Environmental Panel	Data & Analysis Panel	Total Study Group
Total Available Market (Technology/Resource Potential)	9	9	11	9	9/10
Achievable Market (Economic Feasibility)	4/5	10	6/7	6	6/7
Substitution for Exhaustible Fuels	6	2	6/7	2	4
Competing Advanced Technologies	8	7	8	8	8
Resource Requirements	4/5	3	2	5	5
Reliability and Maintainability	7	8	4	7	6/7
Federal Commercialization Support	11	6	9	10	9/10
Legal and Institutional Barriers	3	5	3	3	2
Socioenvironmental Impacts	1	1	1	1	1
Public and Private Perception	2	4	5	4	3
Quality of Program Resources	10	11	10	11	11

Source: Energy Research and Development Administration Inexhaustible Energy Resources Study Panels 1977. Washington, D. C. , April 11.

I. 1), the three most important criteria turned out to be socioenvironmental impacts, legal and institutional barriers, and public and private perceptions.

As a further example, a reputable assessment of energy R&D needs was the Office of Technology Assessment's (OTA) An Analysis of the ERDA Plan and Program (1975), based on the ERDA-48 plan. The OTA study sought to identify "differences between the policy goals mandated by Congress and the programs proposed by ERDA . . . " (Office of Technology Assessment 1975, p. 1). Table I. 3 summarizes the gaps identified by the OTA task groups; many of them involved researchable institutional and policy questions, such as the need for better understanding of the relationships between energy and the quality of life and the need to identify nontechnological constraints on increased energy supply or reduced energy demand (OTA 1975, pp. 30-31). In subsequent Congressional testimony, ERDA Administrator Robert C. Seamans, Jr. called the OTA study "balanced testimony" and agreed that, "There is still a great deal of work to be done in the socioeconomic area" (Seamans 1970, p. 170).

TABLE I. 3

Issues Regarding the Adequacy of the ERDA-48 Plan for Meeting National Energy Policy Goals

Category of Issues	Total Number of Issues	Number of Issues Primarily Economic, Social, Institutional	Number of Issues Involving Social Science Concerns*
Overview	16	11	14
Fossil Energy	16	4	7
Nuclear	18	8	10
Solar, Geothermal, Advanced	17	7	12
Conservation	18	9	10
Environmental, Health	14	3	5
Total	99	42	58

*Economic, social, or institutional issues, plus issues regarding information, resources, or overlaps between socioeconomic issues and technological or environmental issues.

Source: U. S. , Congress. Office of Technology Assessment. 1975. An Analysis of the ERDA Plan and Program. Washington, D. C. : U. S. Government Printing Office, October.

Reasons for the Need

Many of the social and institutional roots of our energy crisis
are quite familiar: the objectives of the Oil Producing and Exporting
Countries (OPEC), the cheapness of energy in the United States, inflation coupled with a decline in economic productivity, uncertainties
about the constancy of government policy, differences of opinion about
what is an equitable distribution of benefits and costs. Some of the
possible remedies for such problems are technological, of course,
but the problems themselves are inherently socioeconomic. We would
have to be fortunate indeed to be able to solve them without understanding more than we do now about the processes that they reflect.

But the heart of the need for social science R&D to support energy policy making lies not in these problems but in two recent fundamental social changes in the United States: a new pluralism in public
policy making and a retreat from a general faith in the capability of
technology to achieve social goals for us.

Consider pluralism. As recently as two decades ago, it was
usually assumed that major decisions in the United States could be
grouped into distinct categories, in each of which a limited number
of groups had a right to participate—usually those with direct economic, regulatory, or technical roles. For instance, it was quite
clear who made oil policy decisions and utility policy decisions and
national defense decisions. As long as the participants were agreed,
an action took place. By the end of the 1950s, in fact, the ability of
these decision-making consortiums—often made up of big business
and big government—was so unbridled that President Eisenhower felt
it necessary to warn the country about the power of "the military-
industrial complex."

But a number of important events during the 1960s, including
civil rights struggles, Vietnam, and the Santa Barbara oil spill, convinced many people that decisions being made within the traditional
frameworks were affecting individuals and groups outside those frameworks. As a result, the demand grew for broader participation in decision making, ranging from pressures for consumer representation
on corporate boards of directors to student participation in promotion
decisions for university professors. The "environmental movement"
was the most visible indicator of this change, but the change involved
more than environmental interests.

As a result, energy policy decisions now involve a wide range
of groups and interests, and it takes a broad consensus among the
parties to take major actions (Kash et al. 1976; Schurr et al. 1979).
This change is probably irreversible, and it is, in many ways, how
a democratic process is supposed to work. But it leaves us with a
serious problem. As Lewis Branscomb (1978) has suggested, our de-

xxiii

cision-making structures—designed for a different time and a different set of conditions—have broken down under the current conditions, and we do not have a new structure to replace them. Without it, we are indecisive, and our traditional adversarial procedures turn disagreement into antagonism.

Since consensus is a social judgment rather than a scientific one and since consensus is a prerequisite to forceful energy policy, social processes must be as thoroughly understood as physical and environmental processes. Political accommodation must be treated as seriously and professionally as engineering cost analysis. This is a part of the R&D challenge.

Consider technology and society. While participation in energy policy decisions has been expanding, many people have been rethinking the role of technology (especially big, technically sophisticated technology) in meeting the country's needs. By itself, this thinking does not represent a fundamental social change, but it seems to be linked to a much more widespread, imperfectly articulated feeling in society that advanced technology can be a mixed blessing.

The reasons for this feeling are not yet well understood, although the point of view is expressed in an abundance of professional literature (for example, Schumacher 1973; Lovins 1977b; Bereano 1976). Perhaps it is partly a reaction to the fact that a period of unprecedented progress in science and technology has not been accompanied by improvements in social indicators (Handler 1979). It may reflect an impression that a high level of technological scale and complexity is associated with an equivalent level of government coordination and control (Henderson 1978; Ryan 1977; Gould and Walker forthcoming). And it is certainly fueled by a belief that some of the people who are closest to the technical details have been "less than candid in telling the whole story" (Handler 1979).

At any rate, there appears to be a consistent difference between the views of energy "technocrats" and many other participants in energy policy making about the mix of energy technologies and incentives that makes most sense. For instance, the U. S. Congress consistently appropriates more money for solar energy R&D than the Department of Energy requests, and it often establishes "rules of the game" that energy officials consider undesirable. Some people believe this to be evidence that a social revolution has taken place, one that our formal techniques for policy analysis are not capable of handling (Ryan 1977; Henderson 1978).

Clearly, one consequence of social changes in the past two decades has been that society's attitudes toward technology options have become less predictable, at least on the basis of our conventional tools for prediction. Like the new pluralism, this situation affects energy policy making directly and centrally; understanding it is one of the tasks of energy R&D.

In summary, energy R&D not only needs to continue under these unsettling (but possibly very creative) new conditions; it needs to address some of these new realities as part of the territory to be investigated. For example, social science research is needed to reduce uncertainties about the future demand for certain energy technologies and the impacts of using them, and it is needed to identify and evaluate social fixes as alternatives to technological fixes.

Types of Needs

As this indicates, the requirements for social science research are far-reaching. They are also diverse, in the sense that a wide range of types of work are essential to the effort. Unless the portfolio of research is balanced among the various types—and linked between them—the needs of energy policy making will not be met very effectively. Such balance involves the several stages of the R&D process, a mixture of attention to issues and problems, and the involvement of a number of research specialties.

Earlier, it was argued that the social sciences are a category of R&D, involving the same sequence of basic research, applied research, and development as hardware R&D. Just as in the physical sciences, ignoring any of the stages of the process can cause other stages to wither.

For instance, although it is recognized that energy policy requires an investment in basic research in fields such as physics, there has been little recognition that competent, effective applied social science research also requires basic research. In fact, the needs may be even greater. "There is . . . less awareness than there should be . . . that the state of existing social science theory imposes severe limits on what one can conclude from [social science research] instruments for assessing or improving policy-making" (National Research Council 1971, p. 48).

Certainly, a limitation on current applied energy research by social scientists and colleagues in related fields is that existing social science theory, methodology, and data are inadequate. Valid applied work in the social sciences depends on a strong base of fundamental scientific research, just as is the case in the other sciences. When there are gaps in the fundamental literature, the applied scientist— usually operating under demanding time constraints—is forced into unrealistic assumptions, unsupported approximations, ad hoc methodologies, speculative judgments, and the use of data with questionable validity. The resulting research conclusions are an exceedingly shaky basis for making energy policy decisions.

In part, the present narrowness and softness of the body of basic social science research for addressing energy questions can be explained by the origin of that basic research in other kinds of questions. There is no reason to expect basic research generated by the needs of particular academic disciplines or other policy fields to be suitable for meeting the needs of applied energy research (Roy 1979). Consequently, some of the basic social science research gaps for energy policy decisions are unlikely to be filled unless the energy research system makes a deliberate decision to fill them. For example, one review of shortcomings of energy supply and demand models indicated the need for research on questions of aggregation versus disaggregation, error/uncertainty factors in forecasting, elasticities, sensitivity analysis as a methodology, and the incorporation of more complex dynamic variables representing "significant forces of change" (Landsberg et al. 1974, pp. 98-111). The importance of some of these subjects of research may be greater for energy policy making than for conventional economic theory.

Other types of imbalance involve the energy data and energy models generated and used by social science research. Investigations by social scientists are often hampered by a lack of data on subjects which have been inadequately treated by the U.S. Census. And when data are in fact collected, they sometimes lack emphasis on questioning whether the right data are being gathered to answer the important questions and making a reliable and credible data base accessible for users (Landsberg et al. 1974, pp. 83-94; Kash et al. 1976, pp. 464-70). Models, in some ways, are one of the Department of Energy's (DOE) major new areas of "technology" development. Their evolution and use should follow the traditional stages of the research, development, and demonstration (RD&D) sequence very closely, and, just as with hardware technologies, they need to be carefully assessed—technical characteristics, benefit/cost relationships, impacts, and appropriate scales for use. But it is not always clear whether they are grounded in basic research and appropriate for the tasks for which they are used. For both models and data, the validation work of the Energy Information Administration will be very interesting to watch.

Energy models usually illustrate the classic problem in social science R&D: that basic disciplinary research and effective policy research are indirectly and indistinctly linked. There is a shortage of bridges between the research communities and the decisionmakers who deal with policy questions. And there is a need for interpreters, because the languages and communication styles of the two worlds are so different.

A different kind of need for balance has been suggested by Joseph F. Coates, who distinguishes between public policy issues and problems. An issue is "a fundamental enduring conflict among or between objectives, goals, customs, plans, activities or stakeholders, which is not likely to be resolved completely in favor of any polar position in that conflict. . . . A problem is a matter of the application of knowledge and choice in a definitive way. Problems can be solved, issues cannot" (Coates 1977, p. 5). For instance, conservation is an issue. Improving efficiency is a problem.

Similarly, in its study published in 1969, the Behavioral and Social Sciences Survey Committee of the National Academy of Sciences and the Social Science Research Council distinguished between social-scientific research and policy research, intended as a guide to action (National Academy of Sciences 1969; also see Landsberg et al. 1974, pp. 6-7; Brim 1969; and Coleman 1972). The latter kind of research "has a different flavor from that found in, say, the economists' tradition" (Landsberg et al. 1974, p. 225).

In this sense, social science research can be viewed as filling three types of need: it solves energy problems through applied and development research; it conducts basic research to strengthen its problem-solving capability; and it contributes to interdisciplinary assessments of issues that incorporate the results of scientific analysis but, in identifying and evaluating alternatives, rely heavily on the collective qualitative judgments of a diverse research team.

There is a general preference—shared by contract managers and most of the social science research community—to conduct research on problems rather than issues (or to treat issues as if they were problems). (See Chapt. 1 for an extended discussion of this topic.) The preference of the social scientist to rely on familiar theories and methods is reinforced by the uneasiness of the contract manager about projects that revolve around qualitative judgments. Consequently, social science research tends to contribute bits and pieces of scientific work that are frequently of limited utility, while too little professional contribution is made to the development of "coherent national doctrines" (Weinberg 1967). For example, the research effort is influenced by the fact that certain "long run outlook considerations are very important but much less academically prestigious" (Landsberg et al. 1974, p. 184).

The Resources for the Future study of energy and the social sciences remarked on the differences between political institutions (responsive to the interests of constituents in making decisions) and technocratic institutions (seeking optimum decisions from objective analysis) Landsberg et al. 1974, pp. 231-32). Although energy is in fact a political policy field, there has been a persistent urge in government and the research community to treat it as a technocratic policy field, characterized by sets of problems rather than by sets of issues. Perhaps it is not surprising, therefore, that some groups in society view certain energy strategies as designed to perpetuate a technocratic elite (for example, Lovins 1977b).

In terms of the various research specialties, in general, social-science related research on energy questions now emphasizes economic modeling and the design of formal models for decision making. (Part of the reason may be historical; economists became knowledgeable about some energy questions sooner than other social scientists.) Without suggesting that this work is unnecessary, it appears that other kinds of needed work are not getting an equivalent level of attention. This includes work in economics as well as work more characteristic of political science, sociology, psychology, and other social science fields. Besides constraining the information available to policymakers about social and institutional factors, this situation produces bottlenecks in the high-priority economic modeling efforts. For instance, the determinants of elasticities and propensities are social and behavioral. And the most likely causes of discontinuities in economic trends are political and environmental. Useful social science work requires a breadth of attention together with a kind of integration of the contributions of different kinds of specialists that is now exceedingly rare.

In addition, focusing research solely on rigorous quantitative analysis may lead to further imbalances. In a 1971 assessment of policy research, the National Research Council criticized "a proclivity to focus experiments or evaluations on what can be measured readily, to use these easily measured effects as indicators of overall program merit and to discount arguments relating to hard-to-measure dimensions that pull the other way" (National Research Council 1971, p. 48).

Priority Needs

Obviously, these social science research needs are so substantial and diverse that their very abundance is a problem because it complicates the establishment of priorities for allocating limited resources for research (Yale University 1976). Lack of agreement on priorities does not mean that the social science research contribution to energy policy cannot be improved; policies can be adopted and actions taken that, regardless of priorities, will increase the likelihood that enough research will be done, that it will be the right research, that it will be integrated into policy making, and that it will be linked to the basic research experience of the social science research community (Wilbanks 1977, 1979, forthcoming).

But, recognizing that priorities will change as the conditions of policy making change, it is possible to identify several critical issues that particularly need social science research attention.

Decision-making structures. We need to improve our understanding of how decisions can be made in our society, and we need to identify new kinds of structures and procedures that enable us to act with resolve. This may involve research on institutional alternatives, and it almost certainly requires differentiating between structures to handle "normal" situations and structures to deal with "emergency" situations. In this book, Helminski and Stubbs point out some of the most important directions for work of this sort.

Equity. A key to reaching consensus on a policy question is assuring that the benefits and costs will be distributed fairly among the impacted groups and individuals. This issue underlies much of our irresolution about energy questions; for instance, it is the fundamental reason for conflicts about the location of new energy facilities, and it is a major factor in the debate about the pricing of energy. As an example of the urgent need for research, consider a significant difference in the state of the art (and the assessment environment) between socioeconomic impacts and ecological/health impacts. For ecological impacts, "critical thresholds" have been established, in most cases beyond which an impact is considered unacceptable; proposers of actions can use these thresholds, which are usually codified in a body of laws and regulations, to assure that their proposals have probable impacts within the range of acceptability, and investigators can use the thresholds as bases for making judgments about acceptability. There is no real equivalent of these guidelines for social and economic impacts (even though socioeconomic conditions are an important determinant of human health). Chapters 2, 4, 5, and 6 are good illustrations of this concern.

Preference functions. We are less certain than we used to be about what people want, about how they would prefer to resolve trade-offs. Public attitudes, for instance, are often at odds with the views of many scientists, to the frustration of both. It is important to focus research attention on risk <u>acceptance</u> as well as risk <u>assessment</u>; it is important to understand how people define comfort and convenience, so that we can achieve energy efficiency without sacrificing quality of life; and it is important to get a better sense of where accommodation can be reached among energy, economic, and environmental goals. Chapters 1, 3, and 7 are examples of steps out into this treacherous terrain.

Other important questions include the effects of failing to meet public expectations regarding energy supply, the ways economies and societies change (how will we make the transition to a future without petroleum and natural gas?), the role of energy and its institutions in society, and the determinants of economic vitality and productivity.

THE INSTITUTIONAL CONTEXT FOR ENERGY-RELATED SOCIAL SCIENCE RESEARCH AND DEVELOPMENT

Closing the gap between the need and the present role of social science R&D will require institutional sensitivity and public support, especially in an era during which policymakers are trying to balance budgets. So far, progress has been slow, but there are a number of encouraging signs that the future may be brighter.

Reasons for the Gap

The gap between need and present social science research has developed for a number of reasons, and it is unlikely to be reduced unless the reasons are identified and examined. One of the reasons, of course, is that changes in U. S. society and the international energy situation have caused the need to increase very rapidly. But other factors have kept the contribution of social science from rising along with the need, including certain constraints on the effectiveness of social science research for meeting energy needs and certain peculiarities in the recent history of the federal institutions most directly involved in energy research.

In terms of constraints, at least one attempt has been made to identify the principal reasons for the gap (Wilbanks 1977), and some revisions of that first effort, based on responses to the report, have been published more recently (Wilbanks 1979). Table I. 4 summarizes the main points of these references, which will not be reviewed in detail here.

Although there are no simple resolutions for any of these impediments, the same references discuss a number of concrete steps that could be taken to enable the energy policy-making system to make fuller use of the potential contributions of social science research. Table 1. 5 shows their major recommendations for Department of Energy policy.

In terms of institutional history, it would be erroneous to imply that energy R&D policymakers have been unaware of a need for research on economic, social, and institutional questions. They have, in fact, supported a great deal of it. Besides the factors previously mentioned, the problem has been that institutional and programmatic R&D roles are often defined in such a way that social science responsibilities and linkages are unclear—gaps result from organizational boundary assumptions.

For example, the national laboratories are intended to be the R&D arms of the DOE, as they were for some of its predecessor agencies: ERDA and, before that, the Atomic Energy Commission (AEC).

TABLE I. 4

Constraints on the Role of Social Science Research
in Meeting Energy Needs

• There is a shortage of social scientists who are knowledgeable about energy issues, when such substantive knowledge is essential if a large proportion of the research is to be useful.

• There is a shortage of policymakers and research program managers who understand how to use social science research.

• The professional competence of some of the current social science research on energy questions (mostly applied, usually done with limited time and resources, and seldom involving careful peer review) is open to question.

• The findings of social science research are especially susceptible to the criticism that they are biased or unreliable.

• Funding support is insufficient overall and predominantly short-term in allocation.

• Funding support is imbalanced in its attention to different types of research needs.

• Every existing institutional setting for research has an Achilles' heel.

• There is a lack of a clear sense of research priorities, when fiscal and human resources are limited.

Sources: Wilbanks, Thomas J. 1977. "The Role of Social Science Research in Meeting Energy Needs." Oak Ridge, Tenn.: Oak Ridge National Laboratory, October. Wilbanks, Thomas J. 1979. "Effective Social Science Research for Energy Policy." Paper presented at the annual meeting of the American Association for the Advancement of Science, Houston, January.

TABLE I. 5

Recommended DOE Actions to Increase the Contributions
of Social Science Research

• Take the lead in developing a source of external support for
types of research that produce more credible results when they are
not managed by a mission agency.

• Assure that social science research support is diversified.

• Undertake a research personnel development program.

• Develop a first-rate in-house social and behavioral research
capability.

• Assure that at least a specified fraction of R&D support is
allocated to research on economic, social, and institutional questions.

• Assure professional peer review of sponsored social science
research.

• Assure that sponsored social science research includes wide
consultation and public access.

• Sponsor a technology assessment at every major research,
development, and demonstration decision point.

• Seek a mix of professional backgrounds and experience among
management personnel.

Sources: Wilbanks, Thomas J. 1977. "The Role of Social Sci-
ence Research in Meeting Energy Needs." Oak Ridge, Tenn.: Oak
Ridge National Laboratory, October. Wilbanks, Thomas J. 1979.
"Effective Social Science Research for Energy Policy." Paper pre-
sented at the annual meeting of the American Association for the
Advancement of Science, Houston, January.

In principle, they provide a series of links between the world of the policy maker and the world of the basic research scientist. The responsibilities of ERDA and AEC for social science research were quite limited, however, which meant that the laboratories did not need a significant social science capability. Other predecessors of DOE, such as the Federal Energy Administration, made extensive use of applied social science work but had very little responsibility (and very little budget) for maintaining and using a full-fledged R&D support system, extending all the way back to basic research support. As a result, their successors, the parts of DOE that most often need social science help, are often oriented toward ad hoc relationships with consultants, while the R&D system itself adjusts slowly to the enlarged scope of the federal agency it serves.

As another example, soon after ERDA was created, the National Science Foundation's (NSF) energy research program was transferred to it. When new energy research needs arose after that time, NSF was hesitant to respond, both because of its own limited resources and because it appeared that such work had been placed very specifically on the other side of its boundary with ERDA. Soon, though, DOE officials were hesitant to support some needed work because they thought it sounded like NSF-type research or inappropriate for a mission agency. Besides tight budgets, both institutions worried about criticisms from external bodies, such as the Office of Management and Budget, the General Accounting Office, or Congressional commitees, that they were encroaching on someone else's turf.

There are other such difficulties as well, but nearly all of them stem from the fact that the federal government is still at a very early stage in organizing itself for energy policy in general and for energy R&D in particular. Social science R&D is not necessarily the most urgent issue as this organizational process evolves, but many of the key questions about responsibility and linkage will be answered by decisions that are made along the way.

The Current Environment

The present situation, then, is one of transition and disorder, as new organizations try to tackle new problems on the basis of new priorities. The day-to-day preoccupations are with the next crisis, the next deadline, the next table of organization. Thinking about long-term R&D needs is a luxury few policymakers can afford.

But the policymakers are pragmatic. They respond to current realities. One of those realities is that they need information about people and their institutions: likely responses to regulations and incentives, determinants of energy demand and market penetration, socioeconomic impacts, ways to make decision making more systematic. Another reality is that a great many groups are telling them that they should be paying more attention to social science research (see General Accounting Office 1978; U. S. Congress 1978b). As a result, the policymakers are trying to find ways to enlarge the commitment to social science R&D. For instance, a plan is under study that would create a small social science program in DOE's Office of Basic Energy Sciences—a largely symbolic but still important recognition that the social sciences are basic energy sciences. Several other parts of DOE (especially Conservation and Solar Energy, the Energy Information Administration, and the Office of Program Coordination for the Assistant Secretary for Environment) are either increasing their support for social science research or proposing to do so. And serious efforts are underway to resolve the DOE-NSF boundary question.

All of these activities, however, are taking place during a period in which a central objective of the federal government is to balance its budget. It is not a good time to be trying to get money for new research initiatives. Since an increase in one area generally means that funds must be taken away from somewhere else, the resistance of the system is stiff. Consequently, the prospects are better for steps that can be taken without adding large new budget lines, such as many of the suggestions in List 3, and for developing a clearer sense of priorities in the work to be done.

Prospects for the Future

Except for constraints related to budgets, however, the future appears bright for those who are patient. Victoria Tschinkel, a member of DOE's Energy Research Advisory Board, has said that the next decade is likely to bring to the field of energy the same kind of growth in social science research that the last decade brought to the environmental sciences (Tschinkel 1979). It is here that the critical issues and impacts will be found. And, when it is carefully targeted and well done, the payoffs for policymakers from social science research are likely to be high in relation to R&D costs.

For reasons already mentioned, the main impetus for this growth will continue to come from outside the energy R&D system for a while, until the social sciences gain a "patron" or two (like DOE's Assistant Secretary for Environment for the environmental sciences and DOE's Director of Energy Research for the physical sciences). But if the social sciences do become a significant category of R&D, a series of turf battles will almost certainly be followed by an organizational response. [2] The challenge during this period of competition and change will be to keep the diverse collection of work linked. For example, the size and social value of the eventual commitment will depend on developing a mission-oriented approach to basic social science research support, in the sense that it is directed toward filling those gaps in theory, methodology, and data that undercut the validity of applied work. If the social sciences succeed in this effort, they may be able to serve as a model of coordination and coupling for some of the other energy sciences.

Most of the research funding will come from the Department of Energy, barring a major reorganization of federal energy programs, but DOE will find that it cannot meet all of its social science research needs by itself. Many kinds of assessments are more credible if they are managed by an organization without a vested interest in the findings—and credibility is a prerequisite for consensus building (Kash et al. 1976). Consider, for example, a study on the acceptance of nuclear power funded by DOE, compared with such a study funded and managed by NSF. In addition, there are very real practical, political, and possibly even ethical limits to the behavioral research that a mission agency will sponsor, regardless of its needs for information. And other agencies and groups will be going ahead with work that will meet some of the needs of energy policymakers (for instance, work on the measurement of equity impacts of federal policies). DOE can benefit from important complementarities if it takes some responsibility for multiagency R&D planning.

This, then, is a critical time. If the institutional issues are resolved, the right directions are selected, and the resulting work is useful, the social sciences will become an important and valued part of the energy R&D picture. Their parts of universities and other research institutions will thrive and, more important, energy policy making will be better. But the future could be much less bright if mistakes are made at key junctures; for example, an experimental R&D program that fails because of a repeated failure to deliver useful results could cast a very long shadow across future prospects.

Consequently, we must recognize that, when given a chance, how well we perform will affect the prospects of others, both our fellow social scientists and the people who are affected by the policies that we influence. And we must remember that our performance will be judged not by the standards of academic disciplines but by whether we help the nation meet its energy needs. In this sense, in our lives as citizens, we will eventually be held accountable for our contributions as social scientists. Fair enough.

Thomas J. Wilbanks

NOTES

1. Lest the concept of parallelism between "hard" and "soft" technology R&D be overdrawn, since it implies that the two lines never meet, remember that they are intricately related to each other. For instance, "hard" technology R&D relies on management and decision-making structures, marketing studies, and impact assessments, while the "soft" technology R&D process depends heavily on communication and computation technologies.

2. According to Don Kash, the first response of government to a policy need is to commission a study or form a committee (which has happened). If that is not sufficient, the next step is to establish a continuing program with its own budget (which is being considered). If the need turns out to be so important and persistent that further action is required, government takes the ultimate step: it creates a new organizational unit (Kash et. al 1976).

PART I
NATURE AND MILIEU
OF THE ENERGY CRISIS

1
PROBLEMS, DILEMMAS, AND THE ENERGY CRISIS

David W. Orr

A remarkable experiment on perception involves two groups of kittens raised in rooms that differed only in that the walls of one were painted with horizontal lines and those of the other with vertical lines. After several weeks, the kittens were moved from one room to the other. Despite the fact that both environments were identical—with the exception of the lines on the walls—both groups suffered severe adjustment problems, including higher mortality rates. The experiment is interesting not so much for what it reveals about cats, but for what it may suggest about perception and adaptability in general. Is it possible that humans under analogous circumstances may experience a similar degree of disorientation? But what analogous circumstances can we envision in a technological society in which humans have become so dominate? Kahn, Brown, and Martel (1976, p. 1) assure us that there are none, and that humankind 200 years hence will be everywhere "numerous, rich, and in control of the forces of nature." This view is built on the belief that there is no limit to what technology can do, nor is there any possibility of altering its directions or slowing its momentum anyhow "even if there are good arguments for doing so" (p. 164).

A different view, which has gained currency lately, portrays the future as one hedged by natural limits, the possibility of social conflict and breakdown, and the likelihood of technological catastrophe (Georgescu-Roegen 1974; Meadows et al. 1972; Mescrovic and Pestel 1974; Falk 1971). While optimists, such as Kahn, regard the future as essentially linear and materially/technologically progressive, this second view depicts a future of major discontinuities and radical changes. The differences between these two approaches represent more than an idle debate among academics; they go to the heart of nearly all important contemporary issues.

4 / DAVID W. ORR

The debate between the optimists and the pessimists is not only about the possible limits of technology or of what Ellul (1964) calls "technique," but are also about the existence of a class of circumstances otherwise known as dilemmas. The optimist's world view admits only problems, which are by definition solvable given the appropriate application of technique and capital. The pessimist's world view, in contrast, includes the possibility that technology itself has created (or intensified) major dilemmas, which are by definition unsolvable. Dilemmas, hence, will force us to make painful choices between equally distasteful options. If there are barriers to human progress that refuse to disappear before the march of science and technology, might not the effects be as completely disorienting as those that beset the cats described at the outset? Indeed, is not the lack of awareness of limitations to technology, and to human capability, an even more serious blind spot in the perceptual makeup of technological humans?

PROBLEMS AND DILEMMAS

The view of the world as a set of problems, characteristic of the technological optimist, rests on two assumptions of modern science. The first is the obvious belief that the world is understandable and that it operates on the basis of laws that can be discovered. From this perspective, science is limited only by our ability to frame questions that can be experimentally tested. But not all questions have yet been asked, and an even smaller proportion have been tested in such a way as to reveal scientific knowledge. Moreover, at least since Heisenberg, science must admit that "God does play dice with the universe" and that there is a certain randomness in all physical relations. Ironically, while the physical sciences have moved toward the recognition of randomness, the social sciences have moved in the opposite direction to occupy terrain abandoned by physics decades ago. This has occurred despite the observations by scientists such as C. H. Waddington that

> There are large areas of human concern, particularly problems about man's own nature, and that of his societies, in which it has been very difficult to formulate questions which can be given clear answers in experiments which it is practical or desirable to carry out. In these areas, science is weak; and non-scientific methods of study, relying on hunches, or experience or intuition, or insight, or empathy or what-have-you, may be the best guide one has available (1977, p. 126).

In political science, for example, the assumption of a Newtonian world leads to severe distortions since, in the words of Almond and Genco (1977, p. 518), "A political science solely concerned with the search for regularities which constrain choice would miss the distinctive aspects of political reality, which is the effort to escape from constraints.

A second assumption of the technological optimist is that reality can be factored into manageable parts in order to enhance our understanding, or our ability to manipulate, without doing excessive damage to either our perceptions or to the system under examination. As Bacon predicted, the payoff in each case is greater control over nature— the chief distinction of a technological society. Problems arise because we inevitably encounter webs of causation we have not considered and of which we may remain entirely ignorant. The current model of science is, in Eugene Odum's word (1977, pp. 1, 289-93), "reductionist," so that we lose a sense of the wholeness of reality amidst the growing pile of thoroughly researched bits and pieces (see also Weizenbaum 1976). It is precisely our knowledge of interrelatedness and systems that is the weakest part of both the physical and social sciences and that poses the greatest threat to the presumptions of the technological optimist.

Nonetheless, there are in this view no unresolvable problems or dilemmas. At most, the optimist would concede only that some problems may take longer than others to solve, but that all are inherently solvable. The failure to do so is more indicative of a temporary lack of knowledge than an indication of limits to technology, science, or of inherent contradictions within either. It is thus standard in scientific reports to call for yet further research, more study, and greater funding. John Platt (1969, p. 1, 117), for instance, after recounting what he describes as a "crisis of crises" attributed to science and technology, could propose that "only more scientific understanding and better technology can carry us through." We are assured that the only limit to progress is our possible loss of nerve at the threshold of the new golden age of cybernetics.

There is a different world view that includes a class of circumstances for which there is purportedly no technological solution. For this view, the informing metaphors are those of the prisoners' dilemma, Rousseau's staghunt, or Garrett Hardin's tragedy of the commons. Each describes a world of pain, collective irrationality, irreconcilable conflicts, and limits to social and natural systems, in a word: dilemmas. First, they can be distinguished from problems in that they require immediate decision, permitting little procrastination. Thus it becomes irrelevant what technology may be capable of doing years hence. Second, dilemmas force the actor to choose between two contradictory paths. To select one is to permanently forego the other. In this regard, a dilemma more closely resembles a cross-road, while problems are more like designing a bridge—which involves applying an existing body of knowledge to the achievement of a specific end. Third, dilemmas are resistant to rational means-ends calculi and methods such as cost-benefit analysis. Dilemmas involve issues that are heavily infused with ethical, moral, and political content and for which there are few generally agreed upon standards. Finally, dilemmas confront the actor with situations in which there is a high degree of uncertainty. They are, by definition, high-risk circumstances in which important variables and outcomes remain concealed from the decisionmaker.

Even if one admits the existence of dilemmas and the possibility that they may constrain technological progress, the question of what to do about them remains. Why not simply deny their existence since there's nothing to be done anyway? Denial would have the advantage of avoiding the social panic that might accompany acknowledgement that the emperor was at least partially unclothed. Why not simply put the best possible face on a no-win situation? This argument has appeal, but only if we equate dilemmas with fate and thereby dissociate them from the realm of human choice. But dilemmas are forced on us less by fate than by the logic inherent within our own philosophies, explicit or otherwise. Dilemmas are by definition unsolvable, but only on their own terms. The old fable of the wise man confronted by the boy inquiring whether the bird he is holding behind his back is dead or alive illustrates the point. Recognizing the dilemma, the wise man simply refused to play the game, responding only "as you wish." There is, as in this instance, the possibility of not playing the game, or of denying its logic by dealing with the situation at a different level, as discussed in de Bono (1973). Dilemmas are unsolvable, not unavoidable or even necessarily unresolvable. There are some courses of action in which they are much more likely to occur than in others. The recognition of this fact ought to lead to their avoidance or to prudently allowing a sufficient margin of error for uncertainty.

Dilemmas are similar to what Thomas Kuhn (1974) has described as unresolvable problems or "anomalies" in science that undermine the logic and assumptions of the dominant paradigm of "normal science." In Kuhn's model, anomalies require the eventual creation of an alternative paradigm resting on a different set of values, methods, and acceptable standards. In human affairs, the occurence of dilemmas may similarly signal radical changes and the need for a new social paradigm with different values, logic, and assumptions. In contrast to the process Kuhn describes, the resolution of social dilemmas depends less on cleverness or methodological virtuosity and more upon that forgotten word of polite academic discourse: wisdom, which implies a sense of perspective, vision, and compassion.

THE ENERGY CRISIS AS A PROBLEM

In no instance is the contrast between the optimist and pessimist more stark than in the present debate on energy policy. Those who view the energy crisis as a problem have constructed their case on three interrelated propositions. First, they unanimously regard energy as the key to future human progress defined in material and technological terms. In the words of Goeller and Weinberg (1976, p. 689) "man must develop an alternative energy source" since "energy will be the ultimate raw material." Kahn and his collaborators (1976, p. 59) similarly argue that "mankind's future well-being is intimately linked to the prospects for an abundant supply of energy at reasonable prices." That these are not people with modest aspirations is suggested by Sterling Brubaker's (1974, p. 5) comment that from an inexhaustible energy base humans might "make a direct attack on entropy . . . or reach for the alchemist's dream of elemental transmutation." If, for whatever reason, we fail to achieve unlimited energy, the future they describe differs little from that depicted by "neomalthusians."

A second and related assumption is that the energy crisis is basically a supply problem and only secondarily one of excess demand. Advocates believe that more energy consumption is good, and that it is directly correlated with economic growth and with the quality of life. Although these are increasingly questionable assumptions, we are nevertheless assured that energy demands are relatively fixed so that energy producers stand in approximately the same relation to consumers as did the sinners once described by Puritan Cotton Mather to his angry god. In either case there is supposedly not much room to mess around—you've got to produce: energy in one case, piety in the other.

The third assumption is that the energy problem can only be solved by the elaboration of the existing technological paradigm. It will require vast outlays of capital and years of research and development, but the lines of progress are clear. In the near term to the year 2000, energy demands can be met by the use of coal and light-water reactors, the development of synthetic fuels, and new fuels including shale oil. In the longer term after 2000, the technological optimists forsee the utilization of such sources of energy as the breeder reactor, nuclear fusion, and satellites to beam energy to earth via microwaves.

Despite lip service given to solar energy, the federal energy priorities are clearly otherwise. In fiscal year 1979, more than 58 percent of the Department of Energy's research budget was consumed by various aspects of nuclear power research; 25 percent was allocated to fossil fuels, but only about 12 percent was directed to solar and most of that was for centralized solar electric (U. S. Congress 1978a). There is little in this pattern to suggest the recognition of fundamental dilemmas or the need to reexamine various options. In the words of one analyst, Lindberg (1977, p. 344), there is "an over-weening faith in progress and a technological optimism that admits of few limitations to the ability of scientific knowledge to solve problems if sufficiently massive investments of capital and manpower are made."

Two features of the technological paradigm are worth noting. First, it represents a commitment only to those forms of technology that are centralized, large-scale, complex, and that demand vast amounts of capital. But the development of such "high" technologies occurs at the expense of other forms and levels of technology and non-technological approaches (see Winner 1977a). It is often mistakenly assumed that technological evolution occurs in a Darwinian world in which all technological possibilities begin on an equal footing and advance or stagnate according to relative efficiency or social merit. This may sometimes be true, but other factors—including government subsidies in a variety of forms and corporate decisions—have played a far larger role in the evolution of energy "policy." Decisions not to price fossil fuels at their replacement rate, to grant depletion allowances and foreign tax credits, and to conduct a nuclear research and development program at public expense explain more about what are perceived as current options than do considerations of efficiency or social merit (see Freeman 1974; Blair 1976; Ford Foundation Energy Policy Project 1974). One recent study concluded that since 1918 the federal government has expended more than $123 billion to encourage and subsidize energy production. (Battelle Pacific Northwest Laboratories 1978, p. 5). Moreover, decisions about energy technology have generally been made by a small elite that shares a faith in high technology. Lindberg (1977, p. 344) suggests that, "policy makers have been petroleum or coal, or oil, or nuclear men. And those within the government tend to share basic orientations with colleagues in industry and the universities. All have a strong supply orientation, a common faith in technology, and an 'engineering mentality.'"

Second, the high technology option, and particularly the nuclear component, is said by its proponents (Weinberg 1972, p. 33; Institute for Energy Analysis 1976, p. 65) to require some version of a "Faustian bargain" by which society presumably receives a perpetual supply of cheap energy in return for yielding political power to a cadre of scientists and their security appendages. Unlike Faust, however, who was ultimately able to renege on the bargain, society must bind itself in perpetuity in the remarkable belief that it can devise social institutions that are stable for periods equivalent to geologic ages. To say, as Alvin Weinberg has, that such stability is something that society is "quite unaccustomed to" seems an understatement. The bargain, if struck, commits society to a path that is essentially irreversible. While we can argue Faustian bargains pro and con, we might wonder what our attitude would be if we were heirs to a similarly constraining bargain struck by Neanderthal man.

Without belaboring arguments made elsewhere, I think that the position of the technological optimist will ultimately collapse for three reasons. First, the optimist has studiously avoided questions of ethics, philosophy, and politics and, consequently, can provide little understanding of the wider issues at stake. Energy policy is reduced to narrow discussions of technology, and this is further confined to consider only those forms that meet the aforementioned criteria. No attempt is made to answer questions about the proper amount or appropriate use of energy. We are simply assured that an expanding supply for whatever source and with whatever effect is a "necessity" (Bethe 1976, pp. 21-31). But we can reasonably ask: For what purposes? For how long? Is there an optimal rate and flow of energy? What are the social effects of various energy options? Which social and human goals are served by a continual expansion of energy consumption and which must be sacrificed? To what extent is present energy consumption in conflict with the legitimate needs of future generations, and how can these concerns be integrated into our decisions?

The narrowness of the optimist's perspective also requires that we discard other equally important political concerns. Who ought to decide? Are nuclear cadres, or is nuclear power itself, compatible with democracy? What happens to those disadvantaged by the expansion of high technology energy supply systems necessary to meet the energy demands of others more numerous and powerful? Is it possible, as charged, that the energy-rich Western states will be reduced to "energy colonies" or that the rights of whole groups that impede energy production will be withdrawn?

These concerns, for which "hard" data seldom exist, are either dismissed from the cost-benefit calculations of the techno-optimist or are filed in a remote appendix under "miscellaneous" (Lovins 1977a, pp. 911-43). Indeed, cost-benefit analysis, which has become the dominant tool for deciding technological issues, is unable to deal with subjective or ethical issues at all. Economist Allen Kneese (1977, p. 111), for example, notes that cost-benefit analysis "cannot answer the most important policy questions surrounding the issue of whether to develop a large-scale world-wide nuclear energy economy. This is so because these questions are of a deep ethical character. Benefit-cost analysis certainly cannot solve such questions and may well obscure them." Krutilla and Page (1976, p. 97) likewise argue that cost-benefit analysis cannot answer questions of optimal supply because "the enormity of the potential costs demands that they be dealt with in the decision-making process," and, further, "The potential redistributions of economic well-being are so great that the problem has become fundamentally an ethical one." The use of elaborate models that deal with the parts of an issue subject to quantification gives an illusion of precision and comprehensiveness that is objectified and preempts political processes (see Hoos 1974). It is at least partially instructive to note that the Vietnam War occurred several years after "rational" cost-benefit methods of decision making were adopted by the U. S. defense establishment.

Secondly, the position of the technological optimist is suspect because of a systematic bias that overstates the economic effects of lowered energy consumption while minimizing the possible effects of disasters caused by accidents, sabotage, or even routine operation of high-technology energy systems. This distortion results from the confusion of low probability/high consequence events with low probability/low consequence events (see Boulding 1976, p. 5). The latter are descriptive of such events as auto accidents, which are both relatively improbable and (from a societal perspective) relatively inconsequential. The Rasmussen Report on nuclear reactor safety, for example, supposedly demonstrated that the probability of any individual fatality from a reactor accident is on the same order as that of being struck by a meteorite. (For a critique, see Hohenemser 1975; Union of Concerned Scientists 1977). Hans Bethe (1976) has used these estimates to argue that an individual's chance of fatal encounter with all sorts of uncommon events is substantially greater than that with a nuclear mishap. Aside from serious questions about the methods, objectivity, and scope of the Rasmussen Report, it is interesting to note that the probability of the sequence of events leading to the blackout in New York in the summer of 1977 has been estimated to be less than one in one billion.

The question remains whether society ought to calculate the safety margins of macro choices in the same way that an individual calculates whether to cross a busy intersection or to smoke a cigaret. The two are hardly comparable. There is at once an obvious discrepancy in the magnitude of consequences. The chances of a nuclear meltdown and a fatal car accident may both be judged to be improbable, but the consequences for society are radically different. Moreover, our knowledge of the causes of individual mortality is based on substantial amounts of data, but our understanding of low probability/high consequence events, on the contrary, is highly conjectural and inconclusive. We have no convincing estimates about the odds of a nuclear meltdown, a liquid natural gas tanker explosion, or the likelihood of CO_2-induced climate changes. Such events may be a great deal more or less likely than estimated because of the problems of dealing with unknown phenomena and the uncertainties of the human/technological interface. How do we accurately predict the likelihood of terrorism, human error, or psychological breakdown? Moreover, the accuracy of estimates of risk declines as the complexity of the system rises.

There is also a high degree of subjectivity built into estimates of energy demands for which we are told we must run certain risks. A few years ago, most energy projections depicted demand in the year 2000 of roughly some 170 quadrillion BTUs, but from the same sources we do not hear that demands will more likely fall in the 101–126 quadrillion range (Institute for Energy Analysis 1976, p. 4). Other estimates are lower still (National Research Council 1978). Energy demand projections in the past were used to justify overbuilding capacity, which then tended to pull consumption upward, justifying yet another round of predictions and frantic building. In effect, energy consumption occurred to meet projections in what Winner (1977a) describes as a process of "reverse adaptation" (see also Daly 1976). Similarly, figures about the economic competitiveness of nuclear, coal, and solar energy depend on shaky assumptions or upon inaccurate data. It seems prudent to be skeptical about aggregate figures and projections that have shown such a high degree of variability in the past. (Oskar Morgenstern (1973) once showed that figures purporting to describe the GNP were only accurate within ± 10 percent range. I doubt that various data about energy use are any more accurate, and there is some reason to think that they may be considerably less so.)

A second problem with the high technologist's approach to risk is his habit of isolating individual risk (r) so that we never know what contribution it makes to the total level of risk (R) to which society is exposed. Should a society with from 60 to 70 nuclear reactors, a large oil industry, and so forth also run the "andromeda" risks inherent in recombinant DNA research? Is there a maximum level of R that we might assign as the outer boundary of social prudence?

Any attempt to aggregate risks arising from different events and processes raises substantial problems of measurement and comparability. Individual risks vary according to magnitude, geographic scope, and time scale. Estimates of r are also likely to fluctuate over time because of "learning," technological changes, changes in the size of the program, and equipment characteristics. Accidents, for example, may become more likely as older equipment fails or personnel become complacent. An increasing number of cases will occur when the consequences of synergistic interactions remain beyond our capacity to assess until damage has already occurred or is irreversible.

A third fallacy in the techno-optimists' approach to risk is the belief that catastrophe would pose only temporary inconveniences to society. Kahn, Brown, and Martel (1976, p. 163–64) argue, for example, that even climate change that resulted in the melting of the polar ice caps "would not tip the balance against progress." They further suggest that while "local disasters are probably inevitable" most people will be content to accept the risk. Presumably, the alleged public willingness to incur risk says something meaningful about the consequences of disaster. In any event, Kahn argues that we do not have much choice since we are "involved in a process that probably cannot be voluntarily and safely stopped or prematurely slowed down significantly." A similar view is expressed by Hans Bethe (1976), who argues that a nuclear accident would be "less serious than most minor wars." For Bethe, the risk of disasters that fall in the category of "most minor wars" is acceptable because of what he describes as the "necessity" of a growing supply of energy.

Whether such views are valid depends on the nature of the event, the diffusion of effects, and the adaptability of society in the face of disaster. In contrast to the mechanistic model of society evident in the work of physicists Kahn and Bethe, Kai Erickson's (1976a) study of the Buffalo Creek disaster demonstrated that the process of recovery from catastrophe is diminished by the overwhelming sense of loss and erosion of morale that afflicts the survivors. After examining the remains of the community of Buffalo Creek, which was destroyed by a dam failure in February 1972, Erickson (1976b, p. 58; see also Erickson 1976a) writes that, "Most of the survivors responded to the disaster with a deep sense of loss—a nameless feeling that something had gone grotesquely awry in the order of things, that their minds and spirits had been bruised beyond repair, that they would never again be able to find coherence, that the world as they knew it had come to an end." These symptoms persisted long after the event, indicating that the effects of disaster are not only immediate physical destruction, but also long-term psychological problems, the loss of community, and social morale. Erickson's study raises questions about the ability of society to recover from large disasters. Recovery may be less likely than many have supposed because the social and psychological wherewithal is more fragile than realized.

The solution to the energy problem proposed by the techno-optimist requires further centralization of both the energy sector and government. Centralization is implicit in the need to organize and manage large supply and distribution networks, to generate large amounts of capital, to maintain security against potential saboteurs, to conduct increasingly expensive research and development on technologies such as nuclear fusion, and, finally, to regulate the entire process. The creation of the federal Department of Energy with an initial budget of $10.6 billion represents a significant step in this direction.

Beyond some threshold, however, there are limits to our capacity to manage complex systems. One result of increasing size is that decisionmakers tend to become more "ignoran(t) of the universe in which they are to act" (Winner 1975, p. 64). According to Kenneth Boulding (cited in Lovins 1977b, p. 164), "The larger and more authoritarian the organization, the better the chance that its top decision-makers will operate in purely imaginary worlds." The management of a large, complex organization is subject to limitations characteristic of pyramidal structures generally. As the size of an organization increases, the need for hierarchically arranged control likewise grows. Growth, however, can serve to lower morale, promote incompetence, impair effectiveness. Organizations can thus become "self-sealing" from their environment and, consequently, unable to "learn" (Argyris 1976 Wilensky 1967). The history of the largest of the auto makers or the largest energy companies or of any government agency ought to caution us against expecting much in the way of flexibility, innovation, or even very accurate perceptions of the "real world."

The causes include not only the pathologies of information and structure, but also the typical procedures of large organizations, which are described as "disjointed incrementalism" (Braybrooke and Lindblom 1970). Government normally divides and subdivides responsibilities and attempts only small changes at the margin of the status quo. The result is that administrators seldom if ever adopt systemic approaches, which we are told will be necessary to resolve the energy crisis. Incrementalism implies not only small adjustments, but also preoccupation with the present. Governments and large organizations do not anticipate problems but, more typically, react long after they have become acute. Quarles (1976, pp. xv-xvi), for example, has written that, "Government action depends on public demand, the government does not begin to attack a problem until that problem has become severe. The government always has to catch up, to find solutions for problems that long before have grown out of control." There is little reason to think that an even more centralized energy department will do much better, and there is some reason to think that it may do worse.

THE ENERGY CRISIS AS DILEMMA

It is time, I think, to admit that we have no good options before us and that the future will be painful no matter what we do. Despite the recent summons to regard the energy crisis as the "moral equivalent of war," the trumpet call to action was highly uncertain. There is a sizeable gap between the magnitude of the impending situation and the program set before the nation, which called for only minimal sacrifices in lifestyle and economic growth. In the words of one critic, the program resembles the captain of the Titanic asking passengers to close their portholes for fear of getting wet. The Senate, however, has demonstrated that even minimal sacrifices may be too much. Nonetheless, there is some advantage in recognizing the lack of easy or painless alternatives. It is undoubtedly true, as Cook (1976, p. 193) has suggested, that a sense of constraint that avoids illusions will make it easier to reach wise decisions. Samuel Johnson once said roughly the same thing, to the effect that "when a man knows he is to be hanged in a fortnight, it concentrates his mind wonderfully." We are still waiting for our collective mind to be concentrated.

But who will do it? Politicians and technologists are both committed to painlessness. Indeed such is the raison d'être of their respective professions. Earlier societies had prophets, oracles, or, sometimes, a dyspeptic preacher such as Reverend Malthus to warn of impending doom. But while technological societies now have computer studies to the same effect, we have also invented elaborate defense mechanisms to avoid reading the printout on the wall. There is a sense in which our faith in technology represents a deeper commitment to the proposition that we can at last eradicate the element of tragedy altogether. The faith that technology can be pushed to this end has become the ultimate form of what Becker (1974) calls the "denial of death."

This faith, however, leads us deeper and deeper into the maw of dilemmas that place the imperatives of expanding energy supply against other values of democracy, safety, public health, ecological integrity, climate stability, economic viability, and international peace. In each of these, we encounter conflict between our short-term interest in preserving the status quo and the prospects we bequeath a decade or more hence. Each dilemma, the optimist assures us, is in fact only a problem waiting to be solved by technology. But, in each instance, the stakes grow higher and the technological feats to be performed become more wondrous and hence more problematic. The proponent of nuclear power offers us electrical energy now but at a price that includes the burden of isolating wastes for 250,000 years, growing prospects for nuclear terrorism, the diffusion of nuclear weapons and a consequent rise in the prospects of nuclear war, an increasing possibility of massive accidents, uncertain economies, and the near certainty of a more authoritarian government (see Keeny et al. 1977; Patterson 1976). The benefits begin now; the costs and uncertainties will be paid on the installment plan with interest.

The plans for utilizing coal proposed in the Carter energy program are only marginally more appealing. The combustion of coal and the resultant release of CO_2 into the upper atmosphere will at some unknown point affect global climate balances, melt polar ice-caps, alter growing seasons, and destabilize ecosystems (National Academy of Sciences 1977). There is at least some evidence that this process may already be occurring (Damon and Kunen 1976). These prospects have led at least one administrative official to suggest the possibility of restriction on the use of coal within the next 40 years (Sullivan 1977). Others are less optimistic. The use of coal imposes other, albeit less dramatic, costs, including the destruction of prime farm- and rangeland, for which reclamation is uncertain, and the adverse health effects caused by pollutants (Scholars 1975, pp. 71-84).

The prospect of a solar civilization, described by Lovins (1977b), Hayes (1977), and Clark (1974) among others, also imposes costs, though of a different sort. While the technological optimist offers near-term advantages, mainly the preservation of the status quo for future costs and risks, the solar option would impose immediate costs but for the eventual prospect of a sustainable, if technologically more modest, future. The costs of the solar option, known or conjectured, include the frontend cost of retrofitting large numbers of buildings and homes with solar equipment, a decline in per capita income and consequently a less materialistic lifestyle, less personal mobility, and the shift to a more labor-intensive economy. (Hannon 1975, 1977). According to some, the solar option also entails the uncertainty that we will be able to harness enough energy to meet the demands of a high-technology society.

Whether such changes could occur without social and political turmoil depends in part upon how the burdens and the gains are distributed (Stretton 1976). It would be necessary to avoid further disadvantaging the low and middle income groups and would thus require greater contributions by corporations and wealthy classes, but this raises other uncertainties. Considering the scope and the speed of the transition Lovins and others propose, there are no historical precedents that come easily to mind. Doubtless, the solar option would also require government centralization, but it would at least hold out the hope that social decentralization and "soft" technologies might eventually minimize the need for authoritarianism.

At this point, however, there is room to doubt whether Lovins and other solar proponents have a sufficiently rigorous theory of social and political change. Is it plausible to believe that a grassroots revolution in energy production could overturn the power of the energy companies? Lovins does not dwell much on politics, so we can only conjecture.

Ultimately, the proponents of a solar society are heirs to the tradition of Jefferson, Gandhi, and perhaps Mao. But the world that they seek to transform was shaped by the ideas of Hamilton, Rockefeller, Ford, and Sloan. The genuine radicalness of the solar option can only be seen in relief—juxtaposed against the outlines of the present—even though its proponents usually speak in quieter tones. We should, therefore, avoid harboring illusions that the ultimate destination of a "soft path" would be anything less than a thorough social transformation of industrial-technological society. But then the implications of the other options would also lead to a future unrecognizable from our current vantage point.

CONCLUSION

It would be presumptuous and beyond the scope of this chapter to say which option or mix of options should be chosen. I will therefore conclude by summarizing four important but ignored components of the energy dilemma. First, the debate is often confined to esoteric descriptions of technological options and is thus dominated by technologists and energy "experts." But beyond analysis and conjecture about the characteristics of particular technologies, the important issues are moral, ethical, social, and political. The choice of technologies is often protrayed as a value-neutral process based on "objective" data. There is no more dangerous illusion. Not only are the "data" often flawed or incomplete, but they seldom include any consideration of the wider effects of technology. These we ignore at our peril.

Second, it is time to rethink the role of energy in society and its relation to quality of life. The demands that we are told are inflexible in large measure result from trivial consumption. While we do not measure that portion of GNP that has no redeeming social virtue, we do know that a sizeable fraction (perhaps as much as half) of the U. S. energy budget is waste. To eliminate such waste by switching from energy-intensive aluminum beer cans or to smaller cars will hardly jeopardize the republic as some charge. Moreover, it is time to consider what Miles (1976, pp. 89-103) has called "the centrifugal social effects" of energy. It is not possible to speak of causation or even of correlation, but we ought to be just a little suspicious of the possible relation between the massive infusion of energy into U. S. society since 1945 and the recent increases of crime, mental illness, broken marriages, drug addiction, alcoholism, and the loss of neighborhood and community. Finally, in light of the fact that the energy input relative to GNP output has fallen by one-third since 1920, we ought to bury the myth that energy/GNP ratio is inscribed on stone tablets somewhere. Paul McCraken (cited in Hayes 1976, pp. 53-54; Institute for Energy Analysis 1978, p. 3), for example, has observed that, "The striking thing about the relationship between the rate of growth in output and the rate of increasing energy consumed is not that it obviously exists, but that it is so variable."

Third, government, industry, and academia are biased in favor of technocracy to the exclusion of the public, which is dismissed as ill-informed and apathetic. In fact, such observations are not only self fulfilling, but also reflect both the lack of opportunity for meaningful participation and the deliberate attempt to keep the public in the dark without full knowledge of the issues. This is somewhat ironic when we first consider that technology has increased possibilities for participation. Advances in computers, fiber optics, and the possibility of video networks have reduced the limits imposed by large numbers of people, costs of information, and physical distance that previously impeded direct participation. Our present plight reflects choices made by technical, industrial, and governmental elites, the "best and brightest," who ironically insist that we need even more of them.

Finally, there are still unresolved and even unasked questions about what level of risk is worth what gain and how each is distributed within and between generations. This is part of a larger question concerning the assessment of technology. There has been a strong bias toward technological can-do macho, evident in the ill-founded enthusiasm for Rube Goldberg devices such as the breeder reactor. Beyond some vague notions of "progress," we have never had a clear idea of where we wanted technology to take us. But, to rework an old saying, if we don't know where we want to go, any technology will get us there. In the words of Winner (1977b, p. 373), we must now acquire "a definite and declared willingness to say 'no'. The hollow optimism and tendency to yield to the 'inevitable' . . . must find a corrective in the courage to recognize and call attention to the untenable."

2
TECHNOLOGY ASSESSMENT:
A SOCIAL IMPACT PERSPECTIVE ON
ALTERNATIVE ENERGY TECHNOLOGIES

Roger P. Hansen

I believe that it is extremely important that we should
learn not to expect of technology more than technology,
by itself, can possibly deliver. The effective formulation of national policies can only be jeopardized by such
excessive expectations. This is so not only because we
will be disappointed and frustrated, but because, by
placing excessive faith in the prospect for a technological "fix," we will fail to explore other measures and
alternatives which may offer greater, or more immediate, prospects for success (Rosenberg 1976, p. 4).

The environmental movement, which burst like a supernova on
the international stage in the 1970s, has been temporarily eclipsed by
the darkening moon of the energy crisis. "Temporarily" is appropriate since the planetary revolution for a quality environment will remain a major social issue for indefinite decades. Scientific evidence
of the increasing degradation of planetary ecosystems is commanding
current headlines. Environmental concern is inextricably related to
concurrent social revolutions for racial justice, freedom from poverty,
and peace in the world.

Technological crisis like the Alaskan Pipeline, Santa Barbara
Oil Spill, the SST, and Silent Spring are predictable because we live
in an era of high technological risks. Our ability to respond to problems with a "technology fix" increasingly outstrips our ability to predict and deal with the undesirable effects of the technology we unleash.
This is true for several reasons.

First, the crisis quality of many of our problems (energy shortages, polluted air, rising cancer rates) appears to demand the crea-

tion of an instant technological response. This results in a technological trigger-happiness that is inconsistent with systematic risk
assessment and long-range planning. For example, the energy crisis is seen by no less than the president of the United States as the
"moral equivalent of war."

Second, relatively few technological innovations are tested on
a small scale long enough to allow their possible effects to be made
known before they are widely deployed. Once an innovation appears
technologically and financially feasible, it is marketed immediately
on a massive scale—whether CB radios, hula hoops, or DDT. The
approach is sell it now and ask questions later. Technology development is often amoral or immoral.

Third, legal and institutional responses are too little and too
late to deal with technologically induced problems. The Clean Air
Act and litigation to stop the dumping of taconite tailings in Lake Superior are years—if not decades—behind the problem. (See United
States vs. Reserve Mining Company 1976.) In the meantime, the
risks of unplanned technology increase exponentially.

And fourth, the enormous gaps in our knowledge (the risks of
uncertainty) preclude advance warning of technological traps that
lie yawning at our feet until it is too late. For example, we understand very little about the effects of hundreds of possibly toxic chemicals and how they are transported through the air, water, and land.
Almost every evening, news programs announce a new chemical crisis—from sweeteners, to hair dyes, to menopause pills.

Long-range planning does not exist. Our society is not organized
legally, institutionally, or technologically to plan much beyond the middle of next week. Much of our "planning" is nothing more than a delayed reaction to fast-moving events over which we have demonstrated
little if any control in the past—urban sprawl, overcrowded airports,
water shortages, run-away inflation. A high percentage of our R&D
effort, public and private, is a reaction to immediate crises such as
kepone, airport noise, and oil embargoes. The Environmental Protection Agency (EPA), for example, is often accused of setting research priorities on a "pollutant-of-the-month" basis.

Joseph Coates (1976) insists that there are only three planning
criteria for opening a Chinese laundry, building Grand Coulee dam,
or siting the Alaskan Pipeline: (1) can you build it?; (2) will somebody
pay the bill?; and (3) is it safe? Safety, however, is probably not that
much of a factor. More likely, the third criterion is what will be the
return on investment?

If we are to have any control over our destinies as a planet, as
a nation, or as individuals, we need vastly improved approaches to
long-range planning. If we are to avoid merely drifting with the tide
and being buffeted by the capricious winds of change on all sides, we

need compasses to help us choose the "best" among alternative futures and to see to it that the future we select becomes a reality. Technology assessment offers some promise of being such a compass.

WHAT IS TECHNOLOGY ASSESSMENT?

Definitions of technology assessment (TA) abound and borrow from each other. Joseph F. Coates (1975) of the U. S. Office of Technology Assessment, a prolific author on the subject of TA, is responsible for the more fundamental definitions, such as:

> Technology assessment is a class of policy studies directed to examining the broadest social implications of the introduction of a new technology or the expansion or extension of an existing technology. It is intended to provide the decision-maker with useful advice and guidance on policies, programs, plans, and alternate actions.

Arnstein (1977) admonishes that TA is not synonymous with such technology-related studies as "technological forecasting, engineering feasibility, clinical trials, market research, cost-benefit or cost-effectiveness studies, environmental impact assessment, or technology transfer and diffusion."

Few insist that TA is or should be a new academic discipline or that institutes of technology assessment or Ph. D. s on the subject should be encouraged. A rigid, academically oriented compartmentalization of TA would stifle its most important characteristic: a holistic,[1] interdisciplinary approach that cuts across such diverse elements as economics, ecology, political science, sociology, engineering, and law. Unless TA as so far practiced and conceptualized is to be destroyed in the process, it cannot be neatly stowed in some academic closet.

Several key philosophical and practical assumptions are inherent in the TA concept. They are expressed by Berg, Chen, and Zissis (1975) as follows.

1. Technological innovation can be both beneficial and disruptive to social and environmental systems;

2. Regulation, control, and planning of technology are necessary, rational, and moral;

3. Technological impacts can be rationally forecasted and controlled;

4. Only some forms of technological growth are necessary and good; and

5. Technological change is necessary for societal survival.

However, the assumptions of Coates (1975) seem even more basic: that the future is not preordained and that we have not only the opportunity but the moral responsibility to select the "most socially desirable" future and to reject less desirable alternatives. If we could only agree on the criteria for the "most socially desirable" future, we might be able to formulate a program to make that particular future unfold. Neither the social nor the biological sciences provide a dependable approach for identifying and describing the "good life" of the future. For the most part, we are limited to public opinion surveys. [2]

BACKGROUND OF TECHNOLOGY ASSESSMENT

Technology Assessment has a social, intellectual, and legislative history. (See Environmental Reporter, August 12, 1977.) From the social value system perspective, there is mounting evidence of a steadily declining credibility problem with the virtues and rewards of "progress" in our society. Too many technological innovations have gone sour: flood control dams that cause floods, pesticides that kill peregrine falcons, computers that invade privacy, SSTs that threaten neighborhood peace and the ozone layer, and oil spills that ruin miles of beaches. The Tennessee Valley Authority (TVA), a lunchbucket and chicken-in-every-pot hero of the 1930s, is seen as an environmental scourge of the 1970s. That glorious American graven image—the automobile—is being degraded as a gas-guzzling polluter. There is a revolutionary recognition that "small is beautiful," that there probably are "limits to growth," and that we may be living on "the late great planet Earth." (See Schumacher 1973; Meadows et. al 1972; and Lindsey 1970.) A rising, vocal public cacophony questions whether we need some technologies at all: nuclear power, genetic experimentation, computerized money transfers. Technological development per se is no longer enough. A new kind of question is emerging: will this or that technology really improve the quality of life, the joy of living? (Wolf 1977).

Studying the effects of technology is not a newly minted intellectual exercise. "Social impact assessment" has been going on for at least 40 years (Wolf 1977). There were studies on TVA relocatees in 1937 (Satterfield 1937) and on war boom communities in 1952 (Carr and Stermer 1952). However, a dramatic legislative breakthrough in 1969 endowed technology assessment with respectability and a much sharper focus.

The National Environmental Policy Act of 1969 (NEPA) has provided major impetus for the more modern versions of TA. (See U. S. Congress 1969, 42 U. S. C. sec. 4321 ff.) NEPA has often been referred to as "social" legislation since it mandates federal agency consideration of the broader societal consequences of agency decisions. The insistence of some environmentalists that "environmental impact" in the NEPA context is intended to be confined to the "natural" environment of trees, grass, wildlife, and scenery indicates a lack of understanding of the intricate interrelationships between socioeconomic human factors and biophysical environmental components. The act recognizes the "profound impact of man's activity on the interrelations of all components of the natural environment" and establishes national environmental goals to:

1. "fulfill the responsibilities of each generation as trustee of the environment;"
2. assure all Americans of "safe, healthful, productive, and aesthetically and culturally pleasing surrounding;
3. attain the widest range of beneficial uses of the environment without degradation;"
4. preserve important historic, cultural, and natural aspects of the national heritage and maintain an environment "which supports diversity;" and
5. "achieve a balance between population and resource use."

Further, NEPA requires federal agencies to "utilize a systematic, interdisciplinary approach which will insure the integrated use of the natural and social sciences and the environmental design arts." Although such an approach has rarely been achieved by federal agencies—and the environmental design arts are generally ignored—the "interdisciplinary approach" is perhaps the most critical component of a technology assessment.

The NEPA provision that has spawned thousands of "environmental impact statements" (EIS) and that is in great part responsible for the growing interest in TA is section 102(2)(C). This requires all federal agencies to include in every recommendation for "major Federal actions significantly affecting the quality of the human environment" a "detailed statement" on the proposed action's environmental impact (emphasis added). [3]

As a response to arguments that NEPA mandates consideration of only the "natural" environment in agency decision making, a line of recent court cases has held that EISs must consider social, economic, and other impacts upon the "quality of life." Such impacts include crime, police protection, schools, hospitals, fire protection, recreation, transportation, and commercial establishments. [4]

Environmental impact statements (a phrase not employed in the legislation) have been justifiably criticized for their poor quality, undue length, inadequacy in identifying impacts, shoddy assessment of social impacts, and use as "justification statements" for projects that should never have been proposed in the first place. Nevertheless, NEPA and its consequent avalanche of environmental analyses, good and bad, provide an excellent background as to the kind of considerations that must go into a comprehensive TA.

Wolf makes a considerable effort to distinguish environmental impact statements and technology assessment from "social impact assessment." He states that social impact assessment (SIA) is "nothing less than that of estimating and appraising the condition of a society organized and changed by large-scale applications of high technology" (1977). This is really nothing more nor less than what technology assessment is all about, called by whatever name. But then Wolf (1977) narrows the SIA concept by defining "social impacts" in this manner: "Social impacts are alterations in behavioral patterns and institutional configurations—the conditions of existence, contents of experience and modes of expression—caused by some natural event or human intervention."

Such psychological, cultural, and even philosophical dimensions are broad enough to include such diverse "topical areas" as industrial development, coastal zone management, weather modification, land use, and energy boom towns.

The dichotomies drawn between "environmental impact assessment," "technology assessment," and "social impact assessment" are often artificial and even fatuous. If one examines what environmental/social impact analyses should be, rather than what they presently are, all of these approaches have a close kinship.

MAJOR TECHNOLOGY ASSESSMENT ELEMENTS

As is true of most if not all approaches to social impact assessment, TA is an evolving state-of-art rather than an exact science and demands maximum flexibility, imagination, and innovation by its practitioners. There is no TA formula and, in fact, the idea that a formula or even a format should be adopted grossly violates the TA concept. Technology assessments offer an opportunity to escape the often rigid conformity of environmental impact statements. Nevertheless, TA approaches contain some generally accepted key elements or components. [5]

Problem Definition

Some technology assessments have been completed without ever having defined with precision the problem to be assessed in all of its parameters. By "problem" is meant the technology, program, or project to be assessed and the issues that flow from it. Problem definition necessarily involves scoping or "bounding" the study. For example, a technology assessment of coal-based electric generation is narrower in scope than a technology assessment of alternative energy sources.

Description of Alternative Technologies

Energy may be derived from a variety of sources, including oil, gas, coal, oil shale, geothermal resources, and the sun. Coal-based energy can be derived from conventional combustion, gasification, liquefaction, fuel cells, and so on. The alternative of not developing or deploying the technology at all—the "no action" alternative legally necessary for an EIS under NEPA—is not appropriate for a TA. A TA must ask: What if this or that technology were developed, modified, or extended?

Impact Identification

Although impacts must be identified before they can be evaluated, these two "steps" proceed more or less simultaneously. A TA must search beyond the obvious, immediate, "direct" impacts and look for "latent, indirect, unintended, and delayed effects" (Coates, n.d.). Many TA practitioners speak of "higher order" impacts, although this designation carries with it the unintended connotation that secondary or tertiary effects are more important than "first order" impacts. Impacts can also be categorized, for example, economic, social, environmental, legal, political. The types of impacts and how they are categorized will vary from one TA to another.

Impact Evaluation

Impact evaluation is the Achilles' heel of technology assessment. This is true, in part, because the magnitude, significance, and manner of distribution of many kinds of impacts cannot be "modeled" in a quantifiable way. Impact evaluation involves scientific and technical data, expert judgment, speculation, interpretation of social values, political insights, and an abundance of creative imagination. It also requires intestinal fortitude to speculate, say, that Western energy development will likely result in increased cancer morbidity in Wyoming in the year 2000.

Decision-making Process Characterization

Who are the decisionmakers who can affect the timing and intensity of the deployment of a technology or program, or whether it will be deployed at all? Are they in government, industry, politics, environmental groups? What is the role of public opinion with regard to the particular technology? In the last analysis, everyone is a decisionmaker and no decision process can be traced with mathematical accuracy. Nevertheless, some understanding of the decision-making process is vital to the policy analysis; it is the illusive decisionmaker who must implement the policy.

Identification and Evaluation of Policy Alternatives

Policy or "action" alternatives that will avoid or mitigate the "undesirable" consequences of a technology—or enhance the "desirable" ones—must be thoroughly examined. This involves several steps: identifying candidate policies, examining implementation strategies, and estimating the consequences of policies if implemented. The mere identification of policy options is insufficient for a TA policy analysis. Policy analysis is the element that most distinguishes TA from other types of social/environmental impact studies.

Involvement of Parties-at-Interest

The strict legal definition of a "party" is the plaintiff or the defendant in a lawsuit. In view of the deluge of environmental litigation since the passage of NEPA, this meaning is perhaps appropriate for a TA. However, a broader definition is "a person concerned or taking part in any affair, matter, transaction, or proceeding" (Black 1951). Whether these individuals or groups are referred to as "parties-of-interest" or "stakeholders" is of no great consequence. Merely identifying those in the private or public sector who may be affected by the technology being assessed is inadequate. Representatives of various interests must actually be involved in the TA process through interviews, workshops, hearings, surveys, conferences, or other techniques. It is imperative that parties-at-interest be consulted for identifying key issues, identifying and evaluating impacts, and analyzing policy options if the TA is to have any credibility.

Scenarios

The term "scenario" was historically used to describe the outline of the plot in a drama or literary work. Moviemakers adopted the term to denote a screenplay. Now, systems analysts, policy planners, and technology assessors have made "scenario" an indispensable ingredient of sophisticated bureaucratese. In energy studies, scenarios are usually (and mistakenly) confined to levels of energy supply or demand. "Context," "what if," "alternative future," "state of society," and "game situation" have all been used in maddening confusion to define "scenario." Vanston et al. (1977) have outlined a 12-step methodology for scenario development. The most important steps are listing of relevant factors (assumptions), selecting themes for alternate scenarios, developing an extrapolative "base case" scenario, and developing alternate scenarios. The selection and construction of scenarios are of critical importance to a TA since impact evaluation and policy analysis flow from (are dependent on) the scenarios.

Communication of Results

Effective communications of the results is a major failing of most public and private research efforts. This is due to several major obstacles. TA papers or reports are cluttered with jargon, words and phrases that are indecipherable to decisionmakers. Due to the peer group syndrome, both written and oral communications often seem intended only for the benefit of other members of the TA inner circle. And many scientists and technicians involved in TA give only secondary or even tertiary consideration to basic communication skills. Government, university, and private organizations conducting TA often have few if any professional writers, editors, or graphics experts. Finally, sponsors of TA, especially government agencies, are often indifferent to the need for "research utilization"—disseminating the results of research efforts, which are often very expensive, to prospective user groups. Most contracts merely specify that the contractor supply so many copies of a final report.

TECHNOLOGY ASSESSMENT METHODOLOGIES

A detailed analysis of the innumerable techniques that can be utilized in TA is beyond the scope of this chapter. Figure 2.1 relates six

FIGURE 2.1

Elements in a Comprehensive Technology Assessment
and Possible Study Techniques for Each Element

Study techniques	Structuring the problem	The systems alternatives	Possible impacts	Evaluating impacts	Identifying decision makers	Identifying action options	Parties at interest	Macro systems alternatives	Exogenous variables state of society	Conclusions and recommendations	Participation of parties at interest	Presentation of results
Historical surveys	●	●	●		●	●	●	●	●	●		
Input/output	●			●			●					●
Compilation of prior work	●	●	●	●	●	●	●	●	●	●		
Cost-benefit	●			●			●		●			●
Systems analysis	●	●	●	●			●		●			
Risk-benefit	●			●				●				●
Systems engineering	●	●	●	●				●				
Simulation	●	●	●	●				●	●		●	●
Expert panels, workshops	●	●	●	●	●		●	●	●	●		●	●
Modeling	●	●	●	●				●		●		
Hearings	●	●	●			●	●	●	●	●	●	●	●
Interpretive structural modeling	●					●		●			●	●	●
Field or on-site investigation	●			●	●	●		●				●	
Signed digraph	●			●	●		●	●					●
Trend extrapolation and analysis				●	●					●		
Physical models				●	●							●
Delphi	●	●	●	●		●	●	●	●	●		●	
Scenarios/games	●	●	●	●	●		●	●	●	●	●	●	
Cross impact	●	●		●	●			●		●		●	
Moot courts			●	●		●		●	●			●	●
Check lists	●	●			●		●	●	●				●
Telecommunication participation			●	●	●		●	●	●		●	●	●	●
Morphological analysis	●	●							●			
Syncons			●	●	●		●	●	●	●	●	●	●	●
Historical analogy	●			●	●	●		●	●		●	●	
Survey techniques				●				●		●	●	●	●
Decision/relevance tree	●	●	●	●	●	●			●		●	●	●
Ballots				●				●		●	●	●	●
Fault tree	●			●	●							●
Decision theory				●			●				●		●
Scaling				●					●	●		●
Brainstorming	●	●	●		●		●	●	●	●	●	●	
Graphics				●						●	●	●
Judgment theory				●		●				●		
Dynamic modeling	●	●	●	●					●			●
KSIM (Kane's Simulation)	●	●	●	●				●	●	●	●	●

Source: Coates, Joseph F. 1976. "Technology Assessment—A
Tool Kit." CHEMTECH (June). Reprinted with permission from
CHEMTECH. Copyright by the American Chemical Society.

27

study techniques to the 12 TA components employed by Coates. A dozen of them, for example, can be employed primarily to secure participation in the TA process by the various parties-at-interest.

Those undertaking a TA would be well advised to select only those techniques with which they are familiar or for which they can hire experienced practitioners. Engaging in such sophisticated techniques as Interpretive Structural Modeling (ISM), computer games, and building relevance trees can be disastrous for the uninitiated. For that matter, organizing an effective workshop or brainstorming session requires meticulous planning and cannot be accomplished extemporaneously.

Finally, technology assessment techniques—as interesting or as much fun as they may be to practice—should not be the tail that wags the dog of the TA analysis and results. There is a tendency among TA practitioners to view "methodology for methodology's sake" and to lose sight of the fact that various pathways are supposed to lead to an ultimate objective. It is possible to conduct a magnificient "crossimpact analysis" and still fail miserably in the identification and evaluation of all of the impacts that should have been considered. Tools and techniques for technology assessment are not ends in themselves.

POLICY ANALYSIS: THE ILLUSIVE
TECHNOLOGY ASSESSMENT BONANZA

The identification and evaluation of policy options for decision-makers is the raison d'être, the bottom line of technology assessment. This is particularly appropriate since everyone, it seems, wants to be a policy analyst—to operate at the "policy level." In the federal government, those at the GS-16 scale or higher are considered to be "policy people," somehow endowed with perceptions and judgments not available to ordinary mortals. What interests so many would-be TA practitioners is that TA is a "policy study" that is somehow superior to more mundane and proletarian environmental analyses—a grossly erroneous impression.

Yet very little of the growing TA literature attempts to define what a "policy" is in the first place. An understanding of what constitutes a "public policy" is taken as a given. Whether a policy is viewed as an action, a decision, a statement of intent, or some combination thereof is not of major importance. What is important is to understand a policy as an implementing, expedition mechanism. A policy is a proposed solution to one or a set of perceived problems.

Kinds of policy options will vary enormously depending on who the decisionmakers or parties-at-interest are. It would seem that the most efficient and comprehensive policy analysis would postulate the greatest number of entities in the policy hierarchy. It would be wasteful and irresponsible, for example, for a TA to frame policy alternatives that could be implemented only by the entity sponsoring the study, for example, the EPA or the DOE. [6]

A policy analysis "hierarchy" of users or audiences for an energy-oriented TA might look something like this:

Federal Agencies
  Energy-related (the departments of Energy and Interior, the Environmental Protection Agency, and so on)
  Peripherally related (the departments of Commerce and Treasury).
State Agencies
  Energy-related (governors' staffs, state environmental protection agencies, and so on)
  Other agencies (natural resources, agriculture, and so on)
Private Sector
  Business and industry
  Public interest groups (environment, consumer, and so on)
  Private research and consulting
  Academia

Of course, policies evolve from the bottom up as well as from the top down. Thus a hierarchical concept should be used only as an organizational device for policy analysis.

If they can meet the challenges, social scientists can make a major contribution to policy analysis that, after all, involves the way human beings perceive and solve problems. However, this is not likely to happen until the bickering among various social science subdisciplines is resolved. Neither is it likely to happen as long as social science literature is filled with jargon that few policymakers can understand. In the meantime, a lot of policy analysis will be done by engineers and dominate the organizations assigned by government agencies to do policy analysis.

PROBLEMS WITH TECHNOLOGY ASSESSMENT

It can be concluded without profound insight that TA is not a panacea for determining the long-range consequences of our technological adventures. It is fraught with a number of perplexing and challenging problems.

Disciplinary Balkanization

As Wordsworth wrote, "we murder to dissect" problems into smaller and smaller airtight compartments. [7] So-called "interdisciplinary studies" are comprised of a forced and uncomfortable multidisciplinary approach that stifles interaction among those of diverse academic backgrounds. Those of different disciplines hold conflicting values and assumptions, and their lack of a common terminology exacerbates the problem. The "holistic" view demanded by TA seems almost impossible to achieve.

"Hard" versus "Soft" Sciences

Some scientists and technologists assume that the social sciences and humanities are populated by unrealistic dreamers. By contrast, engineers, physicists, chemists, and other "hard scientists" are seen as dealing only with "realistic," quantifiable data. But the more recent concern for "morality" and "relevance" in the basic sciences—and the increasing sophistication of social science methodologies—may narrow that dichotomy.

Political versus Scientific

Scientific and technical information is often made irrelevant in determining what becomes a public policy issue. While science is not value-free, a distinction can be made between anticipated technological effects as determined by a scientific examination and as determined by political judgments. We have not yet found a way to balance political considerations and scientific knowledge in decision making. And we cannot afford the luxury of continuing to make energy/environment decisions primarily on the basis of public opinion polls.

Absence of Futures Science

There is not, and never may be, a scientific explanation of how the future is generated and unfolds—who makes what decisions or what circumstances take priority. Inevitably, projecting the future and its consequences involves making estimates, engaging in guesswork, following "wise man" intuitions based on experience, and adopting some "blue sky" protocols. This poses an enormous credibility problem for the futurist since "my guess is probably as good as yours." Yet, a TA demands that we peer ahead into the mists of speculation.

False Dichotomies

Practitioners of actual or de facto TA go to mind-boggling lengths to distinguish technology assessment, social impact assessment, and environmental impact statements. Much of this dichotomy is artificially structured along disciplinary lines. While these approaches are not the same, their differences are more in purposes and applications that in methods that could be employed.

Inadequate Lead Time

Theoretically, TA should be utilized to project the possible consequences of a technology, project, or program before it is deployed or enacted. For example, now would be the time to do comprehensive technology assessments on proposals to break agricultural combines up into 160-acre family farms, tinker with the world climate, or establish a space community on the moon. However, the technology assessors are usually finessed by decisionmakers who want to retrofit a TA on decisions already made.

CONCLUSIONS

Attempting to project and even manage the future is an awesome challenge and a sobering social and moral responsibility. Our implements for the task are crude, and, being mortal, we "see through a glass darkly."[8]

Technology assessment has a vital need for the expertise and, especially, the perception of social scientists. Energy decisions in the next decade, or sooner, will affect the lives of all Americans—and other planetary citizens—in profound and lasting ways. They will necessitate the making of hard choices and the reexamination not only of value systems but also of the whole purpose of life itself. The upward mobility ingredient of the American psyche observed long ago by Tocqueville will have to be reconstituted or excised altogether. Tocqueville (n. d. : 45) observed of Americans:

> As they are always dissatisfied with the position which they occupy, and are always free to leave it, they think of nothing but the means of changing their fortune, or of increasing it. To minds thus predisposed, every new method which leads by a shorter road to wealth, every machine which spares labour, every instrument which diminishes the cost of production, every discovery which

facilitates pleasures or augments them, seems to be the grandest effort of the human intellect.

Today, roads to wealth are longer than ever and many doubt that their construction should be allowed. Labor-saving devices are challenged as consumers of energy and tormentors of the unemployed. Perhaps we are approaching the "posttechnology age" when efforts of the human intellect will have to be drastically redirected.

NOTES

1. Holism is the opposite of atomism. It is the theory that the universe is to be seen correctly in terms of interacting parts. For purposes of a TA, a holistic approach examines not only individual impacts but their synergistic effects.

2. According to an August 1977 Louis Harris poll, 75 percent of Americans would prefer to live in an area with clean air and few jobs rather than in one with dirty air and plentiful job opportunities, and 61 percent believe that modern technology has caused as many problems as it has alleviated (Wolf 1977). This indicates a remarkable change in attitudes toward economic "manifest destiny" and a crisis of confidence in technology to solve historical problems.

3. A "detailed statement" must cover the environmental impact of the proposed action, any adverse environmental effects that cannot be avoided should the proposal be implemented, alternatives to the proposed action, the relationship between local short-term uses of the environment and the maintenance and enhancement of long-term productivity, and any irreversible and irretrievable commitments of resources that would be involved in the proposed action should it be implemented.

4. See Trinity Episcopal School Corp. vs. Romney, 387 F. supp. 2044, 2078 (S. D. N. Y. 1974). North Carolina vs. Federal Power Commission, 533 F. 2d. 702, (D. C. Cir. 1976); Chelsea Neighborhood Associations vs. United States Postal Service, 516 F. 2d. 378, 388 (2d. Cir. 1975) ("human factors" must be considered under NEPA); Hanley vs. Mitchell, 460 F. 2d. 640, 647 (2nd. cir.); Ely vs. Velde, 451 F. 2d. 1130 (4th Cir. 1971); Prince George's County, Maryland vs. Holloway, 404 F. Supp. 1181 (D. D. C. 1975).

5. Coates (1975, 1977) has outlined from 7 to 12 "elements," "components," or "modules" in various articles on TA.

6. As part of the Interagency Energy Environment Program, the EPA Office of Energy, Minerals, and Industry is sponsoring five "integrated technology assessments": Western Energy ITA, Electric

Utility ITA, Appalachian Regional ITA, Ohio River Basin ITA, and National Coal ITA.

7. William Wordsworth, "The Tables Turned." In <u>English Romantic Poets</u>, edited by James Stephens, Edwin Buck, and Royall H. Snow. New York: American Book Company, 1935, p. 18.

> Sweet is the lore which Nature brings;
> Our meddling intellect
> Mis-shapes the beauteous forms of things:—
> We murder to dissect.

8. I Corinthians 13:12.

3

INTERCOUNTRY COMPARISONS
OF ENERGY USE: IMPLICATIONS
FOR U.S. POLICY

Joel Darmstadter

Discussions of energy-conservation potentials in the United
States have frequently taken note of the lower levels of per capita
energy consumption prevailing in other industrialized countries and
have given rise to the assertion—or, at least, the implication—that
these foreign examples validate the case for energy conservation in
this country. A recently completed effort to disentangle some of the
factors accounting for intercountry differences in energy-use patterns
finds that things are more complex than, rhetorically, they are sometimes made out to be (Darmstadter, Dunkerly, and Alterman 1977).
This chapter draws, in large part, upon the contents of that study.

For the United States to manifest what appear to be the energy-
conserving characteristics of, say, an industrialized West European
economy, one or both of two conditions would have to be met. First,
the United States would have to reflect an economic, social, and demographic complexion sufficiently similar to the "model" country to validate the comparison; otherwise, we're comparing apples and oranges.
Second, in those cases in which similar economic or societal activities—say, driving, home heating, or manufacturing processes—are
managed with a lesser energy claim outside the United States, then
the U. S. public, policymakers, or industrial managers would have
to be prepared to take a hard look at, and consider adopting, those
measures governing restrained energy use elsewhere—even though
measures such as higher motor fuel taxes may be unpopular.

ENERGY CONSUMPTION AND ECONOMIC ACTIVITY

Before proceeding with more specific aspects of intercountry
comparisons, let me briefly touch on some basic issues and concepts.

Energy use has tended to show a rather strong, positive correlation with overall economic activity—judging both from the historical experience of different countries as well as from multicountry, cross-sectional circumstances at a specific point in time. But a strong, positive correlation between energy consumption and economic activity by no means implies that a given percentage change in national output is associated with an identical percentage change in energy. The United States, for example, witnessed a steeper rise of energy consumption than of GNP in the closing decades of the nineteenth century and in the early part of the twentieth century. By contrast, for the greater part of the period since the 1920s, U. S. energy consumption, on the average, grew at only two-thirds the annual rate of GNP growth—a phenomenon that, incidentally, accompanied a long-term decline in energy prices relative to other prices.

Apart from the fact that a generally high correlation between economic activity and energy consumption fails to define the respective rates of change ("elasticities") of these two forces, a close look at the quantitative record discloses, moreover, numerous specific exceptions to general trend relationships. These exceptions—dramatically revealed when one compares patterns of energy use and economic activity among different nations—do invite serious thinking about whether there may not be considerable flexibility in future U. S. energy consumption levels, whatever level of national output materializes. The lessons drawn from international experience may thus reinforce judgments about the scope for such flexibility emerging from other evidence and analysis.

Simply stated, America's per capita consumption of energy resources is considerably higher than it is in a number of other advanced industrial countries—for example, France, Germany, Sweden—whose per capita income or output levels cluster within a range not appreciably different from those of the United States. Consequently, the U. S. energy/output ratio exceeds by a considerable margin the ratio in numerous other countries, with the notable exception of Canada, whose ratio is even higher. Why is this so? The importance of the question, as indicated, is obvious. For if something close to the American standard of living were found to be compatible with a fraction of the prevailing level of energy use, that finding could have an important impact on the direction of U. S. energy-conservation and supply-development strategies. The multicountry data shown in Table 3.1 therefore deserve careful examination.

In interpreting intercountry energy/output variability—and particularly in considering the applicability of the findings to the United States—we need to probe the underlying reasons for such differences. Thus, we want to know whether the variability is primarily the consequence of the energy intensity that characterizes given activities within

TABLE 3.1

Per Capita Energy Consumption and Per Capita GDP, Nine Developed Countries, 1972

Country	Per Capita GDP (dollars)	Per Capita Energy (tons oil equivalent)	Energy/GDP Ratio (tons oil equivalent per $ thousand)	Index Numbers (US = 100) Per Capita GDP	Index Numbers (US = 100) Per Capita Energy	Index Numbers (US = 100) Energy/GDP Ratio
United States	5,643	8.35	1,480	100	100	100
Canada	4,728	8.38	1,772	84	100	120
France	4,168	3.31	795	74	40	54
Germany	3,991	4.12	1,031	71	49	70
Italy	2,612	2.39	915	46	29	62
Netherlands	3,678	4.68	1,272	65	56	86
United Kingdom	3,401	3.81	1,121	60	46	76
Sweden	5,000	5.31	1,062	89	64	72
Japan	3,423	2.90	849	61	35	57

Notes: The hydro and nuclear component of primary energy consumption is converted into BTUs on the basis of fuel inputs into fossil-fueled power plants, assuming 35 percent efficiency. Foreign GDPs are expressed in dollars, using a real purchasing-power basis of comparison rather than market exchange rates.

Gross domestic product is the national output measure; it is virtually identical to gross national product for most countries but is the preferred indicator for energy-consumption comparisons, as it excludes that part of a country's income arising from foreign investments and certain other sources.

Source: Darmstadter, Joel, Joy Dunkerly, and Jack Alterman. 1977. How Industrial Societies Use Energy: A Comparative Analysis. Baltimore: John Hopkins University Press for Resources for the Future, p. 5. Reprinted with permission. Some of the indexes are derived from data presented in the table.

36

the respective economies or whether it arises from the fact that there are important "structural" (or "mix") differences among the countries? Aggregated energy/gross domestic product (GDP) comparisons may obscure structural factors highly relevant to the analysis, for it is possible for a country to have a much higher energy/GDP ratio than another solely because of the predominance of such inherently energy-intensive activities as chemicals or metallurgy. Thus, the fact that Canada's energy/output ratio is even higher than that for the United States arises, in large part, from the preponderance of such indus-tries. On the other hand, Sweden's energy/output ratio is lower in spite of a more energy-intensive manufacturing sector.

Both structural and energy-intensity characteristics of an econ-omy may be only the surface manifestations of more deep-seated fea-tures—for example, geography, resource endowment, technology, de-mographic factors, relative prices, and economic policies—to which comparative analysis must address itself. For instance, a compara-tive advantage in steel making (including the ability to export steel to countries lacking that capacity) may have been conferred upon a coun-try through abundant coal and iron ore deposits—scarcely circum-stances betraying energy profligacy. On the other hand, a country's energy consumption may be kept below what it would otherwise be because of such policy decisions as mandatory insulation standards, taxes on motor fuels and on excessive automotive horsepower, or subsidization of public transport facilities.

The comparative findings summarized in Table 3.1 reflect the presence of a number of these elements, which, furthermore, apply in different degrees to various economic sectors of the nine countries included. A few comments on the comparative factors lying behind these aggregate figures may therefore be instructive.

DETERMINANTS OF INTERCOUNTRY DIFFERENCES

When national economic activity and energy use in each country are broken down into principal consuming sectors—residential/com-mercial, transport, industry—it turns out that, by far, the greatest portion of intercountry differences in energy/GDP ratios is due to transportation. Not only are American passenger cars about 50 per-cent more energy-intensive (in terms of fuel per passenger mile) than European cars, but, relative to given income levels, Americans also travel a lot more than Europeans. Indeed, this factor is quantitatively more important than automotive energy intensity in explaining the far greater amount of energy devoted to transportation in the United States compared with Western Europe. To the extent that Americans gener-ate a greater proportion of their passenger miles in urban rather than in intercity highway traffic—as is the case in comparison with, say, Sweden—the tendency for lower U. S. fuel economy is reinforced. (See Schipper and Lichtenberg 1976.) A third contributory element is the proportionately greater share of less energy-intensive public transport modes in the foreign energy mix. These differences are the result not only of the much higher cost (because of taxes) of acquiring and operating cars abroad, but they are also associated with urban density differentials between the United States and other countries and with public policy measures resulting in highly subsidized public transport overseas. From a policy standpoint and especially in a ten- or twenty-year time span, it may be far more promising to work toward greatly enhanced efficiency of automobiles than to strive, in a major way, for the kinds of travel characteristics and mass transit reliance that still prevail abroad. It is worth noting that, in almost all advanced countries except Japan, cars are overwhelmingly the dominant passenger transport mode.

Freight transport also contributes to the higher U. S. energy/GDP ratio. Interestingly, this comes about exclusively by virtue of the high volume of traffic (relative to GDP) that is generated in the United States compared with the grouping of European countries that were analyzed. Indeed, the United States freight modal mix is, more than that of Western Europe, oriented to such energy-saving forms as rail, pipelines, and waterborne traffic. If one argues that size of country and long-distance haulage of bulk commodities (such as ores, grains, and coal) are inherent characteristics of U. S. economic structure and geography, a relatively high U. S. energy/GDP ratio for freight is in no obvious way reflective of comparative energy "inefficiency." In a comparison of freight movement within urban areas only, Sweden recorded less energy-intensive characteristics.

Intercountry differences in industrial energy use also contribute to the higher overall energy/GDP ratio for the United States. The industrial contribution to higher U. S. energy occurs notwithstanding the fact that our industrial sector is proportionately smaller than elsewhere. But the United States exhibits more energy-intensive production processes.

Indeed, if industrial value added were as high a proportion of U. S. national output as it is in most foreign countries, U. S. energy consumption would be still higher. What is true for the industrial sector as a whole appears to be the case in a diverse number of specific manufacturing segments. For example, Swedish manufacturing as a whole and a number of specific manufacturing industries are actually more energy-intensive than their United States counterparts. The paper industry is a good illustration. Within such industries, however, output—product for product—is often less energy-intensive in Sweden than in the United States. This appears to be because technology is newer and conservation is optimized by virtue of considerably higher fuel prices.

It is, however, important to recognize that differences between the United States and other countries in industrial energy intensity need not inevitably reflect differences in the overall economic efficiency of carrying on a given industrial operation. To articulate the relationship between energy intensity and economic efficiency, one would need to explore, in addition to the cost of energy resources, such "inputs" as labor, capital, and nonenergy materials. But the findings, as far as they go, constitute at least a strong presumption that U. S. industrial managers concerned with energy utilization might profitably explore the nature of foreign practices and results.

American households are, relative to income, bigger energy consumers than their foreign counterparts, even after adjusting for climate. In part, this arises from the need to provide space heating (and cooling) for larger, single-family homes. But it is also due to such practices—historically facilitated by relatively cheap fuel prices— as the heating of unoccupied rooms and the maintenance of higher temperatures. Compared with Canada and Sweden, U. S. insulation practices are inferior. Schipper and Lichtenberg (1976) have noted, for example, that at given "degree days" and relative to areas of living space, Sweden appears to consume half as much energy as the United States in space heating.

In summary, a compact list of key factors can be extracted from this range of sectoral findings that operate on and contribute to intercountry energy/GDP variability. This discussion continues to be limited to the United States in comparison with the six European countries combined, since some important elements in the energy/GDP comparison (freight transport, for example) could be dealt with only by using a six-nation European aggregate. We have, moreover, done some rounding and some arbitrary simplification of the quantitative complexity of the analysis. The data in Table 3.2 should be therefore be viewed as an approximate, rather than as a precise, formulation. Yet there is little doubt that these numbers convey the numerical essence of this study, namely, that there is no unique factor that, in quantitative terms, can be singled out as explaining the higher U. S. energy/output ratio. Rather, the 490 tons of oil equivalent by which the United States exceeds the amount of energy associated with $1 million of GDP in Western Europe involves a variety of disparate factors.

Four categories, however, account for more than 60 percent of the energy/GDP variability. In descending rank order they are passenger transport, industry, residential space conditioning, and freight transport. Note also that in three of the sectoral cases shown, the contribution to total energy/GDP variability tabulated in the middle column represents the net item after a balance has been struck

TABLE 3. 2

Contribution of Principal Factors
to Higher Use of Energy per Dollar of Output
in the United States than in Western Europe, 1972

Sector or Activity	Percentage	Tons of Oil Equivalent (per $1 million GDP)
Total passenger transport	28	135
Volume of passenger mileage		58
Energy intensity		52
Modal split		24
Total freight transport	6	30
Volume of ton mileage		75
Energy intensity		−5*
Modal split		−40*
Total residential space conditioning	8	40
Size of units, prevalence of single-family dwellings		30
"Excessive" heating practices		30
Degree-day factor		−20*
Total Industry	20	100
Energy intensity		300
Structure		−200*
Sum of above	62	302
All other (net)	38	188
Total energy/GDP variability[a]	100	490

Note: The West European figures underlying the tabulation represent a six-nation weighted average. Data may not add up to totals due
to rounding. The breakdown in the third column is approximate.

*Negative numbers represent those elements depressing U. S.
energy/GDP below the European ratio.

[a]The figure of 490 is the difference between the U. S. energy/
GDP ratio (1,480 tons of oil equivalent per $ million GDP) and the
West European ratio (990).

Source: Darmstadter, Joel, Joy Dunkerly, and Jack Alterman.
1977. How Industrial Societies Use Energy: A Comparative Analysis.
Baltimore: Johns Hopkins University Press for Resources for the Future, p. 194. Reprinted with permission.

among factors pushing the U. S. energy/GDP ratio above the European ratio (those elements having positive numbers) and those depressing it below the European ratio (those with negative numbers). For example, in the case of space conditioning, the climatic adjustment means that at the colder European temperatures, the U. S. ratio would have been still higher. With the European freight modal mix, the freight energy/GDP ratio would have been much higher. Further, at the European industrial value-added share, U. S. industry's energy/GDP ratio would have been markedly higher (Darmstadter, Dunkerly, and Alterman 1977).

How much of the 302 tons of oil equivalent (or 62 percent) subtotal in the middle and lefthand columns, respectively, can be ascribed with some assurance to intensity factors? It seems reasonable to assume that half of the residential space conditioning component, all of the industrial sector, none of freight transport, and 52 tons of oil in passenger transport are so explained. This amounts to 172 out of the 302 subtotal (or about 57 percent), the balance of 130 tons oil equivalent (or about 43 percent) being accounted for by structural and related characteristics in these four areas of energy use. [1]

This leaves 188 tons of oil equivalent per $ million GDP (or 38 percent of the total energy/GDP variability) not pegged to specific sectors or activities in Table 3.2. This portion of the difference comes from such activities as agriculture, commercial facilities, household uses other than space conditioning, transformation losses, and the utilization of energy sources for purposes other than fuel and power (for example, petrochemical feedstocks and road asphalt). Available data do not permit a precise apportionment of this remaining difference between purely intensity factors, on the one hand, and various other reasons (including structural characteristics), on the other. Our judgment, based on fragmentary information, points to no more than about 30 percent explainable by the intensity phenomenon. If that is correct, combining the identified four categories with the residual energy uses gives a figure of roughly half the energy/GDP variability that is accounted for by intensity factors. Even if the 50 percent share attributable to intensity factors were to some extent an understated figure (see note 1), it is important to recognize that intensity factors alone—that is, higher amounts of energy per unit of activity or output in the United States compared with Europe—clearly leave much of the energy/GDP variability to be accounted for by other characteristics of energy use. One reason this finding is of some importance is that it is perhaps easier (and less presumptuous) to visualize reduced energy-intensity differentials for particular outputs without negative effects on welfare than it is to conjecture about the implications of an energy-conserving change in the mix of final goods and services.

It is worth referring to an alternative method of apportioning energy/GDP differences into the respective contributions of intensity and mix factors. In the previously referred to approach, the results were built up from a separate sector-by-sector analysis. Complementing the sectoral analysis was another approach using input-output, final-demand analysis to get at similar questions in a fashion ensuring a consistent and integrated treatment between energy-using sectors and the rest of the economy. The methodology and detailed findings are discussed in the full Resources for the Future study. Here, it is sufficient to note that the outcome of the input-output work also pointed, unmistakably, to the presence of both significant compositional and intensity characteristics exerting an impact on aggregate energy/GDP differences. The findings of the two approaches are thus in tune with each other.

CONCLUSIONS

Let me turn from these technical and analytical points to a few broader questions. Earlier, I mentioned the impact on comparative energy use of differential prices and taxes, but there are also non-price policy and technological factors to be noted. For example, Swedish weatherization standards for buildings combined with generous mortgage allowances for energy conservation investments have allowed for economizing on the use of heat. In a number of foreign countries, thermal generation of electric power combines heat and electricity production in industries or in communities in which the "reject" heat is used as industrial process steam or "district heat" for multifamily residences. Although the configuration of U. S. locational patterns (both homes and factories) may not be suitable for extensive district heating—for example, because of heat losses in trying to serve dispersed consumption centers—the energy savings from this practice are so impressive that its possible use here deserves a close look.

In the years ahead, new conditions of energy supply and costs, new policies, and new attitudes on conservation and the environment may alter some of the historic U. S. energy-use patterns significantly, such that some of the characteristics of energy use overseas may begin to appear here. More economic automotive practices and space conditioning improvements seem clearcut candidates for enhanced energy utilization. Some notable gains in reducing unit energy requirements in a number of U. S. industrial activities have taken place since 1973. But more appropriate economic signals to energy users are probably a key ingredient in fashioning a U. S. energy picture more nearly like those elsewhere. Certainly, other nations have made much more resourceful use—both prior to and since the 1973 Arab-

Israeli war—of the price and tax instruments that influence energy-associated consumption practices. Generally speaking, the longer the passage of time, the greater the opportunities for substituting energy-saving processes and equipment for energy-intensive practices and capital. In that longer-run sense, even those things that, in a short-term context, may appear to be structurally "frozen" may turn out to be quite flexible. It is worth recognizing that, even where the data point to one country's energy use as more effective than another's, that fact need not define the best attainable practice. U. S. freight transportation, as pointed out earlier, is—overall—less energy intensive than Western Europe's. Yet, U. S. energy intensity in freight might be even lower if, for example, ICC regulations did not dictate an empty backhaul for a northbound trucker of Georgia pecans. Similarly, more economical Swedish heating practices could be still further enhanced if occupants of unmetered apartments served by district heating did not use windows as thermostats.

No tidy final reckoning is possible on the questions I have posed. The research summarized here clearly points to complex and diverse reasons for intercountry differences in energy consumption. Variations in energy/output ratios should not in themselves be viewed as indicators either of economic efficiency or even of energy efficiency. Economic efficiency depends on how energy is used in combination with other resources—particularly capital and labor—and the relative costs of all of these. National energy/output ratios also depend critically on the composition of a country's output and not merely on the energy intensities associated with these component products and activities.

Some of these compositional differences—for example, automotive patterns—appear to be decisively influenced by relative user costs. Changes in these might significantly alter energy-consumption practices. Other notable differences, such as suburbanization, housing, and mobility characteristics—each with marked influence on energy use—might arguably owe some of their historic momentum to cheap energy in the United States and costly levels elsewhere, but they are clearly related to many other impelling forces as well. Whatever their origins, some of these features have become such firmly established elements in American society that it would be unrealistic to expect dramatic change or reversal—even in a new energy-price era. Viewed in this way, energy consumption is, in many of its aspects, essentially a byproduct or, at best, only one element within the wider framework of societal arrangements and choices.

In sum, international experience as well as a reading of our own economic history suggest that the energy consumption required to provide society with a given set of amenities may display considerable flexibility. But thinking that assumes the presence of an energy-conservation ethic and abhorrence of waste "over there" in contrast with the disregard for such things in the United States reflects notions at odds with fact and is simplistic in its view of the world. [2] The need to proceed with energy-conservation strategies appropriate to the United States is too urgent a task to allow ourselves to be too much transfixed by a foreign yardstick that, while intermittently revealing, can also be illusory.

NOTES

1. A somewhat more precise apportionment, recognizing the positive numbers and their negative offsets in the last column of Table 3.2—notably in industry—would result in assigning a greater weight to the energy-intensity component and a lesser weight to the structural component. Such a hypothetical decomposition would necessarily rule out the expositionally attractive device of distributing a 100 percent figure among shares having only positive signs.

2. A number of studies analyzing comparative energy consumption trends and patterns have appeared in recent years. Others are under way. A useful reconnaissance of numerous such efforts is provided by Dunkerley (1978). The interested reader should also be aware of the periodic comparative assessments of member-country conservation efforts and potentials conducted by the International Energy Agency. The latest such survey appears in International Energy Agency (1978).

PART II
SOCIAL AND
HEALTH IMPACTS
OF ENERGY POLICIES

4

INCREASING ENERGY COSTS
AND THE POOR: NEW CHALLENGES
FOR COMMUNITY ORGANIZATION

John W. Hatch and Tony L. Whitehead

During the so-called energy crisis of the 1970s, the cost of fuel and utilities has grown faster than any other necessity (see Table 4.1). While all Americans are affected, those on low and fixed incomes suffer more.

It has been found that while the poor use less energy than the nonpoor (Newman and Day 1975, p. 121), they pay more per unit cost yet have less room for the rapid increase in cost, since the energy

TABLE 4.1

Percentage Increase of Select Consumer Price Index Items, January 1967 to January 1977

Item	Percentage Increase
All Items	75.3
Rent	49.0
Food	83.4
Medical Care	94.1
Fuel and Utilities	94.8

Source: U.S. Senate. Special Committee on Aging. 1977. "The Impact of Rising Energy Costs on Older Americans." Pt. 7. Washington, D.C.: Government Printing Office, April 5, p. 392. Originally published by the U.S. Department of Labor, Bureau of Labor Statistics, Consumer Price Index, January 1977.

they consume is used almost entirely for essentials (Morrison 1977, p. 2). [1] Thus the poor have to make the most critical adjustments in their budgets. These adjustments come primarily from the most vulnerable part of the budget, the food budget. As stated by Archie Gaul, president of the Central Area Agency on Aging in Belfast, Maine, to a special Senate committee on the impact of rising energy cost on older Americans, the accelerating cost of energy will mean a decision by the poor and the elderly in this country to either "heat or eat" (U. S. Senate 1977, p. 249). [2]

Analyses by Herendeen (1974) and Morrison (1977, pp. 2-3), illustrate the following points: all goods and services involve the use of energy either directly or indirectly; necessities such as food, shelter and fuel, which involve both direct and indirect energy use, constitute about three-fourths of the expenditures of the lowest income groups as compared with about one-half or less of the expenses of the highest income groups.

Morrison points out that the greater "income elasticity" of the higher income groups helps to defray the impact of the energy crunch, and he suggests that the very affluent could even gain from the higher prices through investments if profit ratios did not greatly decline (1976, p. 3). [3]

Another way that poor and blue collar workers may be disproportionately affected by the energy crisis is as a consequence of industrial adjustments to the crisis. In order to minimize the cost of production and maximize profits, many industries are choosing to minimize the costs of labor through technological innovations and/or by moving plants to areas in which labor is cheap and environmental quality control is not yet a significant cost item—namely, Third World countries or the southern U. S. Both technology and relocation usually result in a loss of jobs for those with menial skills. Moreover, the rate at which these strategies are employed will only increase as energy costs accelerate.

The energy crisis also affects the ability of the poor to get around—to go "to work, to school, to parties, to supermarkets, to doctors, and to many other places" (Newman and Day 1975, p. 102). The only jobs available to many poor people, who are disproportionately located in inner city communities and rural areas, are many miles away from their homes. Underdeveloped public transportation in most cities and no public transportation in rural areas dictate the use of privately owned vehicles that many of the poor cannot afford or cannot drive, either because of a lack of driving ability or because they can't read well enough to pass the driving test. Moreover, earnings from employment are so low that many of the working poor must hold two jobs in order to survive the rising costs of living (Hill 1971). Places of employment are often in different locations, meaning an increase in transportation costs. [4]

Even while the poor use less energy, their economic situation often forces them into the most inefficient energy consumption patterns. The poor are more likely to occupy substandard housing and to own older cars (if they can afford to own a car), which are more likely to be less efficient in gasoline and oil use. The poor are also less likely to have repairs done that might help to correct these problems, because the cost of such repairs would negatively affect the acquisition of more immediate necessities—particularly food.

SUGGESTED STRATEGIES: PROS AND CONS

Hard Energy Paths

Traditionally, we have tried to tackle our energy problems by simply increasing supplies of energy through centralized high technologies (Lovins 1977b, p. 25), particularly coal-fired electrical power plants and, more recently, nuclear power plants. But as Lovins and many others have pointed out, such "hard technologies" are not only excessively costly, but are also ecologically, socially, and politically risky. It would not only cost hundreds of billions of dollars to continue to build and operate these technologies (Commoner 1975; Freeman 1974; Lovins 1977b, pp. 28-31), but they would also result in a continuous assault on renewable fossil fuels (Holdren and Herrera 1971, pp. 25-50; Illich 1974; Lovins 1977b; Schnaiberg 1975), lead to environmental hazards and massive threats to human health and welfare (Commoner 1975; Fritch 1974, pp. 51-52; Holdren and Herrera 1971, pp. 110-12; Lovins 1977b, pp. 50-51), raise foreign exchange rates in indirect as well as direct energy transactions (Lovins 1977b) and result in increased inequities and tensions among nations (Commoner, Boksenbaum, and Corr 1975; Freeman 1974, pp. 114-37; Holdren and Herrera 1971, pp. 136-38; Lovins 1977b, pp. 54-57, 147-59; Morrison 1976). The prospect of such scenarios has resulted in numerous debates on the broad implications of such "hard" solutions (see Institute for Contemporary Studies 1975; Tavoulareas and Kaysen 1977).

Soft Energy Paths

Conversely, the concept of "soft energy paths," introduced by Amory Lovins (1977b, pp. 38-39) has considerable applicability for the poor, particularly the rural poor. Lovins has outlined four primary characteristics of soft energy paths.

They rely on renewable sources that are always there whether we use them or not, such as sun, wind, and vegetation; that is, they do not run on depletable fuels.

They are diverse in that a number of technologies are used for maximum effectiveness.

They are flexible and easy to understand and use.

They are matched in scale and in geographic distribution to end-use needs; the high quality of wasted energy used to produce a small unit of high quality energy by "hard energy" sources is reduced considerably under soft path techniques.

While Lovins' scheme is appealing and pragmatic, it represents a theoretical conceptualization of methods that have long been used by rural and poor people. People not having access to centralized heating, or even to electricity, have often had to rely on pluralistic energy sources such as the sun, vegetation, wind, and water as well as on other continuous energy sources such as hardened animal and human fecal waste. Urbanization and industrialization have, however, disrupted these patterns through introducing new and sophisticated technologies and/or by reducing the value attached to traditional energy sources.

Despite its advantages, however, there is a possible danger to the poor if Lovins' scheme is adopted without controls on costs. Traditional methods, long depended on by people of low income, will be lost to that economic group if these methods are adopted by the wider society. This is already becoming a problem in North Carolina, where wood has traditionally been a popular means of home heating (Sidbury and Clarke 1978). Conservation and wood-burning heaters have become very popular among the nonpoor, resulting in at least one wood supplier who caters exclusively to the nonpoor. His reasoning is that the higher-income consumer has the ability to purchase larger amounts of wood at a time and to pay cash on delivery. The use of wood as an energy source for industry is also being given a very high priority in North Carolina (Bresee 1978).

This increase in demand will most assuredly be followed by an increase in cost. In fact, wood, coal, and intrastate gas prices have generally increased more rapidly than the price of electricity (U. S. Federal Energy Administration 1976). In Orange and Chatham counties of North Carolina, the cost of wood has doubled since 1974. All of this, of course, has resulted in availability problems for some low-income consumers. Based on spot checks in three North Carolina counties and one Mississippi county, the cost of wood tends to fluctuate more than any other energy source, in part because wood merhants are usually small operators whose capital assets are limited to a pickup truck and chainsaw and who market wood on a part-time basis. When the senior author (Hatch) asked one elderly woman why she did not convert to another source of heating since the price of wood, by her account, was at best equal to the cost of more reliable sources of energy, her response was that she could regulate fuel for the wood stove, while a company was the ultimate regulator of other heat sources. Several other elderly users expressed reluctance to use other sources, fearing explosions, fire, and electrocution. These people said they had always used wood. Yet, of all the energy sources, wood was less readily available and its cost least stable. Nevertheless, whatever the source of energy, one condition was constant: the cost had increased since 1973.

Conservation

It seems that the only action government, regulatory agencies, energy merchants, energy scholars, and citizen groups agree upon is one exhorting consumers to conserve. Aside from tips on beneficcial patterns of personal behavior and the most efficient use of energy converters, however, most forms of conservation cost money. The consumer is informed that a tightly constructed, properly insulated dwelling with storm windows and doors will be more energy efficient. Cost benefit from each action is outlined and investment recovery schedules are estimated. Heating equipment companies recommend proper maintenance and adjustment of equipment as essential to economic operation. While such advice may be very beneficial to those who can afford to take advantage of conservation tips, such measures are often lost on lower income populations. The poor are disproportionately located in inner-city communities, small towns, and rural areas where the percentage of substandard and dilapidated housing is substantial. Fewer housing units are centrally heated, and maintenance is more likely to be neglected. Frequently, the poor rent their housing, and it is difficult to convince landlords that they could improve their properties without personal cost. If the tenants take it upon themselves to make the improvements, not only are they likely to bear the cost, but they might even find their rent increased. Moreover, as Krieger (1970) implies, if conservation strategies become policy, the poor would experience even graver circumstances if some means were not also made to help them absorb the costs of conservation techniques. But even with such economic boosters, any gains that might be made through conservation would be quickly absorbed by continually accelerating energy costs. In any event, while intelligent policies and practices of conservation are necessary, conservation alone is not the answer.

Restructuring Rate Schedules

One of the most popular and logical suggestions for reducing in-equities in energy cost is to restructure rate schedules. As was stated earlier, the pricing policy in most states is based on a declining block structure in which the more energy you buy, the less you pay per unit. Hence industries and other large energy users pay the least per unit of energy consumed, while lower income households pay the most.

Redesigning rate structures to offer more equitable pricing should ideally bring energy cost reliefs to consumers and may even secure industrial compliance to conservation goals, but the imple-mentation of rate restructuring policies alone may not, in the long run, effectively help lower income consumers. As was stated earlier, the additional cost of energy to industry would eventually be passed on to the consumer both through higher prices and through layoffs, industrial migrations, and other adjustments to rising costs. More-over, whereas the restructuring of rate schedules might initially help consumers supplied by utility companies, those dependent on coal, fuel oil, and wood would not benefit from such changes.

Relief Programs

There have been other federal and local actions taken to relieve energy costs to the poor, but these programs often suffer from insuf-ficient funds, get bogged down in local politics, and/or have problems reaching those with the greatest need. To illustrate this point, it is worth examining the Emergency Energy Program (EEP) of the Joint Orange and Chatham Counties (North Carolina) Community Action Program. [5] During the winter of 1976/77, less than half (49 percent) of the 741 families requesting support for assistance in fuel costs were considered eligible for assistance, and then only a $50 maximum per family was allotted to those eligible, as the program was trying to stretch its minimal funds to benefit as many people as possible. For those families needing more money to see them through the win-ter, problem-solving processes including public welfare services, local charities, and other community resources had to be activated. The EEP also has a winterization program, whose primary benefici-aries have been retired homeowners. This program is presently funded at only $25,000 per year. Since average cost per intervention is approximately $400, only sixty-two homeowners could receive en-ergy beneficial improvements during the winter of 1977/78. Yet 307 of the 8,781 homes in the service area are classified as substandard. Most of these are deficient in standards related to energy efficiency. Moreover, those in greatest need—working-poor homeowners and renters—do not benefit from the winterization program. Although community development funds can be directed toward improving heat retention characteristics of housing and the U. S. Farm and Home Administration (FHA) can make low interest loans and, in some situations, offer grants to be used by low income rural families, action taken varies widely and seems related more to the sensitivity and values of the local administrator of the program than to need. In Chatham County, North Carolina, persons with poor credit ratings are excluded from both the loan and the grant programs. It appears that the better-off poor—those who have managed to become homeowners and who have good credit records—are given priority by programs especially designed to meet the needs of poor people.

From interview data of EEP applicants, it appears that most applicants were not aware that utility companies are able to average payments over a 12-month period. Many of these families had reduced their expenditures for food (and food stamps), the most flexible part of home budgets, in an attempt to pay full, partial, or fixed obligation payments for fuel. When such cutbacks in food bills were not enough, other bills went unpaid, including fuel bills. Thus, when most people came to the attention of the EEP staff, they were also delinquent in other accounts. This delinquency in the payment of bills is then considered a cause for disqualification from the FHA loan program.

A final reason that these types of programs do not reach many low income consumers is because consumers themselves see such programs as charity, and many are too proud to accept charity.

The Need for Holistic Strategies

It appears that no single strategy for the energy crisis will work, particularly in regard to the problems of the poor. Strategies must be multifaceted or holistic in nature. Such a holistic program has been suggested by Newman and Day (1975, pp. 195-98) and includes such items as the following:

The introduction of a flat rate structure so that all consumers of energy, that is, those who use less energy and those who use excessive amounts, would pay a constant price per unit.

The introduction of a peak-load pricing system that would make energy costlier at times of higher demand and reduce energy requirements at peak periods, thereby reducing the need for large increases in the number of power plants, holding down costs, and passing the savings on to the consumers.

The support of research to improve the energy efficiency of appliances.

The utilization of technical research results to discover and refer for prosecution manufacturers of major appliances that make products found to be below established limits of performance.

Encouraging legislation that would provide the buyers of all cars, both used and new, with information about car weight and miles per gallon of gasoline.

Encouraging a tax for all cars of more than 2,750 pounds, which would then be used for a public transit fund.

Encouraging the expansion of FHA loan programs to include incentives for the rehabilitation and repair of low and moderate value existing homes with special emphasis on conservation; the building of lower- and middle-income housing (apartments and single-family dwellings) whose designs take energy conservation into account.

Further, Lovins' soft paths solution should be encouraged, accompanied by price control policies that would protect the consumer, particularly the lower income consumer.

While the authors agree with such holistic policies as outlined, we also believe that the dramatic changes that such policies would hope to achieve are highly unlikely without some form of organization on the part of the consumer. Lower income groups must surely organize if their concerns are to be heard and implemented. We suggest three organizational strategies: lower income consumer participation in policy planning; locality development; and consumer education. [6] In each case, community organizers or persons dedicated to the objectives of community organization are necessary to successfully implement these strategies.

COMMUNITY ORGANIZATION STRATEGIES

Consumer Participation in Policy Planning

If the interests of the poor are to be voiced in energy policy, there must be greater representation of the poor in those areas in which policy is made. The poor must not only form pressure and lobbying groups to affect legislative policies, but there must also be a restructuring of decision-making bodies. More consumers must be included in federal and state utility commission boards, while representatives from the energy industry must be dropped because of the great possibility of conflicts of interest (Newman and Day 1975, p. 196).

The inclusion of the poor in decision-making bodies must be beyond utility commission boards, however, because energy affects other areas of life besides energy utilization. For example, energy development and production affects the environment and health. Such important health policy areas as Health Systems Agencies and State Health Coordinating Councils should be encouraged to adopt energy-related policies as an integral part of their plans and programs. [7] At the local level, consumer participation is needed on public health boards; on those planning departments that distribute Housing and Urban Development, community action, and other community development funds; and on such primary governmental agencies as city councils, county commissions, and councils of government. Finally, the participation of low-income persons on the boards of those institutions involved with lending money for energy related purposes should be considered.

Locality Development

Locality development refers to the development or strengthening of resources that already exist in a neighborhood or community. Generally, in studies on the poor, very little attention is paid to the coping mechanisms that already exist. There are few studies that help to identify those strategies that help people with few resources to survive. Scholars have long written about the social disorganization and pathologies of the poor, but we have only very recently become interested in those behavioral and structural patterns exhibited by the poor that have facilitated their survival in economically harsh social environments. Similarly, we know very little about how poor people generally deal with the energy crisis. The authors have observed, however, that economically marginal people in many parts of the world utilize a broad range of methods in taking care of individual and family energy problems. [8] Moreover, there are usually persons who are experts in these lay methods in rural communities and neighborhoods. These are people who might be very knowledgeable, for example, about the range of traditional energy resources available to the community or how to build and/or repair energy efficient homes with scarce resources or who are known in the community as cheap sources of transportation for hire. [9] The community organizer must identify these local resources and enhance their contribution to the community by expanding the number of people they serve. When these local resources themselves cannot be used, their methods can be taught to others.

Community organizers can assist in the development of community and/or neighborhood support groups. These people can learn from one another as well as develop a "resource bank" in which skills related to energy efficiency can be exchanged. These locality development groups may even want to develop a savings or credit union from which members might borrow money for energy concerns. Such groups might also develop car pools or jitney services to defray transportation costs.

Consumer Education

Consumer education is necessary to both of these strategies. In order for lower income consumer participation on policy boards to be a success, board training for all board participants is a vital necessity. In the past, the relationship between nonpoor and poor members has frequently been that of patron and client. These traditional patterns make communication and trust difficult. Lower income board participants might feel that the nonpoor members represent traditional policymakers who are unaware of their needs and who have dominated the planning arena at their expense. The nonpoor, on the other hand, might continue to perceive and treat the poor as too unsophisticated for rational decision making—frequently making demands that cannot be met (Greer 1976, pp. 56-58).

The primary objective of board training would be to socialize professional, nonpoor board members in the principles of democracy and equity by stressing the need for a greater sensitivity to the existence of, and reasons for, conflict and lack of communication; and to socialize lower income members in the history, terminology, and implications of energy utilization and costs. Without such training, goals of equity and fairness would be very difficult to achieve (Steckler, Phillips, and Burdine 1977, p. 23).

Consumer education is also important in locality development strategies. There are three areas of educational need: the education of the general lay public about the correct utilization of energy sources; the recruitment of lay experts and the enhancing of their skills; and either assisting the lay experts in expanding their clientele or diffusing those skills among larger numbers of people.

Educating the lay public about the correct utilization of energy sources is important not only for efficient energy use, but also to ensure the safe use of energy. Wood, coal, oil, and gas heaters are still commonly used energy converters in most rural areas and even among many of the urban poor. The regulation and testing of these types of converters leaves a lot to be desired and are frequently not suited to meet home heating needs (Blocker et al. 1961). Moreover, little information is available on the safety characteristics of some units, and this is usually disregarded by the purchaser when installing the units. These factors all contribute to the fact that the burn morbidity and mortality rate is from three to four times higher among the rural poor than among higher income and better educated families in the same region (Oglesbay 1967; Blocker et al. 1961). The situation is not much better in urban areas. Out of 40,000 oil heater users in Boston in 1960, 15 inner-city residents died as a result of oil heater explosions and another 16 were seriously injured (Brown 1961). All units had been approved by insurance underwriters. We believe that stricter manufacturing legislation, both in terms of energy efficiency and safety, and programs of consumer education would help to alleviate these problems.

Consumer education programs should also work to enhance those skills and resources that people already have. Local structures should be developed and organized for mutual support. Local "lay experts" should be identified and recruited for group leadership, and their skills should be enhanced through some program of specialized training. They would be expected to train the members of the mutual support structures, who would pass on this knowledge to the wider community through various personal networks. In addition to providing information that is directly related to energy efficiency and safety, such training programs should focus on developing the skills necessary to maintain and preserve these support structures, including the skills required to procure external resources.

SUMMARY

At present, we know that poor people and those near poverty are disproportionately affected by rising energy costs. Increases in the cost of home heating, cooking, and transportation took a larger percentage of their budgets than of those of others even before the crisis. At the same time, readjustments by industry to accommodate the rising cost of energy have disproportionately decreased the number of unskilled jobs available. Persons in crisis can find temporary relief in most communities, but there is little evidence of a sharply focused national program specifically aimed at those experiencing the greatest hardship.

The homes occupied by poor people are more likely than others to be inefficient in energy consumption. Upgrading the quality of housing occupied by poor people for conservation purposes would be a step in the right direction, but conservation alone will not, in most instances, reduce the severe economic pressure associated with home-use energy cost. In several years, increasing costs appear likely to absorb any gains through conservation.

While other strategies, such as restructuring rate schedules and changing from hard to soft energy technologies, are welcomed, these methods are unlikely to be of much relief to the poor if they are promoted as solitary solutions. We need a holistic program that would include changes at the policy-making level as well as at the local level. Policies should be developed to take into account the concerns of the consumer rather than those of energy-generating industries. Consumer participation on policy boards, political lobbies, and other decision-making or influential mechanisms are a must. But, even these efforts will be fruitless if self-help activities are not carried out at the local level and if training (consumer education) programs are not implemented through consumer participation policies and self-help programs. Finally, activities carried out at the federal, state, and local levels must be coordinated.

Many persons other than the poor are concerned with the impact of energy cost increases on the lives of poor people and have expressed this concern by mobilizing local resources to meet crisis situations. If some of their efforts could be directed toward legislative action at the state and national levels, it might help to create the milieu of awareness and the type of political environment necessary to promote the development of a national energy program that includes provisions for low income persons.

When President Carter urged the nation to consider the energy crisis as requiring a resolve equivalent to war during a public address in 1977, he might have added that some citizens are already involuntary soldiers in the war and desperately need reinforcements.

NOTES

1. In most states, declining block rate structures reward large consumers and penalize low consumers. In order to promote consumption, the more you buy, the less you pay per unit. Thus, industries and the well-to-do prosper by this pricing system, while the poor suffer (Newman and Day 1975, p. 117).

2. Gaul gives an example of a 78-year-old woman in Waldo County, Maine with a total income of $205.40 per month (including Social Security and a veteran's widow pension). In March, she paid $25.93 for taxes, $116.32 for fuel, $5.50 for kitchen stove gas, $9.40 for Blue Cross-Blue Shield, $14.85 for electricity, $7.68 for the phone, and $5.00 for house insurance—a total of $184.68. With the $20.72 remainder, she had to buy food, medicine, clothing, and other necessities of life, as well as to weather any other rise in costs.

3. Morrison defines this income elasticity of the affluent as the ability to give up some luxuries, defer certain purchases, reduce the use of certain items, substitute cheaper necessities, and to further insulate themselves against price increases through wise investments.

4. While visiting his mother in an inner city area of Washington, D.C., the junior author (Whitehead) was surprised to find so many women who work as domestics by day in the suburbs of Maryland and

Virginia (two hours from home by bus, one and a half by car) and who came back to a second job in the city at night.

5. The objectives of this program are to financially assist low income persons facing crisis situations due to the increased cost of heating, to provide energy conservation consultation to all low income families, and to assist poor and modest income homeowners in making their homes more fuel efficient. Funds are from U. S. Farm and Home Administration grants and low interest loans from the North Carolina Council on Aging. Labor for home improvement is provided by the Comprehensive Employment and Training Act programs. These types of funding are nationally available but must be requested by local community action agencies, churches, civic organizations, and charitable groups.

6. Two of the components of this scheme—locality development and policy planning—are described by Rothman (1970). Rothman does not include consumer education as a major area, however, and we believe that the third part of his model, social action, overlaps greatly with the other two parts and need not be included here.

7. Many of these programs, such as Health Systems Agencies, are required by law to have consumers included in the decision-making process. We thank Allan Steckler, our colleague, for sharing his ideas on the points made here.

8. Field experiences of the authors include West Africa, the Caribbean, the Middle East, the People's Republic of China, and both the urban northern and the rural southern United States.

9. In most developing countries in which only a few people own private cars, owners of private cars put them on the streets as "shared taxis." In a number of cities in the United States, some individuals in inner-city neighborhoods use their cars, called jitneys, in a similar fashion, although they may not have licenses to provide such services.

5
ASSESSING THE SOCIAL IMPACTS
OF ENERGY CONSERVATION

Marvin E. Olsen

Ten years ago, the term "energy conservation" was virtually unknown to the public or to political leaders—or to social scientists. Today, it is a common topic of household conversation, community discussion, political debate, and social science research in the United States and most other industrial nations. Conservation will not provide the final solution to our current energy crisis, caused by overdependence on nonrenewable fossil fuels. Nevertheless, two facts are becoming abundantly clear. First, the United States wastes an enormous amount of energy—estimated to be as much as one-third of its total national energy consumption—that could be saved through effective conservation programs (Schipper and Lichtenberg 1976). The situation is not so extreme in other countries, but opportunities for saving substantial amounts of energy can easily be identified in every sector of every industrial society. Second, energy conservation is the cheapest and easiest means of coping with the current energy situation and of acquiring vitally needed time in which to develop new energy technologies that use renewable resources.

Consequently, it is no longer a question of "should we implement energy conservation programs?" but, rather, "how can we best implement such programs?" and "what will be their social and economic impacts on society?" In a recent survey conducted in Seattle, Washington, for example, 90 percent of the respondents agreed with the statement: "Greater energy conservation must be a vital goal for American society for the rest of this century" (Olsen and Cluett 1978). To date, however, most research and policy writings on energy conservation have focused largely on technological aspects of the problem, assuming that a "technical fix" approach would provide an adequate solution. Relatively little attention has been given to social aspects of energy conservation, and only recently have we begun to realize that, of all the major barriers to implementing energy conservation, "none are strictly 'technical' impediments. The barriers are social, political, economic, and institutional" (Canfield and Sieminski 1975, p. 324).

The purposes of this chapter are to examine the potential for implementing energy conservation in the United States, to review the kinds of social impacts that extensive energy conservation might produce during the next 20 years, and to suggest some ways of studying and predicting these social impacts of energy conservation.

CONCEPTUALIZING ENERGY CONSERVATION

Conservation Definition

Energy conservation can be defined as lowering the rate of energy consumption, as a consequence of either more technically efficient use of energy or of decreased demands for energy usage. It can occur in all sectors of energy consumption, although most conservation efforts thus far have focused on the personal consumption sectors of residential and transportation use, which account for about one-third of all energy consumed in this country. Considerably less attention—in both the professional literature and in President Carter's energy policy—has been given to industrial, commercial, agricultural, and military uses of energy, although these sectors together account for approximately two-thirds of all energy consumption.

Levels of Conservation

This definition refers to lowering the level of consumption, but it does not specify what that lower level should be, since that is a variable policy decision. Alternative goals for energy conservation programs follow:

The rate of growth in energy consumption per capita (6 percent per year from 1950 to 1972 and about 4 percent since then) could be slowed but not eliminated. This is the goal of President Carter's proposed national energy policy, which aims at an energy growth rate of 2 percent per year. It is similar to the "technical fix" scenario of the Ford Foundation's Energy Policy Project (1974).

Or total national energy consumption could be maintained at approximately its current level (74 quadrillion BTUs per year). As described by the Energy Policy Project, this scenario would represent a "steady state" of neither growth nor contraction in energy consumption. If it were maintained in spite of continued population growth, per capita consumption would actually decline somewhat.

Finally, total national consumption of energy could be slowly reduced each year until some specified consumption level were reached. We might aim to match the per capita rate of other highly industrialized societies, about half of ours, or we might be content to remain at some intermediate level of consumption.

POTENTIAL FOR ENERGY CONSERVATION

Since the 1973/74 oil embargo, a number of social science research efforts have focused on social aspects of energy conservation.[1] Most of this work has been only exploratory and descriptive in nature, which is to be expected as a new field of inquiry is first explored, but we have learned a good deal about the potential for energy conservation in this society from these works.

Research Findings

In broad terms, these studies have found, "There have been pervasive but modest efforts at energy conservation on the part of most segments of the public. However, these efforts have not yet gone beyond saving a bit here and there" (Murray et al. 1974). More specifically, the following empirical generalizations concerning the practice of energy conservation in the United States have been fairly well substantiated.

Most people understand the essence of the energy problem. A national survey conducted in April 1976 found that 58 percent of the population responded to the question, "What is your understanding of what the energy problem is all about?" with responses such as "Demand is greater than supply," "Natural resources are being used up," "Energy is being used wastefully," or "U. S. dependence on foreign oil supply." In addition, another 23 percent of the people gave relevant but less precise responses such as "Need to conserve energy," "High costs of energy," or "Haven't developed alternative fuels" (Milstein 1977; Olsen and Goodnight 1977).

Belief in the reality of the energy crisis is fairly widespread. Although figures for the percentage of people believing in the reality of the energy crisis have varied widely among studies, at least half the U. S. population apparently believes that this country faces a serious long-term energy problem (Milstein 1977; Olsen and Goodnight 1977). And that proportion may be increasing, as indicated by a 1978 survey in Seattle, Washington, in which 77 percent of the respondents agreed, "There is a serious energy shortage in the United States at the present time." Further, 81 percent believed that such a shortage would occur within the next 10 to 15 years (Olsen and Cluett 1978).

Most people say they have taken some minimal conservation actions. Following the 1973/74 oil embargo, at least three-fourths of the public reported reducing their levels of home lighting and heating somewhat, and about two-thirds of the population said they drove less, although the actual amounts of reduction were not specified in most of these studies (Olsen and Goodnight 1977). In general, these actions required rather minimal effort and expense and did not significantly alter people's lifestyles. A national survey conducted in January 1976 found that more than half the respondents were making an effort to turn out lights when leaving a room (Milstein 1977), and another national survey conducted during the winter of 1977 reported that one-third of the people claimed to have turned down their furnace thermostats (Harris 1977). However, the latter survey also discovered that the average daytime temperature in all the homes surveyed was still 70° F, which suggests that many people may tend to exaggerate the extent of their conservation actions. Finally, in the 1978 Seattle survey, approximately half the respondents said they had turned down the temperatures on their hot water heaters, and a similar proportion said they had added caulking and weatherstripping to their doors and windows (Olsen and Cluett 1978). Again, however, these practices require only minimal effort and may have been exaggerated.

People are just starting to take major conservation actions. Following the 1973/74 oil crisis, fewer than 10 percent of respondents said they had added storm windows or doors to their homes, installed additional insulation in their homes, or changed their home heating systems (Olsen and Goodnight 1977). The 1976 national survey mentioned earlier reported that only 10 percent of all workers were participating in carpools and that 8 percent were riding public transportation to work (Milstein 1977). During the past year or two there may have been a considerable increase in major conservation actions, however, since half the homeowners in the 1978 Seattle survey claimed to have added additional insulation in their attics, and nearly one-third of them said they had put plastic or glass storm windows on their homes (Olsen and Cluett 1978). Similarly, a national poll conducted in January 1978 found that half of the homeowners said they had added some insulation to their homes (Gallup 1978).

Acceptance of proposed conservation measures is fairly widespread. Surprisingly large numbers of people say they would accept a wide variety of energy conservation measures in the future if that were necessary. The following examples illustrate these acceptance levels: have the government set energy conservation standards for buildings, cars, and other equipment that all builders and manufacturers would be required to follow, 90 percent; lower the temperature and lighting levels in all public buildings, 88 percent; give tax deductions or rebates to people who add insulation or storm windows to theirs, 80 percent; require a mandatory reduction in electricity consumption, 75 percent; give governmental subsidies for mass transit, 52 percent; ration gasoline and electricity, 39 percent; permit only small cars, 35 percent (Olsen and Goodnight 1977; Gallup 1977). As a general rule, nevertheless, the less disrupting a proposed measure would be to current lifestyles, the more likely it is to be accepted by the public (Gottlieb and Matre 1976; Olsen and Goodnight 1977).

Considering the facts that, only five years ago, virtually no one saw energy availability as a problem and most people supported the prevailing national goal of continued energy growth, these research findings suggest that a rather rapid and extensive shift has recently occurred in American public opinion toward awareness and acceptance of the energy problem. They also tell us that the practice of serious energy conservation has thus far not become a significant feature of American life, although many people appear ready to accept rather rigorous public energy conservation policies if and when they become necessary. We can surmise, therefore, that there is vast potential for greater energy conservation in American society.

European Comparisons

Further evidence for the practicability of extensive energy conservation comes from recent studies of energy consumption in several European countries (Darmstadter, Dunkerly, and Alterman 1977). In particular, Sweden has been extensively studied because it is considered to be as "modern" as the United States in terms of industrialization, urbanization, and standard of living. Its per capita income is equal to or higher than that of the United States, and it ranks above this country on almost all noneconomic indicators of the quality of social life, from education expenditures per capita to housing units completed per capita. Yet Swedes consume only 56 percent as much energy per capita as do Americans (Schipper and Lichtenberg 1976).

These energy savings occur in all sectors of Swedish society. Swedish industry uses only 71 percent as much energy per capita as does United States industry, which is accomplished largely through more energy-efficient production techniques, lower process heat requirements, and multiple usage of energy outputs. Commercial buildings in Sweden require only 77 percent as much energy per capita as do American buildings, as a result of better insulation, stricter construction standards, and lower lighting levels. In the residential sphere, Swedish homes require only 50 percent as much energy for heating and 60 percent as much electricity per capita as do American homes, because of better insulation and overall construction standards, smaller living units, more multifamily dwellings with fewer external walls, extensive use of district heating, less use of electrical appliances, and lower lighting levels. For transportation, meanwhile, Swedes consume only 31 percent as much energy as do Americans, since there is only one automobile for every four Swedes (as compared with one for every two Americans), Swedish cars are much lighter and hence more efficient (averaging 24 mpg compared with 14 mpg for American cars), and most urban Swedes use mass transit for intracity travel. In sum, "Swedish methods of energy conservation . . . would result in savings of 30 percent of the total energy used in the United States" (Schipper and Lichtenberg 1976, p. 1,012).

A similar picture can be observed in almost all other industrialized nations. With the exception of Canada, all consume half or less energy per capita than does the United States. A recent comparative study of energy consumption levels and 27 quality of life indicators in 26 industrial societies concluded that energy consumption per capita was totally unrelated to most of these indicators (Mazur and Rosa 1974). It concludes: "So long as America's per capita energy consumption does not go below that of other developed nations, we can sustain a reduction in energy use without long-term deterioration in our indicators of health and health care, of education and culture, and of general satisfaction" (p. 609). The only exception to this generalization was in the production and consumption of material goods such as automobiles, which are directly related to energy use. Quite clearly, Americans could substantially reduce their levels of energy consumption without lowering overall quality of life, even when the cautions expressed in Chapter 3 are taken into account.

Resistance to Energy Conservation

Many people will undoubtedly resist energy conservation practices as strongly and as long as possible, especially in the extensive manner required by the "energy reduction" goal. For instance, it will not be easy to persuade affluent Americans to shift from an eight-room single-family detached house in the suburbs, with two large cars in the garage, to a five-room townhouse located closer to the city center, with just one subcompact car. Nevertheless, rising energy prices and increased energy shortages, coupled with strong public leadership and judicious use of monetary incentives and legal regulations, could likely overcome most of this resistance within a number of years. And there is some evidence that a sizable number of Americans are beginning to consider altering their lifestyles, partially in anticipation of a coming energy shortage (Elgin and Mitchell 1977; Henderson and Voiland 1975).

POSSIBLE SOCIAL IMPACTS

Although energy conservation would not necessarily lower the overall quality of life in this society, any significant reduction in our energy consumption—especially if accomplished within a brief time span—would unquestionably create numerous problems of transition and adjustment. These would be especially acute for the energy-intensive sectors of the economy and for the individuals employed in those sectors. The "zero energy growth" goal would introduce several economic and social modifications into American society, and the goal of "energy reduction" would require numerous changes in employment opportunities, consumption patterns, housing selections, transportation practices, community organization, and many other areas. In short, energy conservation would certainly modify our national lifestyle—or the patterns of activity and ways of living that characterize our society. Whether these changes would eventually enhance or diminish our overall quality of life—or the extent to which we achieve valued collective goals—would depend heavily on how we handled the transition process.

Meaning of Social Impacts

To the extent that widespread energy conservation in the residential, transportation, commercial, and industrial sectors did produce extensive social change in our society, its social impacts could be profound. The term "social" in this context is used generically to include all realms of human affairs: demographic, economic, organizational, community, familial, political, cultural, and so on. Social impacts are alterations in people's living conditions (or lifestyles) that occur in conjunction with a new policy or program and that are seen as significant social events. Since any social system is constantly changing, a first crucial consideration in analyzing social impacts is to identify those alterations that are direct or indirect results of the specific policy or program under examination, apart from all other changes that are occurring in the system from other causes. A second crucial consideration is to determine which of the changes produced by the policy or program are significant enough to constitute meaningful social impacts for the people involved. Third, although social impacts are often thought of as undesirable or detrimental in nature, they may also be desirable or beneficial. Hence impact assessments must always explore the full range of both positive and negative effects of the policy or program being studied.

Socioeconomic Equity Impacts

The one type of social impact that might result from energy conservation programs and that has been examined in any detail is socioeconomic inequity. It has been well documented that low-income people consume considerably less energy than other people, yet spend a disproportionately larger share of their income on energy (Ford Foundation Energy Policy Project 1974, p. 118). For example, in 1973, poor households in the United States were spending almost 15 percent of their incomes for direct energy consumption, compared with 7 percent for middle-income families and 4 percent for affluent families (Newman and Day 1975, p. 122). Any significant reduction in energy availability would therefore impose the greatest hardships on low-income families. A study of the effects of the conservation measures employed during the 1973/74 energy crisis discovered that they were clearly regressive in nature, so that the poor suffered the most (Schnaiberg 1975).

Raising the price of energy as a means of encouraging lower consumption would also severely penalize the poor, since their level of consumption is often already at or near the point considered a minimum standard of living in the United States. With little discretionary use of energy to eliminate, they would be forced to spend an even greater portion of their limited incomes for energy. More well-off families, meanwhile, do have discretionary energy uses they could eliminate, thereby reducing energy expenditures to an even more insignificant portion of their total budgets (Olsen and Goodnight 1977).

This question of the inequitable effects of energy conservation was examined at some length by Denton Morrison (1978) for the Committee on Nuclear and Alternative Energy Systems of the National Academy of Sciences. He noted, "It is self evident that higher energy prices are harder on those who have less money. . . . Chief among such impacts is the fact that, like regressive taxes which make the poor pay at a higher rate than the affluent, higher energy prices, in effect, take away a larger share of the income of the poor than of others" (p. 165).

And, from a broader perspective, environmental and conservation concerns are almost invariably in conflict with the interests of poor people.

> Environmentalists see a quality of life gain in less energy, while this is not the case for those whose energy

use is low. The clear implication of this is that, if environmental policies are to constrain the growth of energy supply, such constraints will be in . . . conflict
with the interests of the poor unless such policies are
explicitly accompanied by policies to redistribute energy use toward the lower income levels—which is, of
course, the same as redistributing income. Thus, a
simultaneous concern for equity and for environment
has profound implications for social change and for social conflict (pp. 185-86).

To go beyond this issue of socioeconomic equity impacts, we
must turn from empirical analysis to writings that are largely speculative in nature, since little or no empirical data are available with
which to test the validity of most predicted impacts of extensive energy conservation. These writings have discussed a diverse array of
such impacts, however, all of which might well be included within all
future studies of the social effects of energy conservation. The following paragraphs describe 35 possible economic, social, and political
impacts of full-scale energy conservation in the United States that
have been proposed by various writers. [2]

Economic Impacts

Increasingly severe economic hardships may be experienced by
low-income people as energy prices rise, since they spend a disproportionately large share of their budgets on energy, while their level
of energy consumption is often already at or near the minimum necessary for survival.

A continual shift from energy-intensive economic production to
more labor-intensive production, using "intermediate technologies,"
may occur.

Production of material goods, especially those that require large
amounts of energy in their manufacture and/or operation may be reduced, but a steady increase in other kinds of economic activity, such
as craft skills, human services, and professional work may occur.

Extensive short-term unemployment may result from these
shifts in the economy, but there would be full employment in the long
run as most economic activities become more labor-intensive.

Severe economic disruption may occur in some communities
that are presently highly dependent on energy-intensive industries,
since these communities could lose much of their economic base.

A somewhat slower rate of overall economic growth, but still
an expanding—and perhaps more stable—economy may result. (The

Ford Foundation's Energy Policy Project [1974, p. 91] concluded that even with zero energy growth, GNP per capita in the year 2000 would still be more than twice as great as in 1973.)

Prices may rise for many material goods, especially energy-intensive goods whose manufacturing processes require large amounts of energy (such as aluminum and steel products), which would raise the cost of living but might lead to lower levels of consumption.

There could be less emphasis on consumption of material goods, a resulting decline in the advertising industry, and more shared ownership of durable consumer goods among friends and neighbors.

Less nighttime operation by factories and stores might somewhat reduce the total volume of business conducted but would also give people more time for noneconomic activities.

Deemphasis on work as one's central life activity might occur, and new values stressing nonmaterial life goals could emerge.

Housing and Family Impacts

Smaller dwelling units, in terms of number and size of rooms, and more multifamily buildings, such as apartments and townhouses, could result.

A lower birthrate and a smaller average family size could result from the decreasing size of housing units.

Population could shift out of metropolitan suburbs into the central city or smaller communities and rural areas.

Extensive collocation of housing with factories, businesses, offices, and stores in relatively self-contained neighborhoods would reduce travel distances.

Cluster housing units, composed of several small family-dwelling units clustered around a number of shared common rooms and facilities, could develop.

Less heating and air conditioning, which may produce some personal discomfort and family conflict over acceptable home temperatures, may occur.

Use of such energy-consuming home appliances as washing machines, dryers, dishwashers, and freezers, may decrease with more housework being done by hand by all family members.

Status equality within the family may result from deemphasis of material consumption and more shared responsibility for housework.

Transportation and Communication Impacts

Personal automobiles may become fewer in number, smaller in size, more expensive, and electrically powered and, hence, would be used much less.

Most transportation within communities could be by walking, bicycles, mopeds, mass transit, people-movers of various kinds, conveyer systems for goods, and so on.

Most transportation, of both people and goods, between communities could be by train, with decreased use of trucks and airplanes.

Reduction in the total amount of traveling could result from greater proximity of housing, work, shopping, and other activities, plus restrictions on both business and pleasure trips.

Multiperson videophones, computer conferencing, and similar electronic communication technologies may enable much work, shopping, visiting, and other activities to be done entirely from one's home, which would further reduce the total amount of transportation.

Two-way mass communications, especially television, could substitute for public gatherings such as organizational meetings, religious services, school classes, and spectator sports.

Mass communications media may become increasingly dependent on governmental or other forms of public financial support as a result of declining advertising revenues.

Interpersonal, Recreational, and Educational Impacts

Family members, friends, and neighbors could interact more on a personal basis as a result of such trends as shared ownership of goods, cluster living, shared housework, less travel, less night work, and so on.

Increased family solidarity and neighborhood cohesion may result from greater interaction and cooperative efforts to cope with common problems caused by energy shortages.

Commercial recreation, especially at night, could decrease with a corresponding increase in personal hobbies and recreational activities.

Massive job retraining programs would be necessary to handle transitional unemployment caused by shifts in the economy.

Education may become a lifetime activity as personal development and avocational activities are increasingly important in people's lives, replacing consumerism and work as dominant social values.

Political Impacts

Urban government may decentralize to neighborhood councils and similar organizations as neighborhoods become more self-sufficient and politically active.

Citizen participation in local neighborhood and community politics may increase as neighborhoods and small communities become more socially viable and cohesive.

Governmental planning and regulation of all spheres of life involving energy production and consumption may increase.

Public anger at the federal government about energy shortages and resulting economic and other problems may occur, followed by much political scapegoating and conflict over governmental energy and economic programs.

New political movements and organizations promoting energy conservation, intermediate technologies, voluntary simplicity, alternative lifestyles, and similar themes may emerge.

Energy Conservation Scenario

This list of potential social impacts of energy conservation suggests that a significant reduction in our level of energy consumption could affect practically every realm of daily living, positively or negatively. This listing does not give an overall picture of what life might be like with less energy, however. For that, we must construct scenarios of possible future societies, which several writers have done. Some of these are extremely pessimistic in tone, suggesting that life would hardly be worth living under such conditions. One example of this genre is an essay by Isaac Asimov (1977, p. 33). The essay—which is dated 1997—concludes with this observation:

> Energy continues to decline and machines must be replaced by human muscle and beasts of burden. People are working longer hours and there is less leisure; but then, with electric lighting restricted, television for only three hours a night, movies three evenings a week, new books few and printed in small editions, what is there to do with leisure? Work, sleep, and eating are the great trinity of 1997, and only the first two are guaranteed.
>
> Where will it end? It must end in a return to the days before 1800, to the days before the fossil fuels powered a vast machine industry and technology. It must end in subsistence farming and in a world popula-

tion reduced by starvation, disease and violence to less
than a billion.

And what can we do to prevent all this now?

Now? Almost nothing.

If we had started 20 years ago, that might have been
another matter. If we had only started 50 years ago, it
would have been easy.

This bleak prophecy of return to preindustrial life could certainly come true. But it is equally conceivable to argue that the quality
of our social life might be considerably enhanced if we were forced by
energy shortages to change some of our living patterns and consumption habits. Let us therefore draw on the Swedish experience with energy conservation to construct a scenario of an energy-conserving
community that would provide many quality-of-life benefits to its in-
habitants. From the studies conducted in Sweden (Schipper and Lichtenberg 1976), we know that energy conservation is promoted when
communities are limited in size and functionally designed to minimize
the necessity of private motor vehicle travel and to facilitate effective
mass transit systems, and when adequately insulated homes contain
less space per person and share common walls.

Each energy-conserving community in our scenario would be
limited to approximately 50,000 people, so that all its neighborhoods
and other sections would be relatively acessible to each other.* Each
community would contain a downtown section consisting of central governmental and administrative offices, cultural facilities, speciality
stores, and other activities serving the total community. The principal functional units of the community, however, would be neighborhoods of from 3,000 to 5,000 people each. Most stores, offices, factories, recreational facilities, schools, churches, and similar structures would be located in neighborhood centers. People would generally live, work, shop, go to school, and carry out most other daily
routines within their neighborhoods, all parts of which could be
reached by walking or riding a bicycle. An efficient and free transit
system would operate among the various neighborhood centers and
downtown, so that automobiles would be totally unnecessary for transportation within the community, and extensive mass transit facilities
would be available for travel between communities. Consequently,
most people would not own automobiles. Rather than bearing the expense of owning and maintaining a car used only occasionally, people

*Most of the ideas sketched in this scenario are developed in
much greater detail by Callenbach (1975).

would find it cheaper to rent a car from the neighborhood rental store when necessary.

Within each neighborhood, dwelling units would be arranged into clusters of approximately 10 units each, housing 25–30 people. Some clusters would consist entirely of units for families with children, some would be designed for couples, some for larger groups of adults, and some for single individuals. But most clusters would contain several different-sized dwelling units to accommodate a variety of family arrangements. A typical dwelling unit would consist of one bedroom per person, a living room, a kitchen-dinette area, and a bath—all relatively small in size. However, each cluster would also contain a number of common rooms, such as a lounge, a television room, a recreation room, a large kitchen and dining room for group meals, laundry and other work rooms, storage rooms, and so on. Consequently, a cluster would contain less volume per person to heat and cool, but it would provide a greater variety of functional areas for its residents than found in most single-family homes.

A cluster might be communally owned by its residents, each dwelling unit might be privately owned as in a condominium, or one person might own the entire cluster and rent out the dwelling units. Regardless of its financial arrangements, however, the cluster would operate as a single functional entity. It would have a central heating/cooling/hot water system, major appliances and equipment would belong to the cluster rather than to individual residents, and purchasing of food and other supplies would be done in bulk. All of these arrangements would reduce the total consumption demands of the cluster dwellers.

This prototype community would clearly achieve the goal of increasing density of living, thereby reducing housing space and automobile travel. The resulting energy savings in consumption of electricity, heating fuels, and gasoline could be enormous. There would also be a considerable reduction in industrial use of energy and other natural resources that would otherwise be required for mass production of durable consumer goods.

What might be the social and psychological consequences of such living patterns? Although we lack adequate empirical data for predicting the full range of potential effects of this proposed community on its residents, studies of partially similar situations—such as Swedish planned communities, American new towns, Israeli kibbutzim, and communes around the world—offer numerous relevant suggestions. A viable neighborhood organizational structure should result in more effective schools oriented toward local needs, more participation in local voluntary associations, increased capability of responding successfully to local social problems, more extensive interpersonal interaction and communication, and greater overall community cohesion.

Cluster living arrangements could provide needed social support for nuclear families, meet many of the social and emotional needs of single and elderly people, free women to participate in the labor force if they wished, and give individuals a sense of belonging to a meaningful social group. These living arrangements should also reduce such personal problems as isolation, loneliness, alienation, alcoholism, mental illness, and deviant behavior because of stronger interpersonal supports and controls and more adequate satisfaction of people's psychological and emotional needs.

PREDICTING SOCIAL IMPACTS

The research on social aspects of energy conservation conducted thus far has focused almost entirely on either the extent to which people are practicing conservation or on the effectiveness of alternative means of promoting conservation (Olsen and Goodnight 1977). There has been much speculation, but almost no empirical research, on the social impacts of energy conservation. This situation is understandable, considering the recency of public concern with energy conservation and the limited extent to which it has been practiced thus far. There simply has not yet been enough energy conservation to have had many significant social impacts that could be studied by social scientists. We can, however, suggest directions that such research might take in the future.

Using Social Indicators

In recent years, a number of social scientists (for example, Bauer 1966) have urged that sets of social indicators be developed and used to measure ongoing change processes. Although economists have long employed such indicators as the GNP, this technique is not widespread in the other social sciences. Social indicators are standardized quantitative measures of specified social conditions that are collected periodically (usually annually) as a time series to describe both current conditions and ongoing change trends. The principal reason for utilizing such standardized, quantitative, time-series measures is to introduce greater empirical rigor, comparability, and temporal awareness into applied research.

My colleagues and I have recently suggested that standardized social indicators would provide an especially useful tool for assessing social impacts (Olsen and Merwin 1977; Olsen et al. 1978). If a common set of social indicators were employed by all researchers studying a particular topic—such as energy conservation—there would be a uniform level of methodological sophistication throughout their research; the results of their studies would be comparable and cumulative; and, perhaps most important, knowledge gained through studies of the impacts of past events could be directly applied to predicting the likely impacts of proposed future policies or programs, since the same indicators would be used for both purposes.

To be most useful as tools for monitoring ongoing change processes produced by energy-conservation practices, these standardized social indicators should be collected and reported for the smallest geographical units possible. Normally this would be counties, which are rapidly becoming the customary units of analysis for impact studies, although, in the case of large Standard Metropolitan Statistical Areas, the entire multicounty area is more appropriate. Collection of data on the local level enables researchers to pinpoint more clearly the causal linkages between conservation programs and their consequences on energy consumption and, thus, to evaluate the effectiveness of such programs. Local data can be aggregated to the state, regional, or national levels as necessary.

Quality of Social Life

Taken by themselves, social indicators are meaningless. They acquire meaning and relevance for social impact assessment only when placed in a broader valuative context. This context is increasingly conceptualized as the quality of social life. Unfortunately, it has no commonly accepted meaning beyond the vague notion of "the good life" or "the general welfare." Perhaps the best we can do, therefore, is to note that all conceptions of "quality of social life" refer in one way or another to what people believe is important in life.

The emphasis placed on this concept in recent years has reflected a growing public awareness that economic growth, by itself, does not necessarily contribute to the overall quality of human social conditions. As expressed in one government document,

> Although the literature offers no consensus on a Quality
> of Life definition, a clear consensus does exist regard-
> ing the importance of the concept. People in business,
> in government, and in the universities are rethinking the
> old tendency to equate a rising GNP with national well-
> being. It is recognized that the paradox of economic in-
> dicators continuing to progress (rising income, increas-
> ing employment) in the face of growing discontent (ghetto
> violence, campus strife, street crime, alienation, and

defiance) must be addressed (U. S. Dept. of Health, Education and Welfare, 1969c).

Despite the widespread attention being given to conceptualizing and measuring "quality of life" (for example, Liu 1975), this notion has not yet been incorporated into the methodology of social impact assessment. Previous impact researchers have frequently implicitly assumed that their assessments should be based on some conception of the quality of life. My colleagues and I (Olsen and Merwin 1977; Olsen et al. 1978) seek to make this linkage explicit by stipulating that the express purpose of using social indicators is to determine the ways and extent to which predicted social impacts will either contribute to or detract from desired quality of life criteria. If the indicators used to measure social changes produced by energy conservation efforts are fully grounded in our conceptions of what constitutes quality of social life, we will be able to directly assess the significance of observed changes as either desirable or undesirable social impacts that should be encouraged or prevented insofar as possible.

Research Goals

The fundamental purpose of social impact research is to enable us to predict the social changes and impacts likely to result from a proposed policy or program—such as energy conservation. To do this, we must determine the patterns, directions, strengths, and temporal sequence of the causal relationships between a proposed innovation and the social conditions that contribute to the quality of social life, as well as the interrelationships existing among all these factors. That is, we need to determine—usually in the following order of increasing methodological sophistication—which factors are related to which other factors, the causal directions of these relationships (both recursive and nonrecursive), regression coefficients for the strengths of these relationships (both unstandardized b's and standardized betas), and the temporal sequences and time lags that occur in this causal process.

Most social science research is still dealing with the first of these tasks, and only recently has any significant headway been made on the second and third tasks. These research limitations can be partially circumvented, nevertheless, by specifying hypothetical patterns of causal relationships in one's theoretical model and then asking the question: If these hypothetical sets of causal relationships did in fact exist, what kinds of impacts would a particular policy or program have on the quality of social life?

Eventually, sufficient research on social impacts and social change processes must be conducted to enable us to express in statistical terms precisely how changes in any given feature of a community or other area will affect all other related social conditions. Only when such regression coefficients become available and are interrelated within complex causal system models will we be able to forecast with any certainty the social changes and impacts likely to result from a proposed innovation such as energy conservation.

A POSTSCRIPT ON VALUES

Social science is never value neutral, and valuative considerations pervade our efforts to assess the social impacts of energy conservation. The selection of factors and trends to be measured and of indicators with which to measure them involves numerous decisions about what is or is not important for the quality of social life. More subtle are the assumptions we make about the direction of measurement with all indicators, determining which direction of change is desirable and which is not. And our evaluations of which expected changes will constitute significant social impacts are largely determined by our social values. Hence we cannot rid social impact assessment of valuative considerations. Nevertheless, social scientists conducting such research can strive to be consciously aware and explicit concerning the value assumptions they make.

Moreover, by grounding our assessments of potential social impacts in explicit quality of life value considerations, we ensure that our research will be directly relevant to public-policy formation. In the case of energy conservation, we can in effect say to policymakers and voters: "The energy conservation programs you propose will have these beneficial social consequences and these harmful effects. To improve our collective quality of life to the fullest possible extent, modify the programs in the following ways." In this process, the social scientist moves from the role of detached researcher to involved policy consultant, in an effort to ensure that his or her scientific knowledge and judgment will be fully incorporated into the formation of public policy. If the potential social impacts of energy conservation are assessed in this manner, the coming energy crisis, now feared, could be used as a vehicle for introducing fundamental social changes into American society. This might greatly improve the quality of social life for all persons in the long run.

NOTES

1. All of this research conducted prior to October 1976 is listed in two bibliographies compiled by members of the Department of So-

ciology at Michigan State University: Morrison et al. 1976 and Frank-ena, Buttel, and Morrison (1976). Much of this literature is summa-rized and discussed in a report prepared for the Northwest Energy Policy Project (Olsen and Goodnight 1977). The results of a series of national surveys of public attitudes toward energy, sponsored by the U. S. Department of Energy, are summarized in Milstein (1977). Finally, a number of papers on social aspects of energy policy have recently been compiled and published (Warkov 1978).

2. Sources of these predictions include the Ford Foundation Energy Policy Project (1974); Henderson and Voiland (1975); Morri-son (1978); Olsen and Goodnight (1977); O'Toole (1976); and Williams, Kruvant, and Newman (1976).

6
HEALTH CONSEQUENCES
OF ALTERNATIVE ENERGY SYSTEMS

Carl M. Shy

This chapter discusses only the health consequences of the two major alternative energy systems available to the U. S. within the remainder of this century—fossil fuel and nuclear. So limiting the discussion to these two systems does not mean to imply that energy in its various other forms (hydroelectric power, wind, tides, direct sunlight, and so on) cannot make an important contribution to our energy needs, even in this century. However, virtually every energy projection forecasts a very limited fraction of total energy being supplied by systems other than fossil fuel and nuclear power before the twenty-first century.

Within the next decade, we will most certainly experience a continuing growth in total energy consumption in the U. S. President Carter's National Energy Plan (Executive Office of the President 1977) calls for vigorous conservation efforts so as to reduce the growth of total energy to below 2 percent annually, down from past growth trends of 3. 5 percent per year. Even under this energy plan, consumption of energy from coal and nuclear sources is expected to double over the next decade. Industry and utilities will be encouraged by taxes on oil and natural gas to convert to coal burning. Coal production is expected to increase from current levels of 600 million tons per year to approximately 1. 1 billion tons by 1985. Even though the president's policy is to defer the U. S. commitment to the breeder reactor, the U. S. will rely on light-water reactors for more electric-generating capacity, adding 75 nuclear plants by 1985. At present there are 63 nuclear plants in operation. Under the National Energy Plan, coal will provide 31 percent of energy consumed in the U. S. by 1985 and nuclear fuel 8 percent, a shift from present consumption patterns of 21 and less than 1 percent respectively (Executive Office of the President

1977). Most of the remaining energy will be derived from crude oil and natural gas.

The significance of these figures, in terms of potential health consequences, needs to be addressed. Increased burning of coal—the "dirty" fuel—and utilization of nuclear power—the "dangerous" fuel—at least imply some degree of risks to public health and safety. I cannot claim the expertise to address the public safety consequences of the use of nuclear power. A number of extensive reports on nuclear safety are available (Nuclear Energy Policy Study Group 1977; U. S. Nuclear Regulatory Commission 1975; American Physical Society 1975). My remarks will be directed specifically to the occupational health and safety risks of the fossil and nuclear energy systems and to the public health consequences of these systems.

In considering the health consequences of energy systems, one must consider potential effects at each stage of the fuel cycle, as shown in Table 6. 1. Occupational hazards are the main concern at the extraction, processing, and generation stages, while public health hazards are largely associated with the generation and waste disposal stages.

HEALTH CONSEQUENCES OF
THE NUCLEAR ENERGY SYSTEM

Since radioactivity is readily measurable and its biological effects extensively studied, it would appear a simple matter to quantify the occupational and public health risks of nuclear energy. Although we know more about the biological effects of ionizing radiation than of any of the chemical pollutants associated with fossil fuel combustion, there are two major reasons for uncertainty in risk estimates. First, most knowledge of human health consequences of ionizing radiation is derived from studies of exposure to very high dose, high intensity radiation. There is a great deal of uncertainty whether we can make quantitative predictions of health effects from these observations to the low dose, low intensity radiation that characterizes population exposure to the various stages of the nuclear energy system operating under normal conditions. Second, nearly all knowledge about the genetic effects of ionizing radiation is derived from animal and insect studies, which cannot be directly extrapolated, at least quantitatively, to human genetic risks.

Information concerning the human effects of ionizing radiation has been obtained from studies of patients who have undergone diagnostic or therapeutic procedures with X rays or radioisotopes; occupationally exposed groups including radiologists, uranium miners, radium dial painters; and the Japanese exposed to the atomic bombs.

TABLE 6.1

Health and Safety Consequences of
Nuclear and Fossil Fuel Energy Systems

Stage of Fuel Cycle	Health and Safety Consequences	Populations at Risk
Mining	Accidents Occupational disease	Workers
Processing	Accidents	Workers
Transport	Accidents	Community
Generation of Energy	Illness and death	Workers
	Malignancy Genetic risks	Community
Waste disposal	Malignancy Genetic risks	Workers Community

Source: Prepared by author.

These studies have been supplemented by extensive animal experimentation.

Risk of Occupational Injury and Disease

Uranium miners exposed to high dose rates from radon and its decay products have experienced excess lung cancers (Lundin, Wagoner, and Archer 1971). Among 3,366 uranium miners followed from 7 to 50 years after they began to work in uranium mines, a 9.4-fold increase in lung cancer, derived by fitting a straight line from origin through observed dose-response levels, was .63 cases of lung cancer per million person years per rem (a measure of absorbed radiation dose) exposure. The risk for cigaret smokers was considerably greater than that for nonsmokers. Extrapolating from these data to the present occupational exposure limit of four working level months per year per worker, we would expect a uranium miner who began work at age 20, worked in uranium for 30 years, and was followed to age 80, to incur an added lung cancer risk of one case per 1,887 miners exposed per year, or .53 per 1,000. For the 620 miners involved in underground uranium mining in 1970, we would expect one excess case of lung cancer in three years. This cancer risk can be placed in perspective against the lung cancer risk of nonsmokers and cigaret smokers in the general population. Doll and Hill (1964) observed a lung cancer mortality rate among nonsmoking British physicians of .07 per 1,000 per year (approximately one-seventh that of uranium miners) and a . rate of 2.27 per 1,000 among smokers of one pact of cigarets per day (approximately four times that of uranium miners).

Risks of accidental death and injury and of excess cancers per 1,000 megawatt of electrical energy (MWe) power plant among the nuclear power work force, have been computed (Table 6.2) by investigators at the Brookhaven National Laboratory (Biomedical and Environmental Assessment Group 1974). These computations are based on the accident experience of the nuclear power industry and on the dose-response relationships for radiation and cancer previously cited. The greatest occupational risk in the nuclear power cycle is associated with underground mining. As shown in Table 6.2, occupationally related accidental death rates are overall nearly twice as great as the risk of cancer; however, the underground miner incurs an equal risk of death from accidents and from lung cancer. Uranium mining shows a health cost per person tenfold greater than any of the other elements of the nuclear fuel cycle. (These estimates are based on an attributed health cost of $1,000 per person-rem, as used by the National Research Council's Committee on Energy and the Environment [1977]).

Risks to the General Population

Somatic risks for general population exposure to low levels of ionizing radiation are obtained by linear extrapolation from effects observed in followup studies of the Japanese survivors of the atom bomb and British patients given radiation therapy for ankylosing spondylitis. These extrapolations were made by the Committee on Biological Effects of Ionizing Radiation of the National Research Council (1972). In each study, radiation dose rates exceeded 1,000 mrem (millirem) per minute, in contrast to projected human exposure to radiation from nuclear reactors that may reach an average of .05 mrem per year in the year 2000, assuming there will be 1,000 reactors in the U.S. (U.S. Environmental Protection Agency 1976).

An increased incidence of leukemia was evident within from two to four years after exposure among the atomic bomb survivors and among patients irradiated for spondylitis. Leukemia incidence rates began to decline within 15 years, but rates still persisted somewhat above that which would be expected 30 years after exposure (National Research Council 1972). Other cancers were found in excess among these exposed populations, including cancers of the thyroid, lung, breast, bone, and gastrointestinal tract. Overall, the committee estimated a cancer risk from ionizing radiation of one case per million

TABLE 6. 2

Nuclear Power Risk of Occupational Injury and Disease
(per year per 1, 000 megawatts of electrical energy plant)

Stage of Fuel Cycle	Accidents		Occupational Disease (excess cancers)
	Deaths	Injuries	
Mining	. 09	3. 50	. 10
Processing	. 05	. 60	. 04
Transport	. 00	. 00	. 00
Reactor	. 01	1. 30	. 02
Waste disposal	No data	No data	No data
Total	. 26	11. 90	. 14

Source: Modified from the Biomedical and Environmental Assessment Group (1974).

person-rem per year, about doubled for persons less than 10 years of age or 50 years and older.

These estimates need to be applied to the situation of continuous population exposure, rather than a one-time event. The committee considered the effects of yearly whole-body radiation doses of 100 mrem/per year on the cancer mortality of the 1967 U. S. population. This radiation dose was chosen because it is approximately equal to the natural background from cosmic and terrestrial sources. These estimates, shown in Table 6. 3, range from 1, 700 to 3, 200 cancer deaths per year. The lower and upper limits are due to uncertainty whether the risk is absolute (that is, a constant absolute increase in the number of cases per rem exposure) or relative (that is, a constant percentage above the expected number of cases in each age group per rem of exposure). Also, it should be noted that the figures in Table 6. 3 are based upon a maximum latent period of 30 years between exposure and complete manifestation of excess cancer. If the latent period were extended to the entire lifetime of the exposed population, the total number of excess cancers under the absolute and relative risk models would range from 2, 000 to 9, 000 deaths per year. To place these figures in perspective, note in the far right column of Table 6. 3 that a total of 311, 000 cancer deaths occur each year in the U. S. population. Table 6. 3 applies to continuous exposure at the rate of 100 mrem/per year, which is 5, 000 times the radiation doses associated with general population exposure to nuclear power plants.

Excess cancer is the only somatic effect associated with occu-

TABLE 6.3

Estimated U.S. Cancer Deaths[1] per Year
Attributable to Continuous Radiation Exposure
(at 100 millirem per year)

Age at Irradiation	Absolute Risk Model	Relative Risk Model	Number of "Natural" Cancer Deaths
In utero	150	110	none
0-9 years	240	800	3,000
10 years and older	1,300	2,200	308,000
Total	1,700	3,100[a]	311,000

Note: This research assumes a latency of from 10 to 30 years between irradiation and development of cancer.

[a]This figure increases to 9,000 if the latency extends throughout life.

Sources: National Academy of Sciences, 1972; U.S. Department of Health, Education and Welfare (1969a).

pational or general population radiation doses that might occur from the normal operation of the nuclear power industry. Other somatic effects, such as the acute radiation syndrome (characterized by bone marrow suppression, gastrointestinal symptoms, radiation pneumonitis) or prenatal deaths, do not occur unless the absorbed radiation dose is at a level between 100 and 1,000 rads, administered as a single dose (Wald 1975). Such doses are well over five orders of magnitude greater than radiation levels from normal nuclear power operations.

Concerning human genetic risks of ionizing radiation, the extensive investigations of children of the Japanese atom bomb survivors have shown no statistically significant effects attributable to their parents' irradiation. Likewise, studies of children of persons exposed by virtue of occupation, therapy, or medical diagnosis have failed to yield evidence of radiation-induced genetic effects. Mutations have been found in human somatic cells after whole-body radiation exposures, but the genetic consequences of somatic cell changes have not been demonstrated.

Almost all information on radiation-induced mutagenic effects has come from animal studies. Mutation frequency increases both with dose and dose rate at high radiation doses. There are no data for mutation frequencies at the low doses or at dose rates associated with normal operations of the nuclear power system. Hence it is necessary to extrapolate from higher doses. Most of the genetic hazard from radiation dose rates at the lower end of the scale of observable effects (that is, doses of between 100 and 1,000 rads at 0.01 to 1.0 rad/per minute) is seen in the male experimental animal. In female animals exposed at low dose rates, the effects are minimal compared with those seen in the male (National Research Council 1977).

In the absence of more precise data on low dose rate effects, there is one useful guidepost—background radiation. Radiation theory tells us that the effects produced by human-made radiation in the range of from 1 to 100 mrem/year will be of the same kind as those produced by the natural radiation to which we and our ancestors have been exposed. It should be emphasized that not all spontaneously occurring mutation comes from background radiation. If anything, background radiation probably contributes only a small part to the frequency of spontaneous mutations. Therefore, if radiation from the nuclear energy system can be kept to a level such that average population exposure is a small fraction of background radiation, we know that the effects will be of a kind and magnitude that should not portend a grave threat to future generations.

Population Exposure to Ionizing Radiation

Sources of population exposure to ionizing radiation are given in Table 6.4. The two major sources are natural radiation from cosmic and terrestrial sources and radiation used for medical purposes. Large fluctuations in radiation dose occur from one location to another and from one individual to another. Population doses from the nuclear energy system are about 0.02 percent of natural background. Even by the year 2000, if 1,000 nuclear plants were operating, population doses would be less than .05 percent of natural background.

These exposure estimates suggest that radiation associated with normal operations of the nuclear energy system does not pose a public health threat. Let me emphasize that this does not take into account safety considerations, such as those related to core meltdown, nuclear diversion, or sabotage. But normal operation of the nuclear energy system, from mining to energy generation and waste disposal, presents some risk to public health, but that risk is relatively small when compared with health risks encountered in everyday living.

TABLE 6.4

Estimates of Yearly Radiation Doses in the United States, 1970

Sources of Radiation	Dose per Person (millirem per year)	Total U. S. Dose (million person-rem per year)
I. Natural		
Cosmic	45	9.7
Terrestrial	60	12.3
Natural radiation in ores, materials, wastes	13	2.7
Subtotal	118	24.7
II. Human-made		
Medical uses	36	7.4
Global fallout	4.0	.8
Nuclear power		
Occupational	.8	.006
Community	.023	.005
Miscellaneous	2.0	.4
Subtotal	42.8	8.6
Total	160	33

Source: U. S. Environmental Protection Agency 1976.

HEALTH CONSEQUENCES OF THE FOSSIL FUEL ENERGY SYSTEM

While the public health risk of nuclear power generation can be attributed to a single agent—ionizing radiation—well characterized in its biological effects, the health consequences of fossil fuel consumption are attributable to a complex array of chemicals that occur as gases, particles, aerosols, and organic and inorganic compounds. We know far less about the biological reactivity of any one of these compounds than of ionizing radiation. And for only a few of the fossil fuel combustion products do we have enough information to draw a dose-response curve of even limited range.

What we do know, however, is that the mining, transportation, and combustion of fossil fuels has exacted a horrendous burden of death and disease in the industrialized societies of the nineteenth and twentieth centuries. It is no exaggeration to state that millions of people have been killed or have died prematurely and that whole populations have suffered adverse health effects in the form of acute and chronic disease, all attributable to the use of fossil fuels. We can only allude to the suffering of children sent into the coal mines of England in the early nineteenth century, to the misery and sickness of coal miners and their families throughout the nineteenth and much of the twentieth centuries, and to the air pollution episodes of London, New York, and other cities even within the past 30 years. Since they have been in operation, the worst nuclear plant failures pale in their effects by comparison with the public health burden of fossil fuel power, a burden that has not been entirely removed.

Risk of Occupational Injury and Disease

Coal mining in the United States has a grim record of safety, which has improved in the past 25 years for two reasons: fewer miners are at risk, and a larger proportion of coal is being obtained from surface rather than underground mining. In the past four decades, 90 percent of fatal accidents in mining have occurred underground (National Research Council 1975). The number of fatal accidents per million tons of coal mined has also fallen progressively since the 1930s, owing to improved mining techniques and increased productivity per working hour. As shown in Figure 6.1, surface mining is clearly safer than underground mining, and these differences hold whether we consider accidents per million tons or accidents per working hours. Of particular relevance to the projected doubling of coal production over the next decade is the observation that less experienced miners run a greater risk of injury (Barry and associates 1972).

Coal workers' pneumoconiosis, black lung disease, is an occupational hazard of underground mining characterized by opacities on chest X rays and chronic respiratory symptoms. Depending on the type of coal mined and the extent of underground mining in a worker's history, from 10 to 40 percent of underground coal miners developed this disease in the years immediately prior to the imposition of a 2 milligrams per cubic meter (2 mg/m^3) dust standard (Morgan et al. 1973). Whether the disease or its progression in a small proportion of afflicted miners to massive fibrosis will be prevented by the coal dust standard is unknown.

Estimates for occupational injury and disease associated with supplying coal for a 1,000 MWe power plant operating at 75 percent capacity have been derived by researchers from the Brookhaven National Laboratory (Biomedical and Environmental Assessment Group 1974). These estimates, presented in Table 6.5, are based on experiences of the 1950s and 1960s. Injury and disease rates may decline significantly if vigorous safety measures are taken and if the coal dust standard of 2 mg/m^3 is achieved and is also protective. Further, a shift to surface mining would appear to diminish the risk to occupational safety and health. Under the president's National Energy Plan, a considerable increase in both surface and underground coal mining is projected. Employment of inexperienced underground miners or mining by inexperienced companies could pose a serious occupational risk.

Extraction, transport, and processing of oil and natural gas have been associated with considerably fewer accidents to workers

FIGURE 6.1

Accidental Fatalities per Million Tons of Coal Mined in the United States, 1907-73

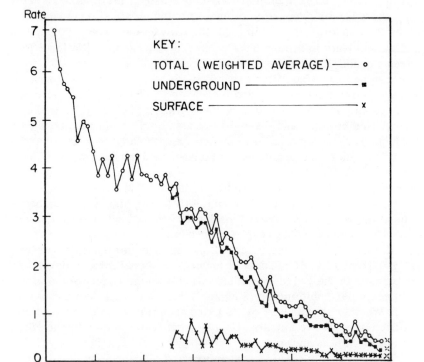

Note: Based on preliminary data.
Source: National Research Council (1975).

TABLE 6.5

Coal-Fired Power Risk of Occupational Injury and Disease
(per year per 1,000 Megawatt of Electrical Energy Plant)

Stage of Fuel Cycle	Accidents Deaths	Injuries	Occupational Disease (Disabled workers/year)
Mining			
Underground	.60	30	.5—7.0
	or	or	or
Surface	.30	13	.5
Processing	.04	3	None apparent
Transport	1.20*	10*	None apparent
Combustion	.01	1.2	None apparent
Waste disposal	No data	No data	No data
Total	1.85 or 1.55	44.2 or 27.2	.5—7.0

*Risk to occupants of motor vehicles rather than to workers in the industry.

Source: Modified from the Biomedical and Environmental Assessment Group 1974.

and with no apparent occupational disease risk (Biomedical and Environmental Assessment Group 1974).

Risks to the General Population

Evidence of the adverse health effects from fossil fuel pollutants has been summarized in the air quality criteria documents published by the U.S. Department of Health, Education, and Welfare (1969a, 1969b, 1970a, 1970b, 1970c) and the U.S. Environmental Protection Agency (1971). More recently, this evidence was reviewed by the National Academy of Sciences (1973, 1975).

The principal hazard to the health of the general population is caused by combustion of fossil fuels with its concomitant emission of gases and particles in many chemical forms. The pollutants of concern include sulfur oxides, nitrogen oxides, particulate matter, carbon monoxide, hydrocarbons, and photochemical oxidants. For the most part, hydrocarbons and carbon monoxide are principally emitted by motor vehicles; hydrocarbons are important in contributing to the

TABLE 6.6

Adverse Effects on Health of Population from
Exposure to Products of Fossil Fuel Combustion

Health Effect	Remarks
I. Acute Effects	
1. Excess mortality in the general population and particularly in persons with preexisting cardiopulmonary disease	Well documented during air pollution episodes
	Apparent, nearly linear relationship between daily mortality and daily concentrations of sulfur oxides/particulate complex
2. Aggravation of asthma	Reported in studies of children and adult panels of asthmatics
3. Aggravation of preexisting chronic respiratory and cardiovascular disease	Reported in studies of patient panels, particularly of elderly persons
4. Nonspecific irritation symptoms; eye, upper respiratory tract, and nose	Most commonly observed effect of short-term exposure to peak concentrations
II. Chronic Effects	
1. Increased risk of death from combined respiratory and cardiovascular causes	Risk estimates based on comparisons of populations in areas of high and low pollution
2. Increased prevalence of chronic bronchitis	Evidence provided in many studies, based on comparisons of disease prevalence in areas of high and low pollution; effect of cigaret smoking is greater
3. Increased risk of acute respiratory disease, particularly observed in studies of children	Evidence derived from many studies of illness rates in areas of high and low pollution
4. Impaired ventilatory function in children and adults	Well established effect found in many studies from Great Britain, United States, Japan, Italy, and elsewhere
5. Miscellaneous alterations in physiological function, biochemical parameters and hematological indexes	Demonstrated in experimental exposures of humans to relatively low pollutant concentrations and in a large number of experimental animal studies

Source: National Research Council (1977).

90

formation of photochemical oxidants. Sulfur oxides and particulate matter are by-products of stationary fossil-fueled electric power plants. The man-made nitrogen oxides are nearly equally derived from transportation and stationary sources.

These pollutants are known to be associated with a variety of acute and chronic diseases of the respiratory and cardiovascular systems. Human responses range from acute irritation of the eyes, nose, throat, and lungs to chronic disease and death. The attention of the medical community to the hazards of air pollution was most dramatically brought into focus by the famous London fog of 1952, when 4,000 excess deaths occurred during four days of intense air pollution. In the previous 100 years, only the influenza pandemic of 1919 had caused as many excess deaths in London over so short a period of time.

The range of adverse health effects attributed to fossil fuel air pollutants is indicated in Table 6.6. Air pollution exposure poses a health hazard particularly to persons with preexisting heart and lung disease. A proportion of these groups—asthmatics, heart disease patients, persons with chronic bronchitis, emphysema, and other chronic respiratory ailments—experience aggravation of their disease states as pollutant concentrations that have little or no demonstrable effect on healthy individuals. There is also ample evidence that young children living in more polluted communities experience higher rates of acute respiratory disease, have poorer lung function, and, as adults, have more chronic respiratory symptoms. Thus it is generally accepted that young children and adults with chronic cardiopulmonary diseases are particularly susceptible to air pollution exposure.

Little is known about health consequences of fossil fuel combustion products. We do not have scientifically convincing evidence that there is a threshold concentration below which susceptible segments of the population will not be affected by air pollution. Illustrative of this lack of evidence is Figure 6.2, depicting the association between sulphur dioxide (SO_2) levels in New York City and 1962-66 daily mortality, adjusted for all the known major determinants of daily variations in mortality (Buechley et al. 1973). The point of the figure is that daily mortality appeared to increase progressively with days of higher SO_2 levels. SO_2 is presented here merely as an index of multiple pollutants related to fossil fuel combustion products. Similar evidence exists for an association between aggravation of disease in asthmatics or in patients with chronic cardiopulmonary disease and daily concentrations of several fossil fuel air pollutants.

There are many gaps in knowledge of dose-response relationships between air pollution and disease effects. The best evidence is provided by animal experiments, which cannot be quantitatively extrapolated to humans. Other good dose-response information has recently been accumulating in several clinical research laboratories in

FIGURE 6. 2

Means of Residual Mortality by Sulfur Dioxide Class
in New York-New Jersey Metropolitan Area, 1962 to 1966
Micrograms per Cubic Meter (1, 826 total days)

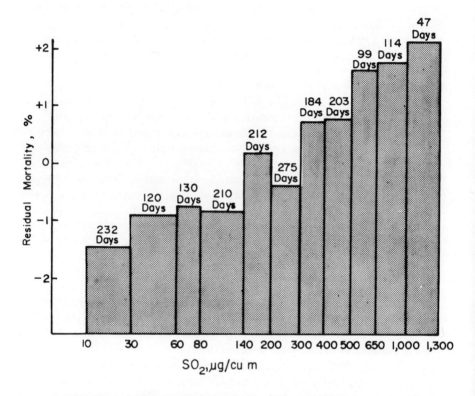

Source: Buechley et al. (1973, p. 137). Copyright 1973, American Medical Association, Reprinted with permission.

which humans are experimentally exposed to different street-level concentrations of chemically specific pollutants. However, these studies are usually performed on healthy young adults; only a few selected acute physiological responses can be measured; and these responses can be related only to pure compounds rather than to the mixture of pollutants as they occur in ambient air. Susceptible population groups in a real-life setting have been studied by epidemiologists, but these studies are limited by the difficulty in measuring the population dose for any one pollutant, by the large array of chemicals in air, only a few of which can be monitored, and by the many coexisting factors that can cause or contribute to the same diseases associated with air pollution.

Many pollutants emitted when fossil fuels are combusted are not ordinarily monitored or otherwise evaluated. These include trace substances, such as arsenic, beryllium, and mercury, and polycyclic organic matter, such as benzo(a)pyrene and numerous coal tar constituents. Some of these compounds, such as arsenic and mercury, tend to accumulate in biological systems and eventually cause severe adverse effects at elevated tissue concentrations. The polycyclic organic compounds are of concern because of their carcinogenic potential. However, most calculations of emission rates from fossil-fueled power plants suggest that trace substances and polycyclic organic compounds do not represent a major public health hazard, particularly when compared with the known adverse effects of sulfur and nitrogen oxides, oxidants, and carbon monoxide. However it is also true that far more is known about the biological effects of these latter pollutants. The toxic trace substances may still be found to be an important contributor to some categories of disease.

At the present time, the health hazards associated with oxides of sulfur and nitrogen appear to present the greatest cause for concern over the projected increase in coal utilization. There is increasing evidence that SO_2 and nitrogen dioxide (NO_2) gas released directly into the atmosphere during the combustion process undergoes atmospheric transformation to submicronic sulfate and nitrate particles. As shown in Maps 6.1 and 6.2, the geographical distribution of atmospheric sulfates closely follows the distribution of fossil-fueled power plants, with a high concentration of both in the midwest and northeast. Sulfate particles remain suspended in air for relatively long periods of several days and in that time can be carried aloft for distances of several hundred miles. These atmospheric transformation products appear to be more toxic than the original gas; they primarily affect the respiratory system, causing diminished airflow through the lungs and aggravation of asthma and cardiovascular disease.

The sulfate and nitrate issues are extremely important in current efforts to assess the health consequences of increased coal consumption. For one reason, achievement of the primary ambient air quality standard for SO_2 and NO_2 does not necessarily protect against the adverse effects of the transformation products of these pollutants. Secondly, while an ambient air quality standard for sulfate and nitrates would be highly desirable, we lack the data base to know whether such standards would protect us. "Sulfates" and "nitrates" are not homogeneous compounds but rather nonspecific anions that, at the same concentration, are known to be more toxic in one chemical form (for example, zinc ammonium sulfate) than another (for example, calcium sulfate). Furthermore, current methods for monitoring atmospheric

MAP 6.1

1970 Sulfate Concentrations, Urban United States
(micrograms per cubic meter)

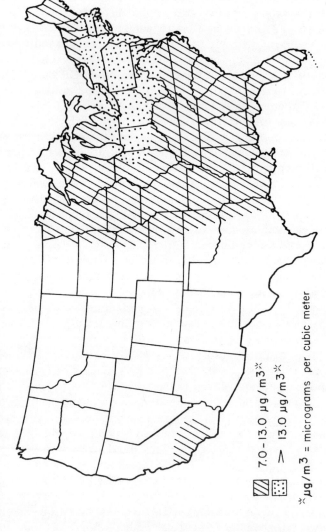

▨ 7.0 - 13.0 µg/m3*

⬚ > 13.0 µg/m3*

* µg/m3 = micrograms per cubic meter

Source: U.S. Environmental Protection Agency 1974.

MAP 6.2

Location of Major U.S. Coal- and Oil-fired Power Units, 1971

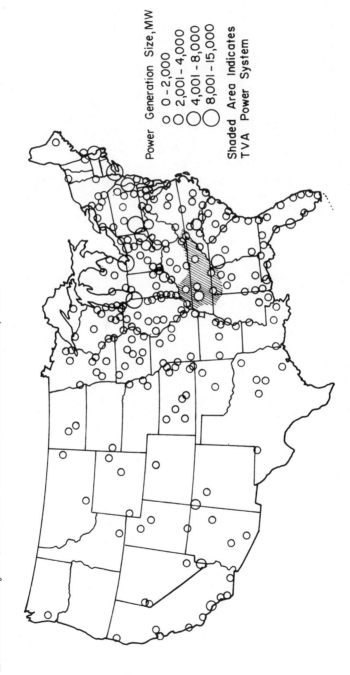

Power Generation Size, MW

○   0 - 2,000
○   2,001 - 4,000
◯   4,001 - 8,000
◯   8,001 - 15,000

Shaded Area Indicates
TVA Power System

Source: U.S. Environmental Protection Agency 1974.

95

sulfates do not provide chemical speciation. Considerable toxicological and epidemiologic research is required to clarify the relationship between atmospheric species of sulfates or nitrates and adverse health effects.

Beyond these public health considerations, we are very uncertain about technological control of atmospheric sulfates and nitrates. A recent report from the National Academy of Sciences (1975) pointed out that there is no direct relationship between control of SO_2 emissions and atmospheric sulfate levels. The transformation of SO_2 to sulfates is accelerated in the presence of an oxidizing atmosphere (which can result from motor vehicle emissions and solar energy) and by certain trace metals in air. Complicating these relationships is the long-distance transport of sulfates. In regions many miles downwind of SO_2 emission sources, stringent control of local emission sources may not appreciably affect sulfate concentrations in the immediate area.

Many estimates have been made of the public health impact of increased emissions of sulfur oxides into our atmosphere, given current pollutant levels. In the National Academy of Sciences (1975) report, Air Quality and Stationary Source Emission Control, the health effects of 1 mg/m^3 annual increment in suspended sulfate levels in the New York metropolitan area were analyzed. An annual excess of from 10 to 50 deaths, 400,000 person-days of illness due to heart and lung disease, 80,000 asthma attacks, and 10,000 cases of respiratory disease in children were associated with the increment. The point of this illustration is not to claim that these projections are accurate but to suggest that small air pollution increments above current levels may result in a large public health burden. There is general agreement within the public health community that sustained increases of existing air quality standards are likely to result in significant disease risks. There is also agreement, though by no means complete, that existing standards are not necessarily protective against all public health risks attributable to air pollution.

CONCLUSION

When we consider the complete fuel cycle—from fuel extraction through conversion into energy and waste disposal—it is apparent that there are occupational and general population health risks even from normal operations of both nuclear and fossil fuel energy systems.

The Nuclear Energy System

Ionizing radiation will increase the risk of lung cancer for uranium miners. At the occupational limit of exposure, miners will be expected to experience the lung cancer incidence between nonsmokers and smokers in the general population. Because there are relatively few uranium miners, this risk does not affect a sizable portion of the population. Nevertheless, miners individually do bear the greatest health risk. Excess cancers are also predicted in the general population from nuclear operations, but here again the magnitude of the public health risk is small because radiation doses to the general population will amount to less than .001 of natural background. Radiation also poses a genetic risk, but, for the same reasons, this risk is small relative to radiation doses from natural background or medical uses.

This assessment of health consequences appears to assign a rather trivial health risk to nuclear power. To the extent that we are evaluating normal operations, expectation of small health risks is appropriate and fully defensible. Concern over the hazards of nuclear power should not be based on health consequences of normal operations.

However, we may have justifiable concern over the possibilities of nuclear sabotage; proliferation of nuclear materials, particularly plutonium that might be diverted to weapons manufacture; certain safety aspects of the transport, reprocessing, and disposal of nuclear fuels; and an excessive exercise of police power that may be required to prevent nuclear theft. Even if these concerns were sufficiently great to warrant a very limited use of nuclear energy, we should distinguish between these rather formidable institutional and sociopolitical barriers and the relatively manageable public health aspects of the nuclear energy system.

The Fossil Fuel Energy System

Mining, transport, and combustion of fossil fuels have exacted an enormous occupational and general population toll in terms of lives lost and disease induced. The public health community tends to agree that present air quality standards, though perhaps very costly to achieve, are necessary for protection of public health. Increased utilization of coal during the next several decades gives justifiable cause for concern in two respects.

First, the air quality standards have not been achieved in several air quality control regions. With the phasing out of poorly controlled emission sources and stricter standards being applied to new sources, we might have expected general improvement in air quality.

However, the national energy plan calls for conversion of many oil and gas fired power plants to coal, and, even with the best available controls, there are bound to be some currently polluted areas that will experience increased emissions of sulfur and nitrogen oxides, with attendant adverse health effects.

Second, atmospheric concentrations of unregulated pollutants, particularly sulfates and nitrates, are a cause for concern. We simply do not have enough knowledge about the determinants of atmospheric transformation of SO_2 and NO_2 into sulfates and nitrates so as to predict what levels can be expected from increased utilization of coal. Emissions of NO_2 are not under good control, from motor vehicles or from power plants. Our country has not pursued a vigorous control strategy for this pollutant class. Yet sulfates and, probably, nitrates are thought to be biologically more reactive than their parent compounds, SO_2 and NO_2. Sulfates and nitrates are submicronic in size and, for this reason, are both transported for long distances and can be inspired deeply into the lung. Some projections of relatively small increases in sulfate concentrations suggest a significant impact on public health in terms of excess mortality and illness episodes. Even if these projections were gross overestimates, the health impact would likely be large because so many people may be exposed to elevated concentrations.

Options for Protection of Public Health

In some ways we are faced with an energy versus public health dilemma. In the short run of from 10 to 20 years, we cannot change lifestyles or implement new energy technologies fast enough to meet the apparent inevitable growth in energy consumption. Our only options to supply this energy, especially in the face of dwindling natural gas and oil resources, are nuclear and coal. While not a public health problem, nuclear energy presents formidable sociopolitical barriers. Coal is an abundant fuel in our country, and we have relatively little choice but to burn it in increasing amounts, probably through the remainder of this century.

Given the potential public health consequences of increased emission of coal combustion products, we need to pursue, as a minimum, a hard-nosed policy of adherence to state and federal air quality standards. Adherence will require costly control technologies, which will be passed on in the form of still higher electricity bills. Technology needs to be pushed beyond present capabilities, to clean up coal before, during, or immediately after combustion. Another economic recession could jeopardize our commitment to these costly control technologies, but the health costs of diminished control should deter us from any reduction of efforts in this regard.

Finally, because of the many unknowns in our assessment of the health consequences of increased coal utilization, we should commit adequate resources to a health monitoring system that will tell us whether we are being protected by our air quality standards. Although the National Energy Plan has affirmed that existing air and water quality standards will not be exceeded, we must recognize that there are unregulated pollutants of concern to health and that "the best laid schemes o' mice an' men gang aft a-gley."

NOTE

1. The expected dose commitment of less than 1,000/person-rem reactor year would correspond to 0.2 cancer deaths/reactor year (Nuclear Energy Policy Study Group 1977).

PART III
POLITICAL AND
SOCIAL CONTEXT
OF ENERGY POLICIES

7

ALTRUISM AND ENERGY CONSERVATION: GENERATING PUBLIC SUPPORT

Elizabeth Martin

Voluntary conservation of energy by Americans is presently seen by the government and by many Americans as essential if the U. S. is to preserve its resources and the environment and to avoid the political vulnerability that arises from dependence on foreign sources of oil. The National Energy Plan (NEP) proposed by the Carter administration in 1977 emphasized the necessity of voluntary conservation by the American public.

> Conservation and fuel efficiency are the cornerstone of the proposed National Energy Plan. . . . Broad public understanding of the energy problem, a commitment to action, and a willingness to endure some sacrifice are all indispensable to the success of a national energy plan. . . . The ultimate question is whether this society is willing to exercise the internal discipline to select and pursue a coherent set of policies well in advance of a threatened disaster (Executive Office of the President 1977, pp. xii, 25).

The energy plan proposed by the administration relied primarily upon price incentives to induce American consumers and industries to use less gasoline. Two measures were proposed:[1]

My thanks to Stanley Presser and Otis Dudley Duncan for helpful comments.

—a graduated excise tax on new automobiles with fuel efficiency below levels required by current legislation, and a rebate on automobiles that exceed the fuel efficiency requirements.

—a gasoline tax to be imposed only if total national gasoline consumption exceeds annual target levels. The tax would begin at 5 cents per gallon and could rise to 50 cents per gallon in 10 years if targets were repeatedly exceeded by large or increasing amounts (Executive Office of the President 1977, p. xvii.)

The authors of the original energy plan were sanguine about the proposed gasoline tax, stating that it is a "highly effective measure for conservation because it affects all cars and all drivers" (1977, p. 38). But is it true that price incentives are the most effective basis for a policy intended to promote energy conservation? Solutions to the problem of how to induce Americans to conserve in the future may be supplied by investigating the reasons they have conserved in the past. A number of factors, such as the price and availability of gasoline, residential location and distance from work, and the availability and cost of gasoline-efficient cars undoubtedly influence gasoline consumption. This chapter explores the additional possibility that conservation may be motivated by altruism. That is, Americans may conserve energy because they are concerned about preserving energy resources and the environment for present and future generations.

The extent to which energy conservation is or can be motivated by altruistic concerns is not known. Indeed, the determinants of public altruism in general are not well understood. Since we do not understand the reasons why people sometimes sacrifice freedom and comfort for the greater good, we do not know how to induce them to do so more often. In the absence of knowledge, it is tempting to ignore or reject altruistic motives for public-minded behavior and to base policies upon the assumption that humans single-mindedly pursue narrow economic self-interest. So, for example, one author concludes, "We cannot instill in Americans an energy conservation ethic as such because people are not interested in saving energy for its own sake. Nor will they save out of patriotism or concern about their progeny. The chance to save money is the most effective incentive in inducing a consumer to save energy" (Milstein 1976, p. 9).

Are the cynicism about public altruism and the faith in monetary incentives expressed by this author warranted? Available evidence supports neither the premise that price incentives are highly effective nor the premise that "altruistic motives" are negligible. The next section of this chapter reviews analyses of the effects of price changes upon demand for one energy source, gasoline, during the 1973/74 Arab oil embargo. Then experimental studies are used to derive hypotheses about the altruistic determinants of energy conservation.

These are tested, using national data on gasoline conservation during the 1973/74 oil embargo. The available evidence cannot be used to compare the relative importance of different determinants of gasoline use—price changes, constraints on availability, and altruism—but the evidence does support the proposition that energy conservation is motivated in part by concern for others. The policy implications of these findings are finally considered.

PRICE INCENTIVES

There is a growing body of evidence concerning the magnitude and nature of consumer response to increases in gasoline price, and it does not uniformly support the optimism expressed by the authors of the NEP. Burright and Enns (1975) review evidence that suggests that changes in the price of gasoline have only small effects upon short-run (one-year) demand for gasoline. Regardless of the data or estimation technique used, estimates of short-run price elasticity are between -.1 and -.3, implying that a 10 percent increase in the price results in a 1 to 3 percent reduction in quantity consumed. The long-run price elasticity of gasoline demand is higher, with estimates ranging between -.65 and -.85. Burright and Enns' analysis implies that a gasoline tax would effectively reduce demand in the long run, with about two-thirds of the increase in price eventually translated into reduced demand. However, this estimate is tentative, in part because estimates of long-run price elasticity are more variable and uncertain than estimates of short-run elasticity. In addition, the estimated time required for consumers to fully adjust to a price increase varies widely, ranging from 2.5 to 12 years (Burright and Enns 1975, p. 11).

Thus, the full effects of a gasoline tax might not be achieved for over a decade. Finally, it is not known how and to what degree American drivers would adjust in the long term to increases in the cost of auto travel brought about by an increase in gasoline price. Stucker and Kirkwood (1977) note that many options are available to offset increases in automobile travel costs. Responses that are economically rational from the consumer's point of view (such as deferring maintenance and driving an older car) do not necessarily result in reduced gasoline consumption. In addition, higher income households account for a disproportionate amount of total gasoline consumption, and these more affluent families can offset greater fuel price increases without reducing total personal travel.

All of these factors raise doubts about the effectiveness of a gasoline tax such as that proposed by the president, leading some authors to argue against its implementation. Peskin and Stopher (1975) argue that gasoline rationing may be a more effective means to reduce consumption than simple price increases. Despite a 40 percent increase in the price of gasoline and the ready availability of alternative means of transportation, Chicago commuters did not respond to the 1973/74 crisis by cutting back on the use of their automobiles to travel to work. (However, as noted below, discretionary travel was reduced. In addition, it should be noted that, even with a 40 percent increase, fuel prices were still relatively low.)

The key determinant of the effectiveness of a gasoline tax, of course, is how American consumers will respond to increasing travel costs. Consumers' adaptation to price increases depends in part upon how much they value lifestyles that depend upon high energy consumption. At present, Americans prefer to live close to services rather than to places of work, to drive alone to work, and to drive full-sized automobiles, all of which require high consumption of gasoline. If present levels and patterns of gasoline consumption reflect strongly held preferences for modes of travel and residential location, as the evidence suggests, Americans may find ways to offset increases in the cost of travel without reducing gasoline consumption. Indeed, the economic analyses of demand suggest that consumers have been reluctant to change travel behavior in response to fuel price changes.

This does not mean that Americans cannot be induced to adapt their lifestyles to consume less energy. To a substantial extent, they did so in response to the oil crisis of 1973/74. Moreover, the reduction in gasoline consumption was immediate and substantial.

A February 1974 Harris poll found that two-thirds of Americans reported that they took steps to reduce gasoline consumption at the height of the shortage (Harris 1974a). Stearns (1975, p. 5) reports reduced driving during the energy shortage, with the mean number of daily auto trips per American adult dropping from 3. 2 in November/December 1973 to 2. 6 in February 1974. The decline was due to reduced discretionary travel rather than reduction in travel to work. Mount and Tyrrell (1977) found a substantial reduction in demand for gasoline during 1974 that was not due to price changes and that they term "non-market conservation." Moreover, conservation was not merely a short-term phenomenon due solely to the restricted supply available for purchase during the gasoline shortage. Mount and Tyrrell found evidence that voluntary conservation continued in 1975, when supplies were no longer constrained. In addition, Murray et al. (1974) report that cutting down on gasoline use is inconsistently related to reports of difficulty getting gas. Americans who reported difficulty getting gas were less likely to conserve in November/December 1973 and more likely to conserve in January/February 1974. These findings suggest that constraints upon gasoline supply account only in part for the reduced consumption during the oil crisis; evidently, voluntary conservation also contributed to the decline.

Whether Americans can be expected to continue to voluntarily conserve dramatically affects projections of future gasoline consumption. Mount and Tyrrell estimate that if nonmarket conservation continued at the same rate between 1974 and 1980, the projected change in the quantity of gasoline consumed would range between -23 percent and +26 percent, depending upon the rate of economic growth and price changes. If Americans do not respond to nonmarket conservation incentives, the projected change in consumption between 1974 and 1980 ranges between -6 percent and +54 percent, again depending on assumptions about other economic changes. Clearly, voluntary conservation has a potentially substantial impact upon future energy use. Therefore, it is important to understand why Americans voluntarily cut back on gasoline use.

SOCIAL AND POLITICAL DETERMINANTS
OF ALTRUISTIC CONSERVATION

Was gasoline conservation during the oil embargo motivated by altruism? If so, the factors that enhance altruistic behavior in general should also enhance energy conservation. Experimental studies of the determinants of interpersonal altruism may be applied to derive hypotheses about the determinants of energy conservation. (Altruism is here defined as an act intended to benefit others. To the extent that energy conservation is motivated by concern for future or present generations, the environment, or society in general, it may be regarded as altruistic.)

Hypothesis 1

Americans who feel a personal obligation to help other people are more likely to conserve gasoline than those who do not.

Experimental studies demonstrate that individuals who feel personally obliged to help are more likely to behave altruistically by, for example, donating blood (Pomazal and Jaccard 1976) or bone marrow (Schwartz 1973). Evidence of a link between altruistic concern and energy conservation is provided by field studies that show that people who are concerned about the environment are more likely to use lead-free gasoline (Heberlein and Black 1976) and to adopt conservation measures (Hogan 1976).

Hypothesis 2

The perceived severity of the energy crisis enhances conservation efforts if the adverse consequences of the shortage are shared; if not, conservation efforts are progressively reduced as the shortage becomes more severe.

Experimental evidence supports the conclusion that empathy with the needs of other people facilitates altruistic behavior. Krebs (1975, p. 1,145) argues, "People are capable of behaving altruistically because they are capable of experiencing empathy," and he demonstrates experimentally that subjects who experienced the strongest empathic reactions were most willing to help another person. In his review of the literature, Krebs (1970) concludes that need and dependency are the characteristics of potential recipients of help that are most likely to elicit altruism. Berkowitz (1970) finds that help is inhibited by self-concern, perhaps because preoccupation with oneself blocks awareness of others' needs.

The fact that altruism is facilitated by empathy with others' needs leads one to expect that gasoline conservation during a shortage would be more likely among individuals who are aware of and concerned about the adverse effects of the shortage upon other people and the harmful effects of their own use of gasoline upon present or future generations of Americans. This suggests that the perceived severity of a shortage should affect individuals' willingness to conserve energy. However, the evidence is inconsistent on this point. Some studies find that Americans who regard the energy shortage as a serious problem are more likely to conserve (see, for example, Murray et al. 1974; Hogan 1976; Doner and Market Opinion Research 1975), while others find no relationship between conservation and beliefs about the seriousness of the crisis (see, for example, Kilkeary 1975; Morrison and Gladhart 1976; Perlman and Warren 1975; Warren and Clifford 1975; Sears et al. 1978; and other references cited by Cunningham and Lopreato 1977).

Several factors may contribute to these inconsistent findings. First, many of the studies are based upon local and/or nonrepresentative samples, so the results are not comparable. In addition, we do not know whether Americans who saw the crisis as severe were primarily concerned about the adverse consequences for themselves or for others. Self-concern might inhibit rather than enhance an individual's willingness to suffer the inconvenience of cutting back energy consumption. Indeed, experimental evidence suggests that empathy and altruism are evoked by a crisis only when the adverse consequences are shared. An experiment by Dovidio and Morris (1975) demonstrates that a threatening situation increases altruism only when individuals face a common threat. When risks are not shared, individuals become more vigilant, and altruism is less likely than in an unthreatening situation involving little risk. The authors interpret their results to mean that an individual's response to a disaster is "very much a function of the similarity of [his or her] losses to those of others in the community" (1975, p. 148).

Thus, according to hypothesis 2, we expect a positive association between the perceived severity of the energy crisis and energy conservation, but only for Americans who believe that other people are adversely affected by the shortage. People who see others as unaffected may actually conserve less according to the degree more serious they believe the shortage to be.

Hypothesis 3

Individuals who believe that other Americans conserve are more likely to themselves conserve.

Macauley (1970) cites findings that show that observing an altruistic model facilitates altruistic acts, such as donating to the Salvation Army. Experiments by, for example, Darley and Latané (1968) also demonstrate the converse: the presence of a model who does not help reduces the likelihood that subjects will intervene to help a person in distress. Altruistic actions by other people may enhance altruism for several reasons. Observing another person give help may increase the likelihood that an observer infers that the situation is one that calls for help. In addition, the behavior of others provides a model that is normative or socially desirable. Finally, demonstrations of goodwill by another person may result in more positive views of people in general. The latter effect is demonstrated in an experiment by Hornstein et al. (1975), showing that altruistic behavior is enhanced by exposure to newscasts of acts of human kindness. Even though they involved the actions of a single individual, the newscasts influenced inferences about social norms and human nature. Subjects exposed to newscasts portraying an altruistic act subsequently viewed people in general more positively and were more likely to help a stranger than were subjects exposed to newscasts involving acts of human malice, harmful acts of nature, or to no newscast at all.

Altruism is enhanced by awareness of others' helpfulness and by a positive and trusting view of people. In general, the maintenance of an altruistic norm depends upon an implicit social contract among the members of a collectivity to share the costs fairly. Willingness to reduce gasoline consumption, for example, may depend heavily on the belief that others are also willing to act in the collective interest by conserving. Any individual effort to conserve may be seen as a futile and insignificant contribution if others do not also conserve.

Trust in the goodwill and fairness of other people is essential to maintain the implicit exchange. Schelling (1970, p. 2) notes that people "may have a limited tolerance to the evidence or to the mere suspicion that others are cheating on the social contract, bending the golden rule . . . " The absence of trust creates powerful incentives to cheat and therefore implies a limited potential for cooperation.

Thus, willingness to sacrifice for the collective good is enhanced to the extent that Americans view the sacrifice as one that is shared by all.

Hypothesis 4

Voluntary conservation is more likely to the extent that Americans trust government leaders and believe that government demands for conservation are fair, legitimate, and based on the collective interest rather than on the self-interests of political or business leaders.

Altruistic or selfish behavior by people in general may facilitate or inhibit altruism; even more important may be the actions and words of society's leaders. Easton (1965, 1975) proposes that citizens' faith in the political system and its authorities influences their willingness to sacrifice to achieve collective goals. In addition, evaluations of political leaders are expected to influence evaluations of the crebibility of official statements concerning the energy crisis and willingness to comply with government directives. This reasoning leads us to expect that political attitudes will influence support for an official government policy calling for energy conservation.

Experimental evidence suggests that the members of a collectivity are more likely to make sacrifices for the collective good when they have faith in their leaders. Michener and Burt (1975) find that cooperation in small groups is affected by evaluations of the fairness of a leader's demands and the leader's contributions to the welfare of the group. Leaders who distribute rewards equitably, who make demands within the defined bounds of authority, or who justify demands on the basis of the group's interest rather than their own self-interest elicit greater group contributions from its members.

One might question whether sacrifices made in response to a leader's demands can be considered altruistic. However, Michener and Burt (1975) find that altruistic leaders elicited greater contributions from members both when they had the power to back up demands and when they did not. In the latter situation, contributions to the collectivity were voluntary and, therefore, may be regarded as altruistic.

Hypothesis 4, derived from experimental studies, is consistent with the more general theoretical position that citizens' faith in the legitimacy of the political system is the basis for their willingness to sacrifice to achieve collective goals. Of course, the winter of 1973/ 74, during which the Arab oil embargo occurred, is a particularly interesting time to test this hypothesis, since it occurred at the height of the Watergate crisis. If citizens cease to act in the national interest when they lose faith in the government or its leaders, one would certainly expect a low rate of altruism in the aftermath of Watergate. Cynicism about the Nixon administration and the oil companies was extreme. Many Americans simply did not believe official assertions that the energy situation was serious and saw the shortage as contrived in order to raise prices. Such beliefs seem likely to have influenced the public's willingness to sacrifice convenience and comfort by conserving gasoline.

Available evidence provides only very limited support for hypothesis 4. In an analysis of the political determinants of gasoline conservation in Los Angeles during the oil embargo, Sears et al. (1978) found that respondents who approved of Nixon were more likely to interpret the crisis as severe and to approve official government policies designed to reduce consumption. However, they found no impact of either general or specific political disaffection upon actual conservation behavior.

ANALYSIS OF SOCIAL AND POLITICAL DETERMINANTS OF GASOLINE CONSERVATION

In February 1974, shortly before the Arab oil embargo was lifted, a national survey conducted by Louis Harris and Associates collected information about Americans' views of the energy shortage and their conservation practices during the previous winter. [2] These data are used to test the previous hypotheses. However, it should be noted that cross-sectional data do not permit strict tests of causal hypotheses, because the causal ordering of conservation attitudes and behavior cannot be established in any unequivocal fashion. Many of the hypothesized causal determinants may just as plausibly be consequences of energy conservation, and, for this reason, the results of this analysis must be considered tentative.

Factors hypothesized to induce gasoline conservation as a form of altruism are a felt obligation to help other people, the belief that the energy crisis is severe and that it affects others adversely, the belief that other Americans are also willing to conserve gasoline, and trust in the legitimacy and fairness of the national leaders who called for conservation.

In order to test these hypotheses, an index of gasoline conservation was constructed to measure the number of steps taken by car drivers to reduce consumption of gasoline. Positive responses (indicating a conservation step had been taken) were summed for ten possible conservation steps, such as reduced driving in metropolitan areas, carpooling, frequent tuneups, and postponing trips. [3]

Table 7.1 presents the results of three analyses of gasoline conservation during the energy crisis. The first equation incorporates demographic characteristics and situational constraints as predictors of altruism. These factors are also included in equations 2 and 3 in order to estimate the net effects of social and political factors upon gasoline conservation.

TABLE 7.1

Predictors of Gasoline Conservation (February 1974)

	Equation		
Predictor Variables	1	2	3
Intercept	6.66*	7.09*	7.51*
	(.28)	(.44)	(.48)
Region of Residence	-.38*	-.26	-.32*
(1 = South, 0 = other)	(.12)	(.14)	(.14)
Income	-.05*	-.10*	-.09*
	(.03)	(.04)	(.04)
Sex	.33*	.35*	.34*
(1 = female, 0 = male)	(.11)	(.12)	(.12)
Race	.62*	.46*	.55*
(1 = black, 0 = white)	(.20)	(.23)	(.23)
Age	-.07*	-.06*	-.06*
	(.03)	(.03)	(.03)
CARUSE	-.25*	-.31*	-.32*
	(.05)	(.05)	(.05)
Availability of Public Transportation	.14*	.15*	.15*
(1 = not at all, 2 = not very, 3 = somewhat, 4 = very)	(.05)	(.05)	(.05)
Distance to Work	-.05*	-.04	-.03
	(.03)	(.03)	(.03)
Blood Donation		.24	.19
(1 = yes, 0 = no or don't know)		(.15)	(.15)
Effect on You		.01	.02
To what extent have you personally been affected by the energy shortage? (1 = hardly at all, 2 = a little, 3 = a lot)		(.10)	(.11)
Effect on Others		.05	.11

To what extent would you say most people you know have been affected by the energy shortage? (1 = hardly at all, 2 = a little, 3 = a lot)		(.13)	(.13)
Duration of Shortage		-.07	-.07
		(.10)	(.10)
Duration x Effect on Others		.11*	.10*
		(.05)	(.05)
Are people you know careful in their use of gasoline? (1 = hardly at all, 2 = not very, 3 = somewhat, 4 = very)		.28*	.25*
		(.07)	(.07)
Rating of Nixon (1 = poor, 2 = only fair, 3 = pretty good, 4 = excellent)			.21*
			(.08)
Watergate			.01
			(.04)
Nixon not Effective			.12
			(.10)
R^2	.08	.13	.14
N	1,334	1,042	1,012

Note: Analyses are based upon respondents who reported that they or their spouses drove cars. For a description of the predictor variables, see Note 3. Coefficients are unstandardized; standard errors are in parentheses.

*Statistical significance at the 0.05 level.

Source: Harris (1974a).

Analysis 1: Demographic and Situational Determinants

Equation 1 tests the effects of demographic characteristics and situational constraints upon gasoline conservation. Southerners, males, whites, older people, and people with high incomes were less likely to reduce gasoline consumption than other Americans. [4]

Situational constraints upon the availability of gasoline and upon alternative modes of transportation also affected the extent to which Americans reduced gasoline consumption during the shortage. The most important predictor of conservation is CARUSE, an index of dependence upon the car to get to work and other places. Equation 1 indicates that Americans who depended on the car to get many places took fewer steps to save gasoline, either because they were unable or unwilling to cut back on consumption. In addition, respondents were more likely to cut back on gasoline consumption to the extent that public transportation was available. Finally, the results indicate that respondents who lived far from their place of work were less likely to reduce gasoline consumption.

Analysis 2: Social Determinants

Equation 2 incorporates variables that permit tests of hypotheses 1-3.

The survey includes no direct measure of the extent to which respondents feel personally obliged to help others. Therefore, a measure of another form of altruistic behavior—unpaid blood donation—was used as a proxy measure of altruistic concern for other people. Equation 2 indicates that respondents who had donated blood during the previous five years were also more likely to have conserved gasoline during the shortage, net of other factors. However, the effect is not statistically significant at the .05 level (p < .10), so the results do not support hypothesis 1.

Despite the weak association between blood donation and gasoline conservation, it is difficult to account for the fact that these two very different behaviors are related at all if they are not jointly determined by a common motive of altruistic concern for the welfare of others.

Indeed, to the extent that gasoline conservation and blood donation are both motivated by generalized concern for and trust in other people, the association between them may be attenuated by including measures of these factors in equation 2. In fact, when measures of the hypothesized altruistic motives for conservation (the perceived duration of the shortage, awareness of the effects of the shortage on other people, and beliefs about others' care in using gasoline) are eliminated from equation 2, blood donation is a statistically significant predictor of gasoline conservation ($\hat{B}$ = .40, s.d. = .13, p < .01). (The analysis, which is not shown, includes all equation 1 variables and blood donation as predictors of gasoline conservation.) Thus, the findings provide some tentative support for hypothesis 1, although better, more direct measures of the extent to which respondents feel personally obliged to help others are required in order to provide a more conclusive test.

By hypothesis 2, gasoline conservation is more likely the more severe the shortage, but only when its adverse consequences are shared. If not, a crisis may lead to vigilance and self-concern, reducing the expression of altruism. This hypothesis implies that Americans who believed that the energy shortage was serious (that is, long in duration) reduced gasoline consumption only if they also believed that other Americans were affected by the shortage.

To provide a test of this hypothesis, equation 2 includes an interaction term between the expected duration of the shortage and its perceived effect upon others. The results support hypothesis 2. The interaction term is positive and statistically significant, indicating that conservation was enhanced when the energy crisis was viewed as serious, but only to the extent that other people were affected by it. Note that the main effect of the perceived duration of the shortage and its perceived effect upon others are not statistically significant. That is, the belief that the shortage would last a long time induced conservation only to the degree that respondents also believed that others were affected.

It is possible that respondents who expected the energy shortage to last a long time were concerned not only about the consequences for others but also for themselves. In order to test the possibility that conservation during the shortage was motivated by self-concern rather than concern for others, a measure of how much respondents felt personally affected by the shortage was also included in equation 2. Net of other variables, the personal impact of the shortage had no effect at all upon conservation, suggesting that the adverse personal consequences of the shortage were not a motive to conserve.

By hypothesis 3, conservation by others establishes conservation as an equitable norm because self-sacrifice is commensurate with sacrifices made by others. This hypothesis is supported by the finding that the perception that others are careful in their use of gasoline is positively related to conservation. This result suggests that altruism is enhanced when it is viewed as normative and when conservation is a shared responsibility.

An alternative explanation for this finding should be noted, however. It is possible that people base their inferences about the behavior of others upon their own behavior. A tendency to "project" one's attitudes and acts to others would result in a positive association between one's own and the perceived behavior of others, even in the absence of the normative influence postulated in hypothesis 3. The cross-sectional data used here do not permit a test of this alternative hypothesis, although the experimental evidence reviewed earlier supports the inference that altruism is enhanced because it is perceived as normative.

Analysis 3: Political Determinants

A third analysis investigates the relationship between political evaluations and Americans' willingness to act in the national interest by conserving gasoline. The experimental literature suggests that members of a collectivity make voluntary sacrifices for a leader who is trusted and whose demands are viewed as credible, legitimate, and based upon the collective interest rather than the leader's self-interest. Once again, the available data do not provide complete measures of the hypothesized political determinants of gasoline conservation. However, the data permit an assessment of whether the widespread

cynicism about President Nixon's role in the Watergate incident reduced Americans' willingness to conserve gasoline. Were the Nixon-
haters the gas-guzzlers? The answer is not clearcut; the results suggest that conservation was enhanced both among Americans who supported Nixon and, to a lesser extent, among those who were cynical
about his role in Watergate.

Equation 3 incorporates three measures of support for Nixon.
The first is an overall rating of Nixon's presidential performance,
the second (Watergate) is a composite index measuring beliefs about
Nixon's dishonesty in perpetrating and covering up the Watergate incident, and the third (Nixon not Effective) measures public perceptions of the negative impact of the Watergate affair upon Nixon's effectiveness. Although the correlations between overall support for
Nixon and each of the two scales measuring negative perceptions of
the Watergate affair are high and negative, all three scales are positively related to gasoline conservation. That is, gasoline conservation was enhanced both by positive overall evaluations of Nixon's presidential performance and by negative evaluations related to Watergate.
Only the effect of overall support is statistically significant, however.[5]

These unexpected findings provide only partial support for hypothesis 4. They suggest several conclusions. First, the results support the hypothesis that a positive overall evaluation of the president
enhanced Americans' willingness to conserve gasoline during the crisis. However, negative views of Nixon's role in Watergate clearly did
not reduce citizens' conservation efforts; if anything, cynicism about
Nixon had a slightly positive direct effect upon conservation. At the
risk of interpreting chance findings, it might be suggested that, under
some conditions, doubts about a leader's effectiveness may enhance
citizens' willingness to act in the collective interest if they believe
that the leader is incapable of doing so.

These findings indicate that one should not assume a simple
model of the effect of the public's evaluations of a national leader upon public behavior. In particular, the results are not consistent with
the simple hypothesis that alienation from political leaders reduces
the public's willingness to act in the national interest. It is possible
that both the cynics and the faithful may act in the public interest, although their motives may differ. The results also suggest that caution
should be exercised when combining different measures of political
disaffection in a single index. Sears et al. (1978) found that approval
of Nixon had no effect upon gasoline conservation in Los Angeles; it
is possible that the difference between their results and those reported
here is due to the fact that Sears et al. combined measures of overall
support for Nixon and cynicism about his role in Watergate in a simple
index of Nixon approval. The findings reported here suggest that the

two types of presidential evaluation had opposite effects upon conservation, so that the combined effect might well be negligible.

CONCLUSIONS

The results presented here suggest that differences in conservation behavior among population subgroups are not substantial, nor are there dramatic differences among regions or between urban and rural areas. Situational constraints imposed by such factors as distance to work, dependence on the automobile to get places, and the availability of alternative means of transportation were important determinants of conservation during the energy shortage.

Although the results are tentative, they suggest that gasoline conservation may be motivated in part by concern for other people and that the social conditions and individual values that promote interpersonal altruism are also related to energy conservation. In particular, the results suggest that the views of other people—whether and how long other Americans would suffer as a result of the shortage and whether others were willing to contribute to its solution— significantly affected individual Americans' efforts to conserve gasoline.

Finally, the results suggest that political conditions may influence Americans' conservation of gasoline. Americans who positively evaluated Nixon's overall presidential performance were significantly more likely to save gasoline. There is no evidence that widespread cynicism about Nixon's role in Watergate had a direct negative effect upon Americans' willingness to cut gasoline consumption; if anything, the opposite effect is found. (It should be noted, however, that although cynicism about Watergate had a positive, insignificant, direct effect upon conservation, the indirect effect may well have been negative, since support for Nixon was much lower among respondents who were cynical about his handling of Watergate.)

The data were not designed to test the hypotheses developed here, so the available measures are not wholly adequate or complete for this purpose. Nevertheless, the results of this exploratory analysis suggest that hypotheses derived from experimental studies of interpersonal altruism may prove useful as possible explanations of impersonal forms of altruism, such as in energy conservation, as well. If so, experimental social psychology may be a rich source of ideas, verified in experimental studies, that may yield a better understanding of the social and political conditions that create or destroy the potential for altruism in society at large. For example, experimental studies suggest that a crisis in itself will not evoke altruistic behavior; its adverse effects must be shared by the members of a collectivity. This experimental finding is replicated in our cross-sectional analysis, implying that it is not sufficient to convince Americans that the energy shortage is serious in order to induce them to conserve. They must also be persuaded that the adverse effects of the shortage are shared by all Americans before they will reduce energy consumption.

Attention should also be directed to the question of what motivates public-minded behavior, such as in energy conservation, if policies that attempt to reduce energy consumption are to be effective. Policymakers tend to assume that narrow self-interest is the only effective basis for policy and structure economic incentives and disincentives accordingly. However, the effectiveness of economic incentives to conserve gasoline may be reduced if present patterns of energy use reflect strongly held preferences for residential location and modes of travel. After all, Americans could already save money by using less gasoline, buying smaller cars, and living closer to work; the fact that they have chosen not to do so suggests that they have been willing to pay a high price for the convenience, freedom, and comfort the automobile provides.

National leaders, in formulating policy, should not underestimate the potential for public altruism in response to national crisis and shortages. The fact that gasoline conservation was widespread during the oil embargo, at the height of public disapproval of the president, suggests a potential for altruism that has yet to be tapped. The findings reported here suggest that future crisis and shortages—of gasoline or of other resources—will enhance or inhibit altruism depending upon the extent to which Americans share an awareness of common needs and a common fate and to which they see one another as interdependent rather than as competitors for scarce resources.

Social conditions that reinforce the common bounds among members of a community or society increase their willingness to sacrifice for the collective welfare. Positive attitudes toward the potential beneficiaries of help—whether an individual, group, government, or cause—increase interpersonal altruism. This suggests that public altruism will not be an effective basis for policies that benefit unpopular groups or causes (for example, busing, prohibition, the oil companies, or the Vietnam War). The conclusion that people who believe in a cause are far more willing to sacrifice to help achieve it seems obvious, but the potential for altruism as the basis for policy is often ignored.

Altruism is enhanced when a community faces a crisis, but only if its members see themselves as sharing the same circumstances and fates. If some people suffer the effects of a shortage more than others or, worse, if some profit from the losses of others, altruism may be reduced. Thus, Americans who believed that other Americans were unaffected by the energy shortage and did not save gasoline were less likely themselves to take steps to conserve. Similarly, data from a March 1974 Harris poll show that Americans who believed that the oil companies profited from the shortages resultant from the 1973/74 Arab oil embargo were less likely to voluntarily conserve gasoline than those who did not view the oil companies cynically (Harris 1974b). These findings suggest that policies intended to promote conservation of energy will be more effective if the costs of conservation—monetary costs, discomfort, inconvenience, and so on—are distributed equitably. In addition, compliance may be substantially heightened by positive examples of conservation; believing that others conserve makes individual actions more meaningful as part of a collective effort.

Neither should national leaders and policymakers ignore the extent to which their own actions may directly and indirectly influence the public's willingness to make sacrifices to achieve collective goals. Americans' approval of their chief executive influenced their willingness to conserve gasoline during the oil embargo. In addition, the extent to which a government policy is viewed as equitable and legitimate, and to which it enhances trust in the honesty and expertise of national leaders, is expected to influence Americans' willingness to make sacrifices required for policy to be successfully implemented. However, the effects of political evaluations and conditions upon public altruism in response to a crisis may be complex, and they are not consistent with the simple hypothesis that alienation reduces altruism. This chapter has only begun to explore the political motives for altruism; hopefully future work will contribute to a broader understanding of both social and political determinants of altruism.

NOTES

1. Ultimately, the National Energy Act passed by Congress in 1978 included provisions for the elimination of the federal income tax deduction for state and local gasoline taxes used for nonbusiness purposes and provided for penalties for manufacturers who build gas-guzzling automobiles.

2. This study uses data from a survey (#2413) of 1,661 adult Americans (18 and older) living in households (Harris 1974a). The analysis is based upon 1,451 respondents who reported that they or their spouses drove cars.

The survey is based upon a national probability sample of 100 blocks or block groups. Approximately 16 interviews were conducted in each block, with interviewers required to fill a sex quota (half male and half female) within each area. If more than one eligible adult was present in a household in the designated area, a randomized procedure

was used to select a respondent. Substitution within households for
the selected respondent was not allowed. However, callbacks were
not required, and interviewers were permitted to substitute one
household for another until quotas were filled. Thus, the survey was
not conducted using strict probability methods.

    3. The items to construct this index and all other variables and
indexes are presented below.

Gasoline Conservation consists of summed responses to the following. "In the past few months, in order to conserve gasoline, have
you (read item from list)?" (1 = have, 0 = have not or don't know.)

    "Limited your speed on highways to a maximum of 55 miles per
hour before any restriction was imposed?"

    "Cut back your driving in downtown metropolitan areas?"

    "Had your car tuned at least every 4,000 miles?"

    "Refrained from using your car one full day a week?"

    "Limited your gasoline purchases to no more than 10 gallons of
gasoline at a time?"

    "Limited your gasoline purchases voluntarily to no more than
$2 worth at a time?"

    "Used public transportation where it's available instead of driv-
ing?"

    "Postponed long trips by car?"

    "Limited your gasoline purchases to no more than 35 gallons of
gasoline per car per month?"

    "Have you or your spouse organized or participated in a carpool
with other people to travel to work in order to conserve gasoline, or
not?" [1 = have, 0 = have not or not sure.]

    CARUSE consists of summed responses to, "Do you (respondent
and/or spouse) usually drive your car to (read item from list)?" (1 =
yes, 0 = no or not sure.)

    "Go to work?"

    "Travel on the job?"

    "Go shopping?"

    "Visit friends or relatives?"

    "Go out in the evening to a movie, restaurant, show or sporting
event?"

    "Go on weekend trips out of town?"

    Distance to Work is the answer to, "About how many miles do
you usually drive round trip to go to work?" (0 = don't drive, 1 = 1
miles, 2 = 1-5 miles, 3 = 6-10 miles, 4 = 11-20 miles, 5 = 21-30
miles, 6 = 31-50 miles, 7 = more than 50 miles, not sure excluded.)

Duration is formed from two questions. "Now let me ask you about specific things. Do you feel there is a very serious shortage of gasoline for cars in the country, a somewhat serious shortage, or not a serious shortage at all?" (If "very" or "somewhat serious"): "How long do you feel the shortage of gasoline for cars will last—a few months, a year, two to five years, six to ten years, or longer?" (0 = not serious at all, 1 = few months, 2 = year, 3 = two to five years, 4 = six to ten years, 5 = over ten years, not sures on either question were dropped.)

Blood Donation: "Now I would like to turn to another topic just for a moment and ask you about giving blood. Have you contributed blood within the past five years or not?" (1 = yes, 0 = no, respondents who were not sure or who contributed to earn money were dropped.)

Rating of Nixon: "How would you rate the job President Nixon is doing as President—excellent, pretty good, only fair, or poor?" (1 = poor, 2 = only fair, 3 = pretty good, 4 = excellent, not sure excluded.)

Watergate is an index of summed responses to the following items. (For each item, 1 = Nixon dishonest/knew about coverup/withheld information/deliberate erasure, 0 = Nixon honest or not sure.)

"Do you feel President Nixon knew about the attempt to cover-up White House involvement in Watergate while it was going on, or do you think he did not know about the cover-up?"
"In his Operation Candor, President Nixon tried to convince the American people that he was not involved in Watergate. Do you feel the President has been frank and honest on the Watergate affair, or do you feel he has withheld important information on it?"
"Now I'd like to read you some statements that have been made about the Watergate tapes. For each, tell me if you tend to agree or disagree. The electronic experts proved that the 18 minutes missing from the tapes were erased deliberately and were not just a mistake. The 18 minutes missing from the tape of the conversation between President Nixon and H. R. Haldeman were deliberately erased because they would have proved Nixon's involvement in the cover-up. The two missing tapes were ordered destroyed because they would have proven Nixon knew about the Watergate cover-up. "
"When all of the investigations and crises have finished, do you think President Nixon will be found to have violated the law, as was true with Vice President Agnew, or don't you think this will happen?

"Now let me read you some statements about President Nixon. For each, tell me if you tend to agree or disagree. He has not been honest about the financing of his houses in San Clemente and Key Biscayne."

Nixon not Effective consists of summed responses to two items:

"He has reached the point where he no longer can be an effective President and should resign for the good of the country" (1 = agree, 0 = disagree or not sure.)

"If President Nixon remains in office for the rest of his term, how serious a handicap in getting the job done do you think the doubts about his involvement in Watergate and about his integrity will be—a very serious handicap, only somewhat serious, or not serious at all?" (1 = very serious, 0 = not or somewhat serious or not sure.)

4. The effects of education and of size of place of residence (suburbs or central city versus small town or rural area) were tested and found to be negligible, so these variables are deleted from equations 1-3.

5. Although the effects of the two Watergate-related indexes are not statistically significant, it is necessary to include them in the equation. If they were excluded, the positive effect of overall support for Nixon would be underestimated ($\hat{B}$ = 0.12, s.d. = 0.06, p < 0.05; analysis not shown).

8
INTERGOVERNMENTAL, INSTITUTIONAL, AND SOCIETAL ASPECTS OF NATIONAL ENERGY PRODUCTION POLICIES

Edward L. Helminski

The United States imports more than eight million barrels of oil a day at an annual cost of billions of dollars. This practice threatens the continuity of our domestic fuel supply and the stability of our national economy. As has been stated by President Carter and past presidents, the United States has no option but to decrease imports. This can be achieved without cyclic economic and social disruptions through a comprehensive national policy of increased domestic production and predictable energy conservation. Because of the inefficient use of presently available energy and the variety of economically developable resources, the United States has the opportunity to develop a multitude of strategies that would result in the establishment of an energy program that would decrease our imports in a planned and nondisruptive manner.

Yet, despite the passage of the National Energy Act, we do not have a recognized national energy strategy. Ironically, one of the major underlying reasons is the multitude of options available. Neither technology nor economics poses insurmountable limiting factors. And, because of the broad spectrum of possible alternatives, the opportunity exists for vested interest constituencies to formulate realizable options and to attempt to impress upon the various decision-making institutions their own perceptions of an achievable national energy program. Additionally, just as the nondeterminative nature of any particular choice lessens the degree to which any group is willing to accept actions that will adversely affect its existing social condition, the same is true for any level of government. Governments are unwilling to acquiesce to a strategy in the "national interest" without a significant role in the decision. Though at least some members of the public agree that the nation is in a crisis because of its level of imports, very few agree that a particular course of action is key to relieving this crisis. Rather than accepting a reasonable degree of adversity that would accompany a particular program, the typical response is to formulate an option under which one's own interests would not suffer.

The lack of a comprehensive national energy policy is therefore due, to a great degree, to an inability to arrive at a national consensus and the lack of recognition within the various decision-making institutions of the effects proposed energy initiatives will have on the social and institutional fabric of the affected "publics." These tendencies suggest that the key to the formulation of a national energy program is not in the hands of the technologists but in the hands of those schooled in the social and institutional aspects of public policy. The purpose of this chapter is to identify some of these social and institutional factors on one side of the energy dilemma—energy production. The intention is to provide the social and behavioral science community with sufficient incentive to focus attention on these problems and to formulate, as a result, research and development agenda and curricula responsive to energy problems.

The first part focuses on the need to establish institutional participatory mechanisms that will allow all publics having either a defined jurisdiction or an interest in the problem to participate in the decision-making process. An attempt is made to define the various categories of decisionmakers and the interests that must be integrated into a participatory process in order to reach acceptable frameworks and criteria for energy production programs.

The second portion identifies and characterizes the social and economic effects of energy production initiatives that pose a significant constraint on the implementation of production policies. The problems identified, for the most part, fall into the category of the traditionally defined social ills that occur when communities experience rapid population growth and economic change. The problems encountered, however, are intensified because the communities experiencing the rapid change are in the remote rural regions of our country, not near urban areas. In many instances, the regions experiencing energy development cannot expect to retain their growth and economic base beyond the life of the exploited resource. Their remoteness generally precludes industrial or commercial diversification that would retain the region as a population center. Though these communities, especially those in the coal-bearing regions, are expected to provide the basis of our national energy production policies, they lack the basic infrastructures needed to function as responsive units of governmental structure.

Finally, guidelines for a solution to the energy crisis—the necessary public participation in the energy decision-making process—

are offered. Further, the distinctive contributions of the social sciences are discussed.

FOSTERING PUBLIC PARTICIPATION
IN ENERGY DECISION MAKING

"If," as many have said, "we can put a man on the moon, we most assuredly can solve our energy problem." To do so requires a National Aeronautics and Space Administration (NASA)-type energy program and past administrations, in fact, have proposed NASA-type energy production policies, such as "Project Independence." Several members of the Conference Committee convened to consider House/Senate action on President Carter's National Energy Plan were espousing a similar initiative—an Energy Trust Fund to infuse massive amounts of capital into energy production initiatives. These approaches relied heavily on new technology, government incentives, and the basic belief that the United States can harness the necessary resources in whatever the period required to solve our energy problems, much as we did in conquering space.

The space program was and remains, however, entirely a federal effort. All the resources emanate from the federal government. The public supported the program as a means of demonstrating the superiority of the American system over the Soviet form of government. President Kennedy was able to harness this attitude to successfully enkindle a patriotic spirit in the American public, which allowed the program to proceed no matter what the cost. President Carter has tried, but has failed, to evoke a similar response to the energy crisis by personally delcaring it the "moral equivalent of war." In contrast with the almost singlemindedness of the public toward the federal space effort, nothing near a consensus attitude exists with regard to national energy policy. As several pollsters have discovered, many Americans are not convinced that a major problem even exists. Those who are beginning to appreciate the precarious nature of present supply/demand situations are in no way forming solid support to effect a solution. A NASA-type energy strategy would require unanimous public commitment, one that does not appear to be forthcoming.

Unlike space exploration, energy resource development is necessarily a multijurisdictional issue. State and local governments, for the most part, have authority over land-use decisions, siting, environmental laws, and regulatory programs that essentially govern development initiatives. An environmental impact statement did not have to be filed prior to the initiation of the space program. The community adjacent to the launching area at Cape Canaveral was not concerned with (nor were they willing to accept, if they knew) the very small probability of a catastrophic accident occurring. Contrast this attitude with the concern over the siting of nuclear power plants in which the possibility of accidents of the order of 1 in 10^{16} are often times brought up in public debates. Cape Canaveralites and intervening communities voiced little concern over the transport of hydrazine, a highly toxic and volatile rocket fuel, while the transportation of spent nuclear fuel rods is a highly controversial issue, with several states now prohibiting such transfer across their lines.

In contrast to the efficiency of the NASA decision-making process, the energy decision process is by necessity more of an open forum, with the public often playing a direct role in the process, via referenda, alongside state and local decisionmakers and the corporate executive. Each participant has, to varying degrees, a vested interest in the final outcome. Indeed, the wide range and intensity of impacts that energy programs necessarily have on the social, economic, and institutional fabric of the host community encourage an intense desire for participation in the decision-making process.

Given the diverse and complex nature of this process, energy production policies will not be effective if framed under a NASA-type mentality. Success will depend on the ability to structure a decision-making process that is cognizant of the present institutional and social environment within which development will occur and that recognizes and openly addresses the direct social impacts of development initiatives.

The need to go beyond present decision-making "structures" stems from several interrelated factors, among them:

- the rather intensive parochial impacts of proposed production initiatives;
- a growing conflict between host and user constituencies on the value of host's own natural resources;
- a more informed and aggressive public;
- the almost complete dominance of the private sector over the financial resources available to invest in development;
- the assertion of local units of government autonomy over their host natural resources;
- the immense geographic and demographic impacts of energy facilities on both the input and output cycles that pay no heed to governmentally defined jurisdictional boundaries.

The Energy Decision-Making Environment

The most important factors affecting the accomplishment of national production policies are the institutional relationships between

the federal government and the state and local governments and between all levels of government with private industry. State and local
governments have the authority to significantly influence almost all
aspects of energy resource development. The states, either on their
own initiative or under the mandate of federal legislation, have primary responsibility for land use, environmental protection, transportation planning, resource allocation, and various other aspects of public policy that directly impact or control energy development. Several
states have instituted energy facility siting mechanisms that specifically outline processes for the licensing and operation of any energy
facility. Though health and safety aspects of nuclear plants remain
under the jurisdiction of the Nuclear Regulatory Commission, the
state and local communities essentially govern nuclear development
by retaining authority over land and water use and other environmental regulations. State and local governments do, in fact, have sufficient authority in most cases to stall or indeed stop any energy development initiative, either through land use management or environmental restrictions.

The Organized Public and the Federal Government

    The complexity of state/federal relationships over energy re-
source development is further complicated by the direct involvement
of the general public through representative public interest groups.
The environmental movement of the 1960s brought the private citizen,
through organized intervenor public-interest organizations, into the
decision-making process.
    The earlier strategies of demonstration, civil disobedience, and
public confrontation have now evolved into sophisticated legal battles
utilizing the courts and structured intervenor processes. The intervenor process is, in fact, no longer an extracurricular activity, having
been institutionalized into the governmental decision-making activity,
The Administration's Nuclear Siting and Licensing Act proposed in
1978 (H. R. 11704) is the most recent example. The bill authorizes
the establishment of "a pilot program for funding intervenors in initial
or renewal licensing proceedings, including site permit, construction
permit, and/or operating license and amendment proceedings" for
nuclear facilities. To be eligible for such funding, criteria are to be
established that demonstrate the intervenor's interest in the matter;
lack of reasonable access to alternative sources of funds; that the intervention would not occur, or would be severely limited, in the absence of federal funds; and that the intervenor's participation will lead
to presentation of substantive arguments that may not be presented
otherwise and lead to fair determination in the proceeding. As a re-

sult of such actions, the "intervenor" is as much, if not more, of a participant in the outcome of national initiatives as the governor, or the mayor, or the county commissioner.

The agenda and character of public interest groups also reflect a social attitude of the populus that must be considered in devising strategies to implement production initiatives. Despite growing unemployment, urban decay, inflation, and a host of other domestic ills, the U. S. citizen has more leisure time and is better paid. This has provided the individual with the opportunity to explore the outdoors, to ski, to take longer vacations, to own a second home in a remote area, and, in general, to be more appreciative of the environment— at least to the extent that he or she is able to keep enjoying it. This sensitivity manifests itself in many ways—from a New Yorker's opposition to a power plant in Utah to Californians and Easterners opposing further lumbering in the redwoods. The interest in maintaining the beauty of the outdoors for the purpose of enjoyment, in addition to concerns about safety, has not only strengthened the support of the intervenors' process but also creates an ambiance not conducive to the development of resources negatively impacting upon this environment.

The Private Sector

Despite the significant role played by the public sector, the corporate structure is primarily responsible for the planning, development, promotion, management, and financing of most energy development. And, though the preservation of the public good may be a reason for or against a particular production initiative, the corporate decisionmaker is not willing to carry out his or her responsibility without applying another criterion in the decision-making process— the degree to which the initiative would profit his company, and, in turn, a select group of the public, the company stockholders.

Our nation relies on the energy corporations to make the necessary judgments with regard to developing energy resources. Federal, state, and local governments may provide incentives or disincentives, but the ultimate decision on a particular initiative rests upon the forecast of potential corporate gains versus losses. The data necessary to support the decision, including statistics on the extent of a particular resource, feasibility of development, and market availability, are compiled by the industry and, for the most part, remain within confidential files. The competitiveness within the energy industry (though many contend that no real competition exists) precludes the release of information to the public. Because of possible antitrust violations, the independent energy corporations are legally prevented from sharing data on many aspects of resource production and distribution, thereby negating the potential for public disclosure. Yet there are data integral to assuring that adequate resources will be developed in a time frame to meet national energy needs. The confidentiality of industry energy resource development information presents particular problems to state and local governments. In order to effectively plan public investment, to support development initiatives, or to develop strategies to protect public health, safety, and the environment, the state/local governments need the data held in confidence by the corporations.

For the most part, our national energy production strategies are determined by the corporate decision-making process outside the public forum. Though a solution to the problem would be a closer working and publicly responsive relationship between the various levels of government and the industry, many oppose such a "mixed marriage" because of the power and influence the corporate resources would have over the involved public officials. Many sectors of the public have complained for many years that industry and all levels of government officials work too closely together, maintaining that this "close" association has adversely affected the general public. Federal and state laws are now being promulgated to terminate industrial and government relationships, so as not to compromise the role of public decisionmakers and to ensure that policies are developed for the public good, not just for the corporate public. The lack of institutionalized mechanisms to effectively link corporate and public decisionmakers further frustrates the formulation of effective national energy policy.

Competitive Interests Within the Federal Government

Adding to complicated, conflicting relationships between the federal government and the states, among the states themselves, and between private sector interests and the public is the general parochial nature and self-preserving attitude of the various federal agencies. Most initiatives aimed at increasing energy supply will fall under the jurisdiction and regulation of several federal agencies and established independent commissions. The siting of an energy facility could necessitate decisions from the following agencies: Department of the Interior Bureau of Land Management and Bureau of Indian Affairs; Environmental Protection Agency (EPA); Council of Environmental Quality; Department of Energy; Nuclear Regulatory Commission (NRC); Department of Treasury; Department of Agriculture. Each of the individual agencies is intent on protecting its own jurisdiction and prerogatives, and interagency conflicts are often the major obstacles to final resolution of an energy initiative.

The Supreme Court was recently brought into one interagency struggle to resolve the problem of whether NRC or EPA had jurisdiction over thermal effluent standards from nuclear power plants. The lack of coordination of federal agencies severely handicaps both the states and private industry from participating in the decision-making process in an effective manner. Intra-agency mechanisms must be established in order to focus federal responsibility for the national decision-making process.

Technology-Driven Relationships

In addition to the state/federal and public/private sector relationships, many other factors condition the energy decision-making environment. It is not the intention of this chapter to discuss them all, but one other does bear mention. For the frequently stated reasons of efficiency, economy and safety, the United States has become a nation dependent on centralized energy generation facilities. This centralization presents a severe impediment toward increasing the utilization of residential solar heating and cooling and is responsible for joining the economies and growth plans of groups of states through electrical grid structures and the need to appropriate massive quantities of natural resources—water, land, and minerals—whose reserves go beyond an individual state's boundaries.

The population and the economy are conditioned to the centralized approach. Above all, so are the relevant bureaucracies. Utilities base their rates and need for new facilities on projected new industrial and residential growth. If new residences used individual solar energy systems rather than hooking up to the utility, rates to the remaining customers would increase. The number of individual homemakers that would turn toward a solar economy has a direct bearing on the rates charged to those that would not. Planners must begin to be cognizant of this impact if residential solar strategies are to be successful. Processes may need to be developed that would integrate an individual's "energy" resource decision into the overall planning process.

Multistate Jurisdiction

Centralization also mandates interstate cooperation in the planning and construction of energy facilities. Multithousand megawatt electric generating stations require large quantities of cooling water, affecting the supply of any state situated along inland waterways. The resultant electricity is sold to a market not restricted by governmental boundaries but regulated independently by those states serviced.

The needed transportation corridors, either of the primary fuel (rail-roads, pipelines) or resultant electricity (high voltage power lines) must necessarily cross several state boundaries. Though a federal framework has been established to govern the existing railroads and natural gas pipeline systems, the present system cannot provide the increased supplies needed. The production and delivery of energy from our most abundant natural resource—coal—from supplier to user states will require the establishment of new corridors, mandating interstate cooperation and planning. The realization of such corridors will re-quire satisfying the demands and interests of the intermediary states, as well as those on the sending and receiving ends. To accomplish such planning and construction in an equitable and responsive manner, regional siting processes will need to be devised that allow states, maintaining their sovereignty, to cooperatively share the responsibil-ity for such development.

The Energy Decisionmakers

The energy decision-making environment can thus be depicted as a multilayered process, taking place in a nonconducive atmosphere more inclined toward preserving the status quo, frustrated by man-dated adversarial roles within the private sector and the ever-present need with the public sector to preserve self-determination at all levels of government. This condition is not a unique feature of energy policy making but of all public policy. The critical nature of our energy sup-ply and the need to increase production has, however, exposed the fragility of the public policy decision-making process. The dilemma that the nation faces is how to provide for a predictable supply to main-tain national growth, balancing the concerns of all constituencies and maintaining the fabric of the federal system of government.

DIRECT SOCIAL AND ECONOMIC EFFECTS
OF ENERGY PRODUCTION POLICIES AND PROGRAMS

The wide range and intensity of the effects of energy production programs on the social, economic, and institutional fabric of affected communities could be classified in the general category of defined so-cial ills that occur when communities experience rapid population and economic change. The national intent to rapidly increase coal produc-tion is the most prominent example of an energy production initiative with associated problems of this nature, and this intent will be exam-ined here. To be illustrative rather than comprehensive, only the so-cial and institutional consequences of increasing our present coal pro-duction are explored.

The most agreed upon approach to providing sufficient energy resources—that of increasing utilization of our domestic coal resources—faces most severe obstacles. Consider, for example, President Carter's goal of increasing coal production to 1.2 billion tons by 1985. According to the administration's estimates (Helme 1978), in order to accomplish this goal:

states would be requested to site 241 new coal-fired electric generating units by 1985;

5,000 new mines would have to be opened over and above increasing production from existing western strip mines;

80,000 new underground miners and 45,000 new surface miners must be hired and trained;

new transportation systems must be developed to deliver the coal, possibly utilizing coal slurry lines, necessitating the granting of interstate rights-of-way;

federal coal-bearing lands must be exploited, heightening the conflict between western states intent to control their destinies rather than have them dictated by federal initiatives;

massive investments need to be made by utilities to assure compliance to clean air regulations.

Labor Management Relations Problems

The increased utilization of coal is intended to cut imports of high-priced imported oil, putting the nation on more stable economic footing by stabilizing our fuel supply and slowing down inflation. The coal industry is, however, one of the least stable industries in the United States and has been for the past 20 years. The major fluctuations in market demand for coal over the past decade have made it impossible to plan to invest for further development. Coupled with the lack of financial stability due to these market fluctuations is the specter of "dismal labor-management" relations, particularly in the Central Appalachian coal field. A recent coal strike vividly demonstrated the fragility of the coal industry and the almost complete inability of the federal government to exert any influence to resolve the work stoppage.

As stated by Helme (1978, p. 12):

Expanding eastern production and bringing in more new miners can only increase labor unrest. Unless major new efforts are made to remedy the socioeconomic conditions in the Appalachian coal fields, this influx of new workers will tax the already substandard infrastructure

to the breaking point. Poor housing and community facilities are likely to contribute to unrest, work stoppages
and wildcat strikes. . . . Private sector efforts to support social services are likely to be curtailed. (This was
the case with the United Mine Workers' Health and Retire-
ment fund cutoff of support for health care needs of miners. The fund was supported by fees on coal production,
and strikes drastically reduced the flow of fees into the
fund.) . . .

Increased labor unrest also will have a secondary
impact that will contribute to further socioeconomic impact problems. Major capital investment in coal mines
will fall short of desired levels as investors shy away
from the uncertain profit picture resulting from labor
problems. While big profits can be made in coal investments, the uncertainty and level of risk tend to discour-
age large institutional investors. On the demand side,
labor problems make long-term contracts for purchase
of coal less attractive to buyers. Potential industrial consumers approach coal with a question mark, preferring
to bide their time rather than make the major capital investments necessary to switch to coal-fired facilities.
As a consequence, it is likely that the coal market will
continue to go through boom and bust cycles.

In order for the switch from oil to coal to be successful, the
problems must be faced at the national level. President Carter has
taken action to resolve the labor-management problems by establishing a coal commission, chaired by Governor John Rockefeller of West
Virginia, to develop recommendations to improve the stability of the
coal industry, particularly labor and production issues.

The Fuel Switch to Coal—Regional Consequences

The particular change that will be experienced by regions as
well as the country as a whole as a result of the switch to coal should
not go unnoticed by social science investigators. The effect of the National Energy Plan is to alter the very foundation of the present energy
structure—switching the nation from an oil and gas economy to one
primarily dependent on coal. The proposed fuel switch would change
the geographic base of fuel supply from the southwest U. S. and (hopefully) the Middle East countries to eastern Appalachia and the Rocky
Mountain west. In both the Appalachian and western states, the social
and economic impacts will be significant. The changing supply base

naturally means a drastic change in the national energy supply route. New energy transportation strategies will have to be devised to carry coal from the west and Eastern Appalachian states to the rest of the country. Though coal transportation routes existed from Appalachia to midwestern and eastern states during our initial industrial development era, these lines cannot, in their present condition, sustain the increased use that would be necessary to meet the demand.

The overall regional economic consequences of the national "switch" are significant. The cost of electricity, for instance, would increase, particularly in those regions depending on natural gas. According to unpublished administrative figures, industry in the central states is projected to increase. These industries will pay increased prices due to the higher price of coal over natural gas and the need to invest in expensive air pollution abatement equipment for coal-fired plants. This, in turn, would trigger increased national electricity costs, which are expected to go up to 17 percent by 1985. Regionally, the increase will vary. The northeast is expected to experience an increase of 5 percent, while the southwest would experience an increased cost of approximately 43 percent. Central and north central states' costs, however, could be increased as much as 30 percent over present costs.

In addition to the generic problems associated with the two regions called upon to serve the nation's coal needs, the Appalachian East and Rocky Mountain West, there are a number of problems that are dictated by the particular conditions of each region. In the recently published report of the Energy Impact Assistance Steering Group (1978), specific problems that are now being experienced by both regions are documented.

> The State of Kentucky has estimated that the increased transportation needs to support coal production will be approximately $151 million per year for capital outlay and $28. 4 million per year for maintenance of a total demand upon Kentucky of $179. 4 million per year over the next 10 years. In Colorado, the State Department of Highways has estimated that the existing coal and uranium mines, plus those new mines expected to be placed in production in the near future (including a low level of oil shale production), will require a minimum of $279 million in capital outlays for transportation improvements by 1990.
>
> The State of West Virginia estimates that approximately 35, 000 new miners will be required by 1985 to support an increase in coal production of 170 million tons in the State. The State has estimated that the related new

population associated with this development in need of infrastructure services will be 225,000. The cost of providing seven basic infrastructure needs of this new population
is estimated at from $1.2 to $1.4 billion (based on a per
capita cost of $5,518 and $6,098, respectively). The State
estimates that the cost of providing housing will be an additional $3.7 billion (p. 23).

The report also specifically delineates the extent and variety of
social and economic impacts associated with coal production within
various counties of each region.

In Rock Springs, Wyoming, a very large coal-fired power
plant was put under construction in 1972, with one month's
prior notice to local government. Simultaneously, the exi-
isting trona (natural soda ash) mining industry was expanding both its mining and processing operations. With
population growth rates of over 15-20 percent per year,
Rock Springs and nearby Green River faced inadequate
law enforcement services, overcrowded schools, inability to go beyond constitutional bonding limits to build
schools at a rate fast enough to accommodate enrollment
increases, and hesitance on the part of voters to bond
themselves to accommodate a boom of uncertain duration.
These factors, combined with other boom town problems
led to productivity declines in the existing mining industry of 25-40 percent, and similar shortfalls in expected
productivity in the energy development activity.
   The doctor-patient ratio went from 1/1100 to 1/
3700 within two years, because of the difficulty of attract-
ing additional health services professionals to this boom
community. At the height of Rock Springs' growth, 30 percent of the population indicated that they were obtaining
health services from Salt Lake City, 200 miles away. The
construction of a new supermarket required two years instead of the anticipated six months in Rock Springs because
of the malfunctioning labor market and the difficulty of
maintaining construction workforces in a boom situation.
Local merchants found it extremely difficult to obtain capital for inventory expansion, much less for new facilities,
until the boom had been underway for approximately two
years. As a result of such problems, a survey found 31
percent of the new residents, e.g., the newcomers who
were generating employment turnover rates of 100-150
percent annually, were saying they would leave town with-

in a year if there were not substantial improvements made in shopping facilities. Sixty percent were planning to leave if there were not substantial improvements in health services.

Similar problems occur in most of the isolated, rural localties where energy development is anticipated. The only variation is in the effectiveness of individual State economic development programs, and their flexibility in assisting commercial development in growth areas instead of the declining areas they are usually concerned with (Appendix A, pp. 2-3).

A Coal Economy

The coal extractive industry is, by the nature of the industry, a limited growth industry. Towns that grow up around specific mines will last only as long as the resource lasts. This is particularly a problem in Appalachia, where most coal is deep-mined and transportation corridors are not adequate to enable easy transport of workers within the region. The west has less of a problem in this respect, primarily because of its lesser dependency on workers (most of the coal is strip-mined) and because of the vast nature of the strip mines. Most workers do not live near the operation but in residential enclaves. Both regions must, however, plan to some degree for a boom/bust cycle. Economies must be based on resources of limited lifespan. The limited lifespan of the resource, including rapidly fluctuating population changes both in size and makeup, may completely overhaul local economic structures.

Social Consequences of Other Production Scenarios

Although coal production was selected as illustrative of an energy production initiative that necessarily involves immense social and economic changes, other energy production initiatives have similar impacts. The more rapid the development, the more rapid the population change. The degree of population impact would, of course, be dependent on many factors, including the degree to which the particular industry is dependent on technology, requiring the importation of a sophisticated staff. The negative aspects of such a rapid growth phenomenon could far outweigh its economic/social benefits. The character and extent of the population growth pose enormous problems in both the fabric of the community and the stability of the individual—problems that can be addressed and mitigated through well-planned community development scenarios.

CONCLUSION

The social and behavioral science community can serve the national need to establish responsive energy production policies by intensifying traditional programs and directing their research focus to rural and remote energy-rich areas of the country.

There is a pressing need for both practitioners and researchers in the fields of governmental management, planning, and administration; social work; law enforcement administration; community psychology and public health administration; and educational administration. Programs designed to train such individuals need to be skewed toward the particular complexities of energy production programs that are being implemented both in the far west and in Appalachia.

Moreover, the social science behavioral community needs to explore ways by which representative publics can better communicate among themselves and with decisionmakers, both in the private and public sector, toward the formulation of acceptable development criteria on specific projects. Innovative processes need to be devised that will allow for constructive dialogue among public and private decisionmakers above and beyond existing mechanisms that are usually of an adversary nature. Managers, policymakers, and administrators must be more effectively schooled in the various methodologies that could be employed to enhance public participation and consensus building, which would enhance their leadership rather than weaken it.

Since the impact and output of energy production projects ordinarily cross several jurisdictional boundaries, there is also a growing need to explore means by which regional institutions, both interstate and intrastate, can be established to effectively plan projects, share responsibility for development, and formulate effective and systematized governmental permitting procedures. The importance of establishing processes that "allow the development of consensus" toward the building of a national energy policy was the major conclusion of Kash et al. (1976, p. 5) on the role of research, development, and demonstration in reaching a national consensus on energy supply.

> After two years of research . . . we have come to one overriding conclusion: coping with the shortfall between domestic energy production and consumption is intimately tied to a broadened scope of participation. Only when ways are found to accommodate the varied interests that will be participating in decisionmaking will the energy crisis be resolved.

The solution to the energy crisis, then, lies in establishing various types of "negotiation" processes, involving all affected parties, in a manner such that all have sufficiently participated in the decision-making process toward the final resolution of specific energy initiatives. Although the type and degree of participation of the interested parties would depend on the particular initiative, to be successful such participatory systems should at least:

recognize the jurisdictional authority of states over their territories and the states' responsibility to protect the health and safety of their citizens, allowing governors of the states to be the principals in the process;

assure the education of the public on all relevant issues to enable interested parties to participate intelligently in the process;

allow for public hearings in a manner to assure responsive and timely input;

allow for redress by all affected parties to the highest levels of government, assuring that the final decision responds to the fullest degree to the concerns of the various publics and to the national interest;

facilitate cooperation and the exchange of relevant information and data between private and public sectors;

establish a single federal agency responsible to the fullest degree practicable for final resolution of decisions in specific energy policy areas.

The design and institutionalization of participatory decision-making processes along such guidelines, allowing the national interest to be served while safeguarding the interests of selected publics, demands the expertise of individuals schooled in behavioral sciences and legal and political processes.

In order to significantly contribute toward the establishment of such processes, the social and behavioral science community must first identify and characterize the major interests affected by specific energy production initiatives. Attention has to be given to understanding potential roadblocks to establishing an interactive participatory process. Among these would be anti-trust regulations; the private sector's need for confidentiality; the lack of an informed public; the lack of an institutional framework to provide for binding decisions between jurisdictional units of government; and an overly complex planning process.

To begin to design participatory processes to address the inter-jurisdictional nature of energy projects will require the study of interstate and intrastate relationships. Success will depend on the ability to "educate" and convince state and local officials, industrialists, and interest groups of the value of such interactive processes. It will require the social scientist to be more attentive to the practical real-world politics of the day, necessitating increased contact with decisionmakers.

The best and most effective way that this can be achieved will be through active involvement. Social and behavioral science departments and institutions need to establish programs, such as sabbatical leave programs, that allow individuals to have direct contact with and involvement in the energy decision-making environment. Only through such contact will the appreciation of the varied interests involved in energy decision making be obtained; and, through such appreciation, the potential of particular participatory processes evolve.

9
GOVERNMENT ROLES IN ENERGY MANAGEMENT: A RESEARCH PERSPECTIVE AND AGENDA

Anne D. Stubbs

The limited success of the United States in slowing its rate of energy consumption raises serious questions of public willingness and governmental capability to address complex problems in a comprehensive, noncrisis manner. Since the 1973/74 oil embargo, "energy" has become a priority topic of discussion, research, and analysis. Numerous studies have established the importance of energy resources to the economic well-being of modern industrial societies. Yet, with the impasse over federal energy policy, it is apparent that the government's role in energy management, and its capability to address energy management effectively, is less well defined. As a public policy area, energy management may be viewed as having three distinct components: delineation of the nature of the energy problem and articulation of policy objectives; knowledge of specific measures and actions that contribute to energy management objectives; and policy strategies and program measures most likely to lead to adoption of specific energy management actions. Government's role in energy management is most visible in the third area, but, in order to be most most effective, policies and programs must be closely and explicitly tied to an understanding of both the problem and the specific means to address it.

If policy research is to benefit both the analyst and the decision-maker, it must assume new directions. Since initial analyses of energy policy preceded technical studies of comprehensive energy sys-

---

I wish to thank Susan E. Clarke for her valuable comments on this paper.

140

tems, these analyses were frequently descriptive of government policy activities or prescriptive of options government should consider. Intensive research on technical, economic, and environmental aspects of energy systems is now generating empirical information and analysis of the energy problem and the means to address it. Future policy research must address itself, therefore, to bridging the gap between technical research on energy systems and management techniques and to empirical policy research on government's capability to address energy issues effectively.

It is the premise of this discussion of research needs that research on the means by which government can undertake energy management is premature if it is not preceded by and based on analysis of the relevant characteristics of energy and governmental systems. The structure of these two systems—one primarily physical and economic (albeit with broader implications), one primarily political and legal—and the dynamic relationship between them is a critical dimension for policy research. The following review of the dominant structural characteristics of each system suggests both a focus and agenda for research that is directed to the interaction of the decision-making processes of the energy and governmental systems.

ELEMENTS OF ENERGY MANAGEMENT

The concept of energy management incorporates two major elements: the patterns of energy flows in the economy; the decisional processes that affect the patterns of supply, demand, and price. Energy management, broadly defined, is a dynamic and deliberate process through which readjustment occurs in the relationship of energy supply, energy demand, energy-use efficiency, environmental factors, economic activity, and lifestyle. Energy management involves institutional adjustments within the governmental system, the private sector, and in public-private sector interactions. It also requires adjustments in the decision-making processes of government, of the private sector, and of the individual citizen. The basic premise of an energy management program is that it must be directed at supply and demand and that it requires actions that are both short- and long-term in their impacts. But the pervasiveness of the energy issue has government on the horns of a dilemma. Efforts to alter energy flow patterns have repercussions in other policy areas. Goals to change energy flow patterns and any subsequent actions to change the existing energy-economic mix are difficult to attain since they are directed at the basic order of American society. For example, a policy goal of reducing national dependence on imported oil by encouraging or mandating conversion to coal appears to conflict with the equally important objectives of environmental quality and continued economic growth. Also, the policy approach of reducing energy use and of generating energy capital investment funds with market- or tax-induced price increases is constrained by the equity and inflationary impacts of rapid price increases.

Government's role in energy management is influenced by the intergovernmental structure of the political system and by the interdependencies of policies and programs created by the intergovernmental system. Federal, state, and local governments have their respective authorities, sometimes distinct but frequently shared, which enable them to undertake energy management responsibilities. This overlapping structure of authority sets an important parameter for government's decision-making process for energy management. Differences in problem definition, for example, can be partially attributed to differences in the perspectives of decisionmakers at the federal, state, and local levels. At the federal level, supply issues focus on the aggregate national supply of various energy resources. Concern at the state level is further directed to the allocation of supply and the prices at which energy supplies are made available. Economic and social impacts associated with changes in supply availability and price are particularly sensitive issues at the state and local levels, where impacts are immediate and cannot be averaged over the nation as a whole.

As an end user of energy, government faces some of the same difficulties as the individual consumer or business in changing its use patterns. Government may use its regulatory and taxing authority to increase the level of domestic supply or to restrain the growth rate of energy consumption. Yet, through its policies and programs on transportation, housing, and public infrastructure, government can concurrently facilitate a steady rise in the rate of energy use.

Government's current indecisiveness on energy management programs can be attributed to informational gaps in the state of the art on management techniques as well as to institutional problems in addressing complex issues. One recent examination of the institutional question underlying energy management suggested that existing government decision-making mechanisms are unable to address the energy issue due to a lack of knowledge about energy flows, long lead times to increased supply, increasing size and centralization of energy facilities, and loss of incrementalism in decision making (Bensky and Armstrong 1975). In short, characteristics of both the energy system and the governmental system create problems for the development of coherent, effective energy management policies and programs.

THE STRUCTURE OF ENERGY
DECISION-MAKING PROCESSES

The basic objective of energy management programs and policies is change in the energy flow patterns of the economy through adjustments in supply-demand relationships. Achieving this objective involves influencing decisions made by users and suppliers of energy resources. The structure of various energy decision-making processes is an important focus for research on government's capability to manage the use of energy. Breaking the energy decision-making process into its component parts, the questions of "where and by whom" become critical. In other words, energy decision making can be viewed as a continuum, ranging from highly centralized to extremely fragmented structures, depending on the nature of the decision. In modern industrial societies, the decision pattern for energy demand is more fragmented than the decision-making structure for energy supply. Each point along the overlapping energy decision-making process (producer, intermediate and end users) represents a potential leverage point at which various governmental entities can attempt to influence the demand and supply patterns and interactions. The decisions of where and how to exert leverage are based upon several factors: energy fuel or resource to be managed, the energy use sector, impact considerations, and the unit of government attempting to exert leverage.

At one extreme and for certain energy uses, the relevant energy demand decisionmaker is the individual consumer, whose decisions on work, residence, and lifestyle in the aggregate contribute to energy demand. These decisions may be made with little thought or knowledge of their implications for energy consumption, although individual consumer demand may, in effect, be substantially determined by a centralized economic system. For other energy end uses, the critical decision may be highly centralized and more energy conscious. Product manufacturers of home and heating appliances, automobiles, and building components may willingly or under duress produce a product that uses energy more efficiently. Decisions on energy use in industrial processes are also more centralized and deliberate. While plant or corporate managers may be sensitive to energy availability and prices, they are also constrained by such factors as technological capabilities, environmental considerations, capital availability, and the economic feasibility of retrofitting an existing plant.

The decision-making structure for energy demand permits an interplay of governmental roles for energy management. The authority and institutional capability of federal and state governments are well suited to demand management programs. While the state has limited resources and legal authority to affect energy supply and prices, it does have appropriate powers to adopt and implement energy conservation strategies (Bensky and Armstrong 1975; Council of State Governments 1976a).

Approaching demand management policies and programs from a state or regional perspective has certain advantages. From the state perspective, data analyses can be more sensitive to the diverse mix of economic sectors, markets, geographic and climatic variables, and social behavior that affect energy use patterns. Policies based upon nationally aggregated demand and supply patterns and uniform program regulations are unlikely to be sensitive to the extreme number and diversity of "entry points" through which public policy can affect energy demand. In contrast, at state and regional levels, the design and administration of demand management policies and programs can be more flexible and responsive to energy and economic patterns. In developing a series on energy information, researchers often find that the regional level of analysis is a more effective approach to energy research (Brainard et al. 1976). For example, the northeastern states are attempting to build their individual capabilities to address energy related issues through a better understanding of the regional energy context within which their economies operate (New England Regional Commission 1976a, 1976e).

Decisions on energy supply, both type and level of energy resource, are made in a relatively centralized decision-making structure in the current "hard path" scenario (Lovins 1977b). Even with new emphases on solar and other forms of site-generated energy, U. S. economy continues to rely upon a centralized, integrated energy network for generation, distribution, and ownership. Energy companies, within the parameters of government regulation and market forces, make critical decisions about production levels, about exploration for new energy sources, and about the level of investment in research and development for alternate technologies and energy resources. National and international energy resource companies present a sharp contrast to the individual consumer. While supply decisions do react to demand, centralized decisions on the level and allocation of energy supplies greatly affect patterns of demand, both by sectors and by regional areas of the country since regions within the U. S. exhibit differing patterns of energy supply dependence (oil, gas, hydropower, coal). The oligarchic nature of energy companies and the national network of energy development and distribution systems effectively precludes any governmental entity other than the federal government from addressing supply and price variables. State governments can indirectly affect energy availability through policies and laws affecting energy siting and public utility regulation and through development of ports and related transportation networks (Council of State Governments 1976b; New England Regional Commission 1976b). The dominant federal role in supply and price issues is reinforced by federal preemption of authority over regulation of major energy distribution systems (natural gas, Alaskan oil, electric transmission lines).

Most of the land and water areas on which new energy resources can be exploited lie solely or primarily within the federal domain. Only the federal government's taxing authority is sufficiently broad in its reach to affect energy resource companies' activities. Finally, only the federal government has the necessary financial resources to support major research and development of alternate renewable energy resources.

ENERGY MANAGEMENT: A RESEARCH AGENDA

The pervasiveness and complexity of the energy, economic, and environmental relationship lead to three basic questions that must be addressed by policy analysts and decisionmakers: What is the nature of energy management—what are the major elements and how do they interrelate? What are appropriate and viable government roles in energy management? Which units in the intergovernmental structure are best suited to perform various energy management functions?

In short, government can develop and implement effective policies and strengthen its institutional capability to address energy management only to the extent that it understands the nature of the energy management problem and its own structural strengths and weaknesses. For optimal policy effectiveness, government's decision-making structure for energy management should be designed for close interaction with other energy decision-making processes.

Energy management policy research is a series of building blocks to which social science research can now productively contribute. The wealth of information on energy flows and specific management techniques being generated by technical and scientific research does not ensure that government will use this information effectively. Energy data must be complemented by social and policy sciences research on government's capability and role in energy management.

Energy management is not a policy area in which government objectives can be achieved directly through delivery or expenditure programs or by direct legal action. Government must direct its efforts to inducing those behavioral changes in the economic and social systems that lead to desired adjustments in energy flow patterns. Academic researchers have the responsibility and liberty to examine a full range of policy and program options theoretically available to government. In contrast, the practitioner who develops and implements policies must deal with limits on government's ability to act. The practitioner is best served by research that enhances his or her ability to make effective use of the resources available to government (money, workers, legal authority, suasion) by harnessing those resources in support of policies and programs with the potential for optimal impact.

Research contributing to this information need is characterized by empirical analysis and dynamic systems evaluation. To aid in policy and program development, empirical studies and multivariate analyses are needed to examine the dynamic relationship of energy supply, demand, and price factors to each other and to levels and changes in economic activity, employment, environmental factors, and income/expenditure patterns. Research findings drawn from hypothetical/situational studies and modeling analyses must be complemented by case studies and monitoring/evaluative research of ongoing programs. Finally, research must be directed to empirical analyses of the political, legal, and resource constraints within which government must operate.

The following research agenda is directed to identification and analysis of optimal leverage points and program tools for government to bring about desired changes in the energy system. Descriptive and analytical research on energy flows must continue and must be refined to meet the informational needs of policy analysts at each level of government. But research on energy flows must be complemented by analysis of the institutional aspects (structural, functional, process) of government's capability for energy management.

REFINEMENT OF ENERGY-RELATED DATA SYSTEMS

Continued refinement of energy data collection and analysis is a requisite for policy development. Current energy management analysis is hampered by the absence or incompleteness of data on energy flows and interactions at the national and subnational level of aggregation and by limited emphasis on monitoring/evaluative research designed to validate energy-related data generated by hypothetical analysis and modeling.

Initial efforts to develop an energy data base focused on readily available national data (Federal Energy Administration 1976a, 1976b; National Science Foundation 1975). These nationally aggregated data cannot reflect regional and state diversity of energy flows nor variations in supply and demand among regions and use sectors. Since energy management decisions and impacts occur at the local, state, and regional levels, data at the subnational level of aggregation are required for policy research. Efforts underway to develop baseline data on energy flows and supply/demand curves at the regional and state levels (New England Regional Commission 1976d; Brainard et al. 1976; Pacific Northwest Regional Commission 1976) should be expanded to identify and analyze energy distribution networks within and between geographic regions and regional economic interdependencies created by these distribution systems.

The types of data required for policy development include the level and distribution (by fuel type and region) of energy supply; technical data on energy management techniques (hardware and practices); geographic/climate data relevant to energy use; level and distribution of energy use at the household, substate, and state levels; economic and environmental impacts of energy management measures; and social indicators describing attitudinal and behavioral changes related to energy management techniques and policies.

Reliable indicators of energy variables and management impacts should be developed when a complete data base is not available for each level of policymaking. State-of-the-art modeling techniques for demand and supply prediction for various energy sources (electricity, oil, gas, coal, alternate sources) must be examined to determine whether current techniques make adequate allowance for management efforts and technological advances and whether anticipated demand is distinguished from anticipated need (Daly 1976). Since utility investment is regulated by government, research is needed to determine the type of information on future capital expenditures that can be extrapolated from demand models.

As baseline data are developed and management programs implemented, data collection and analysis must also incorporate monitoring and evaluation of actual changes in energy flow patterns. Management techniques may be developed by hypothetical analysis, but their effectiveness is verified by causal analysis of actual changes in energy flow patterns. Monitoring is necessary to identify the magnitude and direction of change in each variable. Information generated by such research is vital for assessment of impacts of management techniques and for refinement of policy approaches devised from hypothetical analysis.

Multivariate Analysis

The emphasis on energy flow dynamics shifts the research focus to economic, technological, social, environmental, and political variables associated with energy flows. With a multivariate approach, various leverage points for inducing changes in either the supply or demand side of the energy equation can be identified, and actual or hypothesized outcomes of changing one or more of the energy variables can be analyzed. Such research provides actual or predictive

information on critical questions for policymakers, namely, whether
a given change in one or more of the energy variables will affect the
supply-demand relationship, at what cost, over what time period,
and with what environmental, social, and economic consequences
(New England Regional Commission 1976c, 1975b; Krutilla and Page
1976; Baughman and Hnyilicza 1976; Enzer 1975; Jorgenson and
Houthakker 1973).

The energy-environment-economic-social relationship has been
asserted more than demonstrated. Thus, case studies, modeling, and
regression analysis can contribute to more informed policy analysis
by providing a better understanding of these relationships. The economic concept of opportunity costs can be incorporated in proposals
to achieve energy objectives through manipulation of any given variable. Further attention must also be paid to the economic and social
equity consequences, to individuals and to government, associated
with changes in energy patterns.

Energy Management Techniques and Policy Implementation

Analysis of the means to change energy patterns permits identi-
tification of policy options available to government to affect energy
flows (Ahern et al. 1973; Seidel, Plotkin, and Reck 1973; Kalter and
Vogely 1976; Energy Research and Development Administration 1975).
Since energy management policy must address immediate and long-
term changes in energy patterns, research on management techniques
must assess the lead time required for adoption and outcomes of various techniques.

In the area of supply management, policy research must build
from basic and still debated studies on the scientific, technological,
economic, and environmental feasibility of developing renewable and
nonrenewable energy resources (Decision Sciences Corporation 1973;
U. S. Environmental Protection Agency 1973; Portola Institute, n. d.).
Analyses of the government's role in managing energy supply under
soft path conditions are essential. Federal policies and regulations
on taxation, energy distribution systems, and environmental protection as they affect energy system decision making have received some
research attention (Mitchell 1976; Tietenberg 1976; Breyer and Mac-
Avoy 1974) and would profit from further development.

A major focus of energy management research is on the techniques to slow or reduce the growth rate in energy demand. Demand
management research has been directed to management techniques in
those sectors accounting for a major portion of the nation's energy
consumption. These include load management in the utilities industry
(Federal Energy Administration 1975a, 1975b); increased energy ef-

ficiency in buildings (American Institute of Architects 1974; Moyers 1971; Little 1976; Hittman Associates 1975), price elasticities for demand in various sectors (Askin and Kraft 1976; Jorgenson 1976); and solar energy systems and onsite generation (Scott, Melicher, and Sciglimpaglia 1974; Duffie and Beckman 1974).

Constraints on Techniques and Strategies
for Energy Management

Research and analyses offered in support of policy and program options frequently fail to account for the constraints within which government decisionmakers must act. To a researcher, these political, economic, and institutional factors are variables whose change is one research objective. To a decisionmaker, these constraints are situational variables over which he or she has limited control at any given point in time.

Data on total exploitable energy resources and energy savings possible through technical changes or demand management techniques are frequently inflated by "best case" scenarios. The optimistic findings frequently result from research assumptions that fail to account for economic, social, and institutional constraints. These constraints may be inadequate research and investment capital for resource development, limited elasticity of demand or supply to price changes, legal or market constraints to adoption of management techniques, or lack of public responsiveness to voluntary, incentive, or disincentive programs to change energy use patterns. Approaching policy and program development through analysis of potential obstacles provides the decisionmaker who must target limited resources with important information and valuable insights (Hagel 1976; Macrikis 1974; Olsen and Goodnight 1977; Schipper 1975).

Governments' Policy Responses to Energy Management

Federal and state governments have addressed energy management capability with a diverse array of organization, policy, and legislative initiatives. Federal and state energy offices have been created with responsibility for regulation, research, information dissemination, and/or program development (Council of State Governments 1976c; Federal Energy Administration 1975b). Legislative and administrative actions set in place policies and programs that were regulatory, voluntary, and informational in nature (Council of State Governments 1976b). Examination of government's capability must begin with an assessment of its responses. The various program responses should be monitored and evaluated for information on the scope and impacts of these policy approaches and programs and on the relative effectiveness of each policy approach in reaching the target audience. With this information, policy analysts can better determine how effectively available energy information is being utilized in the design and implementation of policies and programs and the extent to which additional research efforts should be directed to refinement of energy information or to improvement of government's capability to act effectively.

The organizational response of creation of special agencies for energy matters should also be carefully assessed. This response raises anew the public administration issue of whether a separate organization for an issue as pervasive as energy management will enhance or detract from the capability for energy management. A separate energy office may bring greater attention to the concern for energy management by creating an advocate agency, but it may isolate these program efforts from the large number of government agencies and decisions affected by energy flows. The debate between structure and process leads to the need for research on mechanisms to encourage the inclusion of energy management objectives and programs in decisional processes of key functional agencies (New England Regional Commission 1975a; Duga, Malone, and Davis 1975).

Structural and Functional Roles of Government

The analysis of governmental organization must be broader than the relative benefits and disadvantages of a separate energy office. The pervasiveness of energy issues requires that policy research focus on governmental structure as a whole and its interaction with the energy system and on the interaction of government structure with nonenergy policies and programs. Examining the structure of government (formal authorities, resources) in light of the energy decision-making structure suggests a role specialization within the intergovernmental system. This policy focus, by highlighting the interactions among agencies within and between each level of government (horizontal and vertical interactions), increases research finding sensitivity to the vulnerability of a given governmental entity in respect to decisions and actions made within a separate government context. This approach to organizational analysis contributes to optimal interaction of the energy and governmental systems.

A further refinement of role specialization results from analysis of the functional roles and policy approaches available to each level of government, in light of the energy decision-making system and the factors contributing to changes in energy flow patterns. These functional roles include regulation, financial incentives and disincentives, public education, voluntary actions, and public suasion. Breaking government involvement into its component parts and analyzing the functional roles available to each governmental entity in light of the energy system structure and process has several advantages for analysis. It permits the policy analysts to target government's activities to the policy objectives and program measures most appropriate to the formal authorities and available resources of each actor at the federal, state, and local levels (Bensky and Armstrong 1975; McLane 1974).

Once the discrete energy management roles of government have been identified and analyzed, they must be reassembled for integrated structure and processes necessary to optimal policy effectiveness. Energy management must become a routine component of planning and decision making in government. Energy use and supply considerations must become a factor in the tradeoff process of public decision making in those areas where such decisions influence or determine subsequent energy flow patterns. These include transportation, environmental programs, land use, public capital investments, and economic development programs.

A major area for policy research is identification and analysis of both conflicts and complementarity between energy management objectives and measures and related areas of environmental, economic, and social policies. Analysis of policy and program conflicts has an intergovernmental dimension that must be explored. Regional differences in economic, environmental, and energy impacts of national policy, which heighten these conflicts at state and regional levels, may effectively negate program implementation at those levels. Since conflicting policy goals and programs will not likely be eliminated, research should address the means to minimize conflict through modification of policy objectives and approaches and of program measures.

Complementary programs that are adjuncts to formal energy management measures should be identified and developed. Long-term energy management objectives may be best achieved by program efforts that are only indirectly energy management techniques. Urban development and rehabilitation programs, including housing, antiredlining, mortage/rehabilitation loan programs, public services, zoning, and public transit facilities should be examined for their roles in supporting or detracting from efficient energy use patterns.

CONCLUSION

In summary, social science research on energy management policies needs to take into account the structural and decisional pro-

152 / ANNE D. STUBBS

cess characteristics of the current patterns of energy flows in the economy and the private and public sector units whose decisions affect the patterns of supply, demand, and price. How such characteristics might vary under different hard and soft path conditions is an important dimension of this perspective.

Attributes of both energy flow systems and governmental policy-making systems contribute to difficulties in development of coherent, effective energy management policies and programs. The degree of fragmentation in energy decision-making structures appears to differ among governmental units and between supply and demand perspectives. This variation affects the types of policy research called for and the manner in which research questions are formulated. As noted, policy research at the regional level of analysis appears to be especially useful to state policymakers, whereas information on nationally aggregated demand and supply patterns is of critical importance to national policymakers.

To ensure that governments can effectively guide desired adjustments in energy flow patterns, policymakers need further social science analyses of the economic, social, and environmental impacts of various energy technology options, feasible and viable policy instrumentalities for achieving agreed upon objectives, and studies of nontechnological impediments to effective energy management policy implementation. Priorities on a social science energy research agenda include issues of regional energy data collection and validation; development of energy-relevant social indicators; economic and social equity consequences associated with changes in energy patterns; evaluation of the effectiveness of supply and demand management techniques; institutional barriers to development of alternative energy technologies and energy policy implementation; organizational modes for energy programs; and policy interdependencies, particularly of economic, environmental, and energy policies. Both the research methodologies and the behavioral perspective of social science research are valuable contributions to contemporary energy policy formulation.

BIBLIOGRAPHY

Ahern, William, Ronald Doctor, William Harriss, Albert Lipson, Deane Morris, and Richard Nehring. 1973. Energy Alternatives for California: Paths To the Future. Santa Monica: The Rand Corporation.

Almond, Gabriel A. and Stephen J. Genco. 1977. "Clouds, Clocks, and the Study of Politics." World Politics 29 (July: 518).

American Institute of Architects. 1974. Energy and the Built Environment: A Gap in Current Strategies. Washington, D.C.: The American Institute of Architects.

American Physical Society. 1975. "Report to the APs by the Study Group on Light-Water Reactor Safety." Review of Modern Physics 47: Suppl. No. 1.

Argyris, Chris. 1976. "Organizations of the Future." In Improving Urban Management, edited by W. Hawley and D. Rogers, pp. 175-208. Beverly Hills: Sage.

Arnstein, Sherry R. 1977. "Technology Assessment: Opportunities and Obstacles." Institute of Electrical and Electronics Engineers Transactions on Systems, Man, and Cybernetics SMC-7 (August).

Asimov, Isaac. 1977. "The Nightmare Life Without Fuel." Time Magazine, April 25, 1977, p. 33.

Askin, A. Bradley and John Kraft, eds. 1976. Econometric Dimensions of Energy Demand and Supply. Lexington, Mass.: Lexington Books.

Barry, T. and Associates. 1972. Fatality Analysis Data Base Development. Prepared for U.S. Bureau of Mones, June 30, 1972.

Battelle Pacific Northwest Laboratories. 1978. An Analysis of Federal Incentives Used to Stimulate Energy Production. Seattle: Battelle Human Affairs Research Centers.

Bauer, Raymond A., ed. 1966. Social Indicators. Cambridge: Massachusetts Institute of Technology Press.

Baughman, Martin and Esteban Hnyilicza. 1976. "System Interdepencies and Government Policy." In Energy Supply and Government Policy, edited by Robert J. Kalter and William A. Vogely. Ithaca: Cornell University Press.

Becker, Ernest. 1974. The Denial of Death. New York: Free Press.

Bensky, Lawrence and John R. Armstrong. 1975. Energy: The Institutional Question. Madison, Wis.: State Planning Office, Department of Administration.

Bereano, P. L., ed. 1976. Technology as a Social and Political Phenomenon. New York: John Wiley.

Berg, Mark R., Kan Chen, and George J. Zissis. 1975. "Methodologies in Perspective." In Perspectives of Technology Assessment. Jerusalem: Science and Technology Publishers.

Berkowitz, Leonard. 1970. "The Self, Selfishness, and Altruism." In Altruism and Helping Behavior, edited by J. Macauley and L. Berkowitz. New York: Academic Press.

Bethe, Hans. 1976. "The Necessity of Nuclear Fission." Scientific American 234 (January: 21-31).

Biomedical and Environmental Assessment Group. 1974. The Health and Environmental Effects of Electricity Generation: A Preliminary Report. BEAG-HE/EE, BNL 20582. Upton, N.Y.: Brookhaven National Laboratory.

Black, Henry Campbell. 1951. Black's Law Dictionary. St. Paul: West.

Blair, John. 1976. The Control of Oil. New York: Pantheon.

Blocker, T. G. Jr., W. W. Washburn, S. R. Lewis, and Virginia Blocker. 1961. "A Statistical Study of 1,000 Burn Patients Admitted to the Plastic Surgery Service of the University of Texas Medical Branch." Journal of Trauma 2 (July): 409-23.

Boulding, Kenneth. 1976. "The Importance of Improbable Events." Technology Review 78 (February): 5.

Brainard, Joel, Harry Davitian, Richard Goettle, and Philip F. Palmedo. 1976. A Perspective on the Energy Future of the Northeast United States. Upton, N. Y.: Brookhaven National Laboratory.

Branscomb, Lewis. 1978. Testimony before a joint hearing of the U. S. Senate Committee on Commerce, Science, and Transportation and the U. S. House Committee on Science and Technology, Washington, D. C., February.

Braybrooke, David and Charles Edward Lindblom. 1970. A Strategy of Decision. New York: Free Press.

Bresee, James C. 1978. "Memorandum to all Recipients of Requests for Proposals to Conduct Research into the Potential of Wood Energy for Commercial and Industrial Use." Research Triangle Park, N. C.: North Carolina Energy Institute, September 22.

Breyer, Stephen G. and Paul W. MacAvoy. 1974. Energy Regulation by the Federal Power Commission. Washington, D. C.: Brookings Institute.

Brim, Orville G., ed. 1969. Knowledge into Action: Improving the Nation's Use of the Social Sciences. National Science Board, Special Commission on the Social Sciences. Washington, D. C.: National Science Foundation.

Brown, Edwin. 1961. "Space Heater Hazards." New England Journal of Medicine 265 (October 19): 794-95.

Brubaker, Sterling. 1975. In Command of Tomorrow. Baltimore: Johns Hopkins University Press.

Buechley, Robert W., Wilson B. Riggan, Victor Hasselblad, and John B. Van Bruggen. 1973. "SO_2 Levels and Perturbations in

Mortality: A Study in the New York–New Jersey Metropolis."
Archives of Environmental Health 27 (American Medical Association Specialty Journals): 137.

Burright, Burke K. and John Enns. 1975. Econometric Models of the Demand for Motor Fuel. Rand Report R-1561-National Science Foundation/Federal Energy Administration, April. Washington, D. C.

Callenbach, Ernst. 1975. Ecotopia. Berkeley: Banyan Tree Books.

Canfield, Monte, Jr. and Adam E. Sieminski. 1975. "If You're So Smart, Why Ain't You Rich?" Public Administration Review 35 (July-August): 322-27.

Carr, Lowell J. and James E. Stermer. 1952. Willow Run: A Study of Industrialization and Cultural Inadequacy. New York: Harper.

Clark, Wilson. 1974. Energy for Survival. New York: Doubleday.

Coates, Joseph F. 1977. "What Is a Public Policy Issue." Paper presented at the Symposium on Judgment and Choice in Public Policy Decisions, annual meeting of the American Association for the Advancement of Science, Denver, February 23.

_____. 1976. "Why Think About the Future: Some Administrative-Political Perspectives." Public Administration Review 36 (5): 580-85.

_____. 1975. "Technology Assessment at NSF." In Perspectives of Technology Assessment. Jerusalem: Science and Technology Publishers.

_____. N. d. "Technology Assessment—What It Means to You, Your Profession, Your Corporation, Your World." Washington, D. C.

Coleman, J. S. 1972. Policy Research in the Social Sciences. Morristown, N. J.: General Learning Press.

Commoner, Barry. 1975. "How Poverty Breeds Population (And Not the Other Way Around)." Ramparts 13 (August): 21-25.

Commoner, Barry, Howard Boksenbaum, and Michael Corr, eds. 1975. Energy and Human Welfare: The Social Costs of Power Production. New York: Macmillan.

Cook, Earl. 1976. Man, Energy, Society. San Francisco: Witti Freeman.

Council of State Governments. 1976a. Energy Conservation: Policy
Considerations for the States. Lexington, Ky.: Council of State
Governments.

____. 1976b. Energy Legislation Update: 1973-76. Lexington, Ky.:
Council of State Governments.

____. 1976c. State Energy Organization Charts. Lexington, Ky.:
Council of State Governments.

Cunningham, William H. and Sally Lopreato. 1977. "Annotated Bibliography of Energy Attitude Surveys." In Energy Use and Conservation Incentives: A Study of the Southwestern United States,
edited by W. H. Cunningham and S. C. Lopreato. New York:
Praeger.

Daly, Herman E. 1976. "Energy Demand Forecasting: Prediction or
Planning?" The American Institute of Planners Journal (January: 4-15.

Damon, Paul E. and Steven M. Kunen. 1976. "Global Cooling?" Science 193 (August 6): 447-53.

Darley, John M. and Bibb Latané. 1968. "Bystander Intervention in
Emergencies: Diffusion of Responsibility." Journal of Personality and Social Psychology 8 (April): 377-83.

Darmstadter, Joel, Joy Dunkerley, and Jack Alterman. 1977. How
Industrial Societies Use Energy: A Comparative Analysis. Balti-
more: Johns Hopkins University Press for Resources for the
Future.

de Bono, Edward. 1973. Lateral Thinking. New York: Harper & Row.

Decision Sciences Corporation. 1973. Economic Evaluation of Total
Energy: Guidelines. Washington, D. C.: U. S. Department of
Housing and Urban Development, July.

Doll, Richard and Austin B. Hill. 1964. "Mortality in Relation to
Smoking: Ten Years Observation of British Doctors." British
Medical Journal 1: 1,399-410.

Doner, W. B., Inc. and Market Opinion Research. 1975. Consumer Study—Energy Crisis Attitudes and Awareness. Lansing: Michigan Department of Commerce.

Dovidio, John F. and William N. Morris. 1975. "Effects of Stress and Commonality of Fate on Helping Behavior." Journal of Personality and Social Psychology 31 (January): 145-49.

Duffie, John A. and William A. Beckman. 1974. Solar Energy Thermal Processes. Somerset, N. J.: John Wiley.

Duga, Jules J., David W. Malone, and Richard M. Davis. 1975. Energy: The Policy Planning Framework in State Governments. Columbus, Ohio: Batelle Columbus Laboratories.

Dunkerley, Joy, ed. 1978. International Comparisons of Energy Consumption. Proceedings of a workshop sponsored by Resources for the Future and the Electric Power Research Institute. Washington, D. C.: Resources for the Future.

Easton, Dennis. 1975. "Toward A Reassessment of the Concept of Political Support." British Journal of Political Science 5 (October): 435-57.

_____. 1965. A Systems Analysis of Political Life. New York: John Wiley.

Elgin, Duane S. and Arnold Mitchell. 1977. "Voluntary Simplicity: Life-style of the Future?" The Futurist 11 (August): 200ff.

Ellul, Jacques. 1964. The Technological Society. New York: Vintage Books.

Energy Impact Assistance Steering Group. 1978. Report to the President: Energy Impact Assistance. Washington, D. C.: U. S. Department of Energy, Office of Assistant Secretary for Intergovernmental and Institutional Relations, March.

Energy Research and Development Administration. 1975. A National Plan for Energy Research, Development, and Demonstration: Creating Energy Choices for the Future. Vol. 2. Washington, D. C.: Program Implementation (ERDA-48).

Environmental Reporter. 1977. "EPA Reports Data on Industry Effort." Edited by John D. Stewart. 8 (August 12): 565-66.

Enzer, Selwyn. 1975. Some Societal Impacts of Alternate Energy Policies. Menlo Park, Calif.: Institute for the Future.

Erickson, Kai. 1976a. Everything in its Path. New York: Simon & Schuster.

____. 1976b. "Trauma at Buffalo Creek." Society 13 (September-October): 58.

Executive Office of the President. 1977. The National Energy Plan. Washington, D. C.: U. S. Government Printing Office.

Falk, Richard A. 1971. This Endangered Planet. New York: Random House.

Federal Energy Administration. 1976a. Monthly Energy Review. Washington, D. C.: National Energy Information Center.

____. 1976b. National Energy Outlook. Washington, D. C.: National Energy Information Center.

____. 1975a. The Challenge of Load Management: A Convergence of Diverse Interests. Washington, D. C.: Office of Utilities.

____. 1975b. Directory of State Government Energy Related Agencies. Washington, D. C.: National Energy Information Center, September.

Ford Foundation Energy Policy Project. 1974. A Time To Choose: America's Energy Future. Cambridge, Mass.: Ballinger.

Frankena, Frederick L., Frederick H. Buttel, and Denton E. Morrison. 1976. "Energy/Society Annotations." Supplement to Morrison et al. 1976. Prepared for the Sociopolitical Risk/Impact Panel of the Committee on Nuclear and Alternative Energy Systems. Washington, D. C.: National Research Council of the National Academy of Sciences.

Freeman, S. David. 1974. Energy: The New Era. New York: Vintage Books. New York: Walker.

Fritch, Albert J. 1974. The Contrasumers: A Citizens Circle to Resource Conservation. New York: Praeger.

Insulation. Princeton: The Gallup Organization.

_____. 1977. The Public's Behavior and Attitudes During the February 1977 Energy Crisis. Princeton: The Gallup Organization.

General Accounting Office. 1978. The Multiprogram Laboratories. Washington, D. C. : General Accounting Office, May 22.

Georgescu-Roegen, Nicholas. 1974. The Entropy Law and the Economic Process. Cambridge: Harvard University Press.

Goeller, H. E. and Alvin M. Weinberg. 1976. "The Age of Substitutability." Science 191 (February): 689.

Gottlieb, David and Mark Matre. 1976. Sociological Dimensions of the Energy Crisis: A Follow-up Study. Houston: The Energy Institute.

Gould, Leroy C. and Charles A. Walker, eds. Forthcoming. Too Hot to Handle: Public Policy Issues in Nuclear Waste Management. New Haven: Yale University Press.

Greer, Ann L. 1976. "Training Board Members for Health Planning Agencies: A Review of the Literature." Public Health Reports 91 (1): 56-61.

Hagel, John. 1976. Alternate Energy Strategies: Constraints and Opportunities. New York: Praeger.

Handler, Phillip. 1979. "Science, Technology, and Social Achievements." Paper presented at the Edison Centennial Symposium, San Francisco, April.

Hannon, Bruce. 1977. "Energy and Labor Demand in the Conservor Society." Technology Review 79 (February): 47-53.

_____. 1975. "Energy Conservation and the Consumer." Science 189 (July): 95-102.

Harris, Louis and Associates, Inc. 1977. Harris 1977 Carter Energy Plan Survey #3739. New York: Louis Harris and Associates (Producer); Chapel Hill, N. C. : The Harris Data Center, University of North Carolina (Distributor).

Gallup, George. 1978. A Survey of Homeowners Concerning Home

____. 1974a. Harris February 1974 Energy Shortage Survey #2413. New York: Louis Harris and Associates (Producer), Chapel Hill, N.C.: The Harris Data Center, University of North Carolina (Distributor).

____. 1974b. Harris March 1974 Survey on the Energy Shortage #7484. New York: Louis Harris and Associates (Producer), Chapel Hill, N. C.: The Harris Data Center, University of North Carolina (Distributor).

Hayes, Denis. 1977. Rays of Hope. New York: W. H. Norton.

____. 1976. Energy: The Case for Conservation. Washington, D. C.: Worldwatch Institute.

Heberlein, Thomas A. and J. Stanley Black. 1976. "Attitudinal Specificity and the Prediction of Behavior in a Field Setting." Journal of Personality and Social Psychology 33 (April): 474-79.

Helme, Edward A. 1978. National Energy Plan Coal Production Goals: New Responsibilities for the States. Washington, D. C.: National Governors' Association/Center for Policy Research.

Henderson, Floyd M. and Michael P. Voiland, Jr. 1975. "Possible Effects of Energy Shortages on Residential Preferences." The Professional Geographer 27 (August): 323-26.

Henderson, Hazel. 1978. "Science and Technology: The Revolution from Hardware to Software." Technological Forecasting and Social Change 12 (December): 317-24.

Herendeen, Robert A. 1974. "Affluence and Energy Demand." Mechanical Engineering 9 (October): 18-22.

Hill, Robert. 1971. The Strength of Black Families. New York: Emerson Hall.

Hittman Associates, Inc. 1975. Technology Assessment of Residential Energy Conservation Innovations. Washington, D. C.: Department of Housing and Urban Development, May.

Hogan, Mary J. 1976. "Energy Conservation: Family Values, Household Practices, and Contextual Variables." Ph. D. dissertation, Michigan State University.

Hoheumser, Kurt. 1975. "The Failsafe Risk." Environment 17 (January/February): 6-10.

Holdren, John and Philip Herrera. 1971. Energy: A Crisis in Power. San Francisco: The Sierra Club.

Hoos, Ida. 1974. Systems Analysis in Public Policy: A Critique. Berkeley: University of California Press.

Hornstein, Harvey A. , Elizabeth Lakind, Gladys Frankel, and Stella Manne. 1975. "Effects of Knowledge about Remote Social Events on Prosocial Behavior, Social Conception, and Mood." Journal of Personality and Social Psychology 32 (December): 1,038-46.

Illich, Ivan. 1974. Energy and Equity. New York: Perennial Press.

Institute for Contemporary Studies. 1975. No Time to Confuse: A Critique of the Final Report of the Energy Policy Project of the Ford Foundation: A Time to Choose America's Energy Future. San Francisco: Institute for Contemporary Studies.

Institute for Energy Analysis. 1978. Economic and Environmental Implications of a U.S. Nuclear Moratorium, 1985-2010. Oak Ridge, Tenn.: Institute for Energy Analysis.

International Energy Agency. 1978. 1977 IEA Reviews of National Energy Programmes. Paris: Office of Long-term Co-operation and Policy Analysis.

Jorgenson, Dale W. , ed. 1976. Econometric Studies of United States Energy Policy. New York: Elsevier.

Jorgenson, Dale W. and Hendrik Houthakker, eds. 1973. Energy Resources and Economic Growth. Cambridge: Ballinger.

Kahn, Herman, William Brown, and Leon Martel. 1976. The Next 200 Years. New York: William Morrow.

Kalter, Robert J. and William A. Vogely, eds. 1976. Energy Supply and Government Policy. Ithaca: Cornell University Press.

Kash, Don E. , Michael D. Devine, James B. Freim, Martha W. Gilliland, Robert W. Rycroft, and Thomas J. Wilbanks. 1976. Our Energy Future: The Role of Research, Development, and Demonstration in Reaching a National Consensus on Energy Supply. Norman: University of Oklahoma Press.

Keeny, Spurgeon M., Jr. 1977. Nuclear Power: Issues and Choices. Nuclear Energy Policy Study Group of the Ford Foundation. Cambridge: Ballinger.

Kilkeary, Rovena. 1975. The Energy Crisis and Decision-making in the Family. Springfield, Va.: National Technical Information Service, U.S. Department of Commerce (PB38783).

Kneese, Allen V. 1977. Economics and the Environment. New York: Penguin Books.

Krebs, Dems, L. 1975. "Empathy and Altruism." Journal of Personality and Social Psychology 32 (6): 1,134-46.

____. 1970. "Altruism—An Examination of the Concept and a Review of the Literature." Psychological Bulletin 73 (4): 258-302.

Krieger, Martin. 1970. "Six Propositions on the Poor and Pollution." Policy Sciences 1 (3): 311-24.

Krutilla, John V. and R. Talbot Page. 1976. "Energy Policy from an Environmental Perspective." In Energy Supply and Government Policy, edited by Robert J. Kalter and William A. Vogely, pp. 76-98. Ithaca: Cornell University Press.

Kuhn, Thomas. 1974. The Structure of Scientific Revolutions. Chicago: University of Chicago Press.

Landsberg, Hans H., John J. Schrenz, Jr., Sam H. Schurr, and Grent P. Thompson, eds. 1974. Energy and the Social Sciences: An Examination of Research Needs. Washington, D.C.: Resources for the Future.

Lindberg, Leon. 1977. "Comparing Energy Policies: Political Constraints and the Energy Syndrome." In The Energy Syndrome, edited by Leon Lindberg, pp. 325-356. Lexington, Mass.: Lexington Books.

Lindsey, Hal. 1970. The Late Great Planet Earth. Grand Rapids, Mich.: Zonderdan.

Little, A. D., Inc. 1976. Energy Conservation in New Buildings: An Impact Assessment of ASHRAE 90-75. Washington, D.C.: Federal Energy Administration.

Liu, Ben-Chieh. 1975. Quality of Life Indicators in U. S. Metropolitan Areas, 1970: A Comprehensive Assessment. Kansas City, Md. : Midwest Research Institute.

Lovins, Amory B. 1977a. "Cost-Risk-Benefit Assessments in Energy Policy. " The George Washington Law Review 45 (August): 911-43.

_____. 1977b. Soft Energy Paths: Toward a Durable Peace. San Francisco: Friends of the Earth International. Cambridge: Ballinger.

Lundin, Francis E. , Joseph K. Wagoner, and Victor E. Archer. 1971. Radon Daughter Exposure and Respiratory Cancer: Quantitative and Temporal Aspects. Report from the epidemiological study of U. S. uranium miners. National Institute of Occupational Safety and Health, Joint Monograph No. 1. Washington, D. C. : U. S. Public Health Service.

Macauley, Jacqueline R. 1970. "A Shrill for Charity. " In Altruism and Helping Behavior, edited by Jacqueline R. Macauley and Leonard Berkowitz, pp. 43-60. New York: Academic Press.

Macrikis, Michael S. , ed. 1974. Energy: Demand, Conservation, and Institutional Problems. Cambridge: Massachusetts Institute of Technology Press.

Mazur, Allan and Eugene Rosa. 1974. "Energy and Life Style. " Science 186 (November 15): 607-10.

McLane, James. 1974. "Energy Goals and Institutional Reform. " Futurist 8 (October): 239-42.

Meadows, Donella H. , Dennis L. Meadows, Jorgen Randers, and William W. Behrens III. 1972. The Limits to Growth. New York: University Books.

Mesarovic, Mihajlo and Edvard Peste. 1974. Mankind at the Turning Point: The Second Report to the Club of Rome. New York: E. P. Dutton and Reader's Digest Press.

Michener, H. A. and Martha R. Burt. 1975. "Components of 'Authority' as Determinants of Compliance. " Journal of Personality and Social Psychology 31 (April): 606-14.

Miles, Rufus. 1976. Awakening From the American Dream. New York: Universal Books.

Milstein, Jeffrey. 1977. "How Consumers Feel About Energy." Unpublished report available from the U. S. Department of Energy, Office of Conservation and Solar Applications, Division of Buildings and Community Systems, Washington, D. C.

_____. 1976. "Attitudes, Knowledge, and Behavior of American Consumers Regarding Energy Conservation with Some Implications for Governmental Action." Unpublished document of the Federal Energy Administration, Washington, D. C.

Mitchell, Edward J. , ed. 1976. Perspectives on United States Energy Policy: A Critique of Regulation. The American Enterprise Institute for Public Policy Research. New York: Praeger.

Morgan, W. Keith C. , Dean B. Burgess, George Jacobson, Richard J. O'Brien, Eugene P. Pendergrass, Robert B. Reger, and Earle Shoub. 1973. "The Prevalence of Coal Workers' Pneumoconiosis in U. S. Coal Miners." Archives of Environmental Health 27 (October): 221-26.

Morgenstern, Oskar. 1973. On the Accuracy of Economic Observations. 2nd ed. Princeton: Princeton University Press.

Morrison, Bonnie M. and Peter M. Gladhart. 1976. "Energy and Families: The Crisis and the Response." Journal of Home Economics 68 (January): 15-18.

Morrison, Denton E. 1978. "Equity Impacts of Some Major Energy Alternatives." In Energy Policy in the United States, edited by Seymour Warkov, pp. 164-189. New York: Praeger.

_____. 1977. "Equity Impacts of Some Major Energy Alternatives." Paper presented at the annual meetings of the American Sociological Association, Chicago, August-September.

_____. 1976. "Growth, Environment, Equity and Scarcity." Social Science Quarterly 57 (September): 292-306.

Morrison, Denton E. , Virginia Bernis, Frederick L. Frankena, Frederick H. Buttel, Joseph Galin, Olivia Mejorado, and Jay Cardinal. 1976. "Energy/Society Reference Update: A Bibliography of Recent Social Science and Related Literature." Prepared for the Sociopolitical Rise/Impact Resource Group of the Risk/Impact Panel of the Committee on Nuclear and Alternative Energy Systems. Washington, D. C. : National Research Council of the National Academy of Sciences.

Mount, Timothy and Timothy Tyrrell. 1977. Energy Demand: Conservation, Taxation, and Growth. Cornell Agricultural Economics Staff Paper #77-33, Appendix to chap. 6 of the Report on the Panel on Energy Demand and Conservation of the Committee on Nuclear and Alternative Energy Systems. Washington, D. C.: National Academy of Sciences/National Research Council, August.

Moyers, John C. 1971. The Value of Thermal Insulation in Residential Construction: Economics and the Conservation of Energy. Oak Ridge, Tenn.: Oak Ridge National Laboratory, December.

Murray, James R., Michael J. Minor, Norman M. Bradburn, Robert F. Cotterman, Martin Frankel, and Allen E. Pisaiski. 1974. "Evolution of Public Response to the Energy Crisis." Science 184 (April): 257-63.

National Academy of Sciences. 1977. Energy and Climate. Washington, D. C.: National Academy of Sciences.

_____. 1975. Air Quality and Stationary Source Emission Control. A Report by the Commission of Natural Resources, National Academy of Sciences, National Academy of Engineering, National Research Council. Prepared for the Committee on Public Works, U. S. Senate. Committee print, serial no. 94-4. Washington, D. C.: U. S. Government Printing Office.

_____. 1973. Proceedings of the Conference on Health Effects of Air Pollutants. Prepared for the Committee on Public Works, U. S. Senate. Committee print, serial no. 93-15. Washington, D. C.: U. S. Government Printing Office.

_____. 1969. The Behavioral and Social Sciences: Outlook and Needs. Englewood Cliffs: Prentice-Hall.

National Research Council. 1978. Committee on Nuclear and Alternative Energy Systems, Demand and Conservation Panel. "U. S. Energy Demand: Some Low Energy Futures." Science 200 (April 14): 142-52.

_____. Committee on Energy and the Environment. 1977. Implications of Environment Regulations for Energy Production and Consumption. Vol. 6 of Analytic Studies for the U. S. Environmental Protection Agency. Washington, D. C.: National Academy of Sciences.

_____. Committee on Mineral Resources and the Environment. 1975. Mineral Resources and the Environment. Washington, D. C. : National Academy of Sciences.

_____. Committee on the Biological Effects of Ionizing Radiation. 1972. The Effects on Populations of Exposure to Low Levels of Ionizing Radiation. Washington, D. C. : National Academy of Sciences.

_____. Division of Behavioral Sciences. 1971. Policy and Program Research in a University Setting. Washington, D. C. : National Academy of Sciences.

National Science Foundation. 1975. Energy Information Resources. Washington, D. C. : American Society for Information Science.

New England Regional Commission. 1976a. Energy Flows in New England: Historical and Projected. Boston: New England Regional Commission.

_____. 1976b. Energy Policy and Legislation: Collected Staff Papers. Energy program technical report 75-0. Boston: New England Regional Commission.

_____. 1976c. An Energy Strategy for New England: Objectives and Implementation. Energy program technical report 76-4. Boston: New England Regional Commission.

_____. 1976d. New England Energy Information Management Systems. Boston: New England Regional Commission.

_____. 1976e. New England Power Pool: Description, Analysis, Implications. Boston: New England Regional Commission.

_____. 1975a. Decision-making for Energy Facilities in New England: Institutional and Legal Processes. Energy program technical report 75-7. Boston: New England Regional Commission.

_____. 1975b. Petroleum Development in New England: Economic and Environmental Considerations. Boston: New England Regional Commission.

Newman, Dorothy K. , and Dawn Day. 1975. The American Energy Consumer. Cambridge: Ballinger.

Nuclear Energy Policy Study Group. 1977. Nuclear Power Issues and Choices. Cambridge: Ballinger.

Odum, Eugene. 1977. "The Emergence of Ecology as a New Integrative Discipline." Science 25 (March): 1,289-93.

Oglesbay, Floyd B. 1967. "Preventing Clothing Ignition Burns Through Health Education." Course major paper, University of North Carolina, Chapel Hill.

Olsen, Marvin E., and Christopher Cluett. 1978. Evaluation of the Seattle City Light Neighborhood Energy Conservation Program. Seattle: Battelle Human Affairs Research Centers.

Olsen, Marvin E., Martha G. Curry, Marjorie R. Greene, Barbara D. Nelber, and Donna J. Merwin. 1978. "A Social Assessment and Management Methodology Using Social Indicators and Planning Strategies." Report RAP-18. Seattle: Battelle Northwest Laboratories.

Olsen, Marvin E. and Jill Goodnight. 1977. Social Aspects of Energy Conservation. Portland: Northwest Energy Policy Project of the Pacific Northwest Regional Commission.

Olsen, Marvin E. and Donna J. Merwin. 1977. "Toward a Methodology for Conducting Social Impact Assessments Using Quality of Social Life Indicators." In Methodology of Social Impact Assessment, edited by Kurt Finsterbusch and C. P. Wolf, pp. 43-63. Stroudsburg, Penn.: Dowden, Hutchinson & Ross.

O'Toole, James. 1976. Energy and Social Change. Cambridge: Massachusetts Institute of Technology Press.

Pacific Northwest Regional Commission. 1976. Northwest Energy Policy Project. Portland: Pacific Northwest Regional Commission.

Patterson, Walter. 1976. Nuclear Power. Baltimore: Penguin Books.

Perlman, Robert and Roland L. Warren. 1975. Energy Saving by Households in Three Metropolitan Areas. Waltham, Mass.: Brandeis University, Helier Graduate School for Advanced Studies in Social Welfare.

Peskin, Joseph Schofer and Peter Stopher. 1975. The Immediate Im-

pact of Gasoline Shortages on Urban Travel Behavior. Final
Report. Washington, D. C. : U. S. Department of Transportation,
April.

Platt, John. 1969. "What We Must Do. " Science 166 (28): 1,117.

Pomazal, Richard J. and James J. Jaccard. 1976. "An Informational
Approach to Altruistic Behavior. " Journal of Personality and
Social Psychology 33 (March): 317-26.

Portola Institute. N. d. Energy Primer: Solar, Water, Wind, and
BioFuels. Fremonts, Calif. : Pricke-Parks Press.

Quarles, John. 1976. Cleaning Up America. Boston: Houghton-Mifflin.

Rosenberg, Nathan. 1976. "Thinking About Technology Policy for the
Coming Decade. " In U. S. Economic Growth from 1976 to 1986:
Prospects, Problems, and Patterns, vol. 9, p. 4. U. S. Congress, Joint Economic Committee, Technological Change. Washington, D. C. : Government Printing Office.

Rothman, Jack. 1970. "Three Models of Community Organization
Practice. " In Strategies of Community Organization: A Book
of Readings, edited by Fred M. Cox, John L. Erlich, Jack
Rothman, and John E. Tropman, pp. 20-36. Itasca, Ill. : F.
E. Peacock.

Roy, Rustum. 1979. "A Contemporary Justification for the National
R&D Budget and Process. " Paper presented at the annual meet-
ing of the American Association for the Advancement of Science,
Houston, January.

Ryan, Charles J. 1977. "The Choices in the Next Energy and Social
Revolution. " National Technical Information Service. Cambridge: MIT, PC A03/MF A01.

Satterfield, M. Harry. 1937. "The Removal of Families from Tennessee Valley Authority Reservoir Areas. " Social Forces 16
(December): 258-61.

Schelling, Thomas C. 1970. On the Ecology of Micro-motives. Working paper, Public Policy Program, Kennedy School of Government. Cambridge: Harvard University.

Schipper, Lee. 1975. Energy Conservation: Its Nature, Hidden Benefits, and Hidden Barriers. Berkeley: Energy and Environment Division, Lawrence Berkeley Laboratory; and Energy and Resources Group, University of California, June 1.

Schipper, Lee and Allen J. Lichtenberg. 1976. "Efficient Energy Use and Well Being: The Swedish Example." Science 194 (4269): 1,001-13.

Schnaiberg, Allan. 1975. "Social Synthesis of the Societal-Environmental Dialectic: The Role of Distributional Impacts." Social Science Quarterly 56 (June): 5-20.

Scholars, Leonardo. 1975. Resources and Decisions. North Scituate: Mass., Duxbury Press.

Schumacher, Ernst F. 1973. Small is Beautiful: Economics as if People Mattered. New York: Harper & Row.

Schurr, Sam H., Joel Darmstadter, Henry Petty, William Ramsey, and Milton Russell. 1979. Energy in America's Future. Baltimore: Johns Hopkins.

Schwartz, Shalom H. 1973. "Normative Explanations of Helping Behavior: A Critique, Proposal, and Empirical Text." Journal of Experimental and Social Psychology 9: 349-64.

Scott, Jerome E., Ronald W. Melicher and Donald M. Sciglimpaglia. 1974. Demand Analysis: Solar Heating and Cooling of Buildings. Washington, D.C.: National Science Foundation.

Seamans, Robert C., Jr. 1976. Testimony before the Subcommittee on Energy Research and Water Resources of the U.S. Senate Committee on Interior and Insular Affairs, Washington, D.C., October 1.

Sears, David O., Thomas Tyler, Jack Citrin, and Donald R. Kinder. 1978. "Political System Support and Public Response to the Energy Crisis." American Journal of Political Science 22 (February): 56-82.

Seidel, Marquis R., Steven E. Plotkin, and Robert O. Reck. 1973. Energy Conservation Strategies. Washington, D.C.: U.S. Environmental Protection Agency, Office of Research and Monitoring, Implementation Research Division, July.

Sidbury, Gary A. and Susan E. Clarke. 1978. "Carolina Commen-
   tary." University of North Carolina Newsletter 63 (October): 33.

Stearns, Mary D. 1975. The Social Impacts of the Energy Shortage:
   Behavioral and Attitude Shifts. Final Report #DOT-TSC-OST-
   75-36. Prepared for the U. S. Department of Transportation,
   Washington, D. C., September.

Steckler, Allan, Harry T. Phillips, and James J. Burdine. 1977.
   "The Concept of an Ideal HSA Board." American Journal of
   Health Planning 1 (July): 19-24.

Stretton, Hugh. 1976. Capitalism, Socialism and the Environment.
   New York: Cambridge University Press.

Stucker, J. P. and T. F. Kirkwood. 1977. The Economic Impact of
   Automobile Travel Cost Increases on Households. Rand Re-
   port R-1842. Washington, D. C.: National Science Foundation/
   Federal Energy Administration, July.

Sullivan, Walter, 1977. "Climate Peril May Force Limits on Coal
   and Oil, Carter Aide Says." New York Times, June 3, 1977,
   p. D13.

Tavoulareas, William P. and Carl Kaysen. 1977. A Debate on a Time
   to Choose. Cambridge: Ballinger.

Tietenberg, Thomas H. 1976. Energy Planning and Policy: The Political Economy of Project Independence. Lexington, Mass.:
   Lexington Books.

Tocqueville, Alexis de. N. d. Democracy in America. Volume 1.
   Translated by Henry Reeve. New York: Arlington House.

Tschinkel, Victoria J. 1979. "Report of the Social Science Subcommittee of the OSTP/DOE Working Group." Paper presented at
   the annual meeting of the American Association for the Advancement of Science, Houston, January.

Union of Concerned Scientists. 1977. The Risk of Nuclear Power Reactors. Cambridge: Union of Concerned Scientists.

U. S., Congress. House. Committee on Science and Technology. 1978a.
   1979 Department of Energy Authorization. Hearings before the
   House Committee on Science and Technology, 95th Cong., 2d.
   sess.

_____. Office of Science and Technology Policy. 1978b. Report of Working Group on Basic Research in the Department of Energy. Washington, D. C.: Government Printing Office, June.

_____. Office of Technology Assessment. 1975. An Analysis of the ERDA Plan and Program. Washington, D. C.: Government Printing Office, October.

_____. Senate. Special Committee on Aging. 1977. "The Impact of Rising Energy Costs on Older Americans." Pt. 4. Washington, D. C.: Government Printing Office, April 5.

_____. 1969. National Environmental Policy Act.

U. S., Department of Health, Education, and Welfare. 1970a. Air Quality Criteria for Carbon Monoxide. National Air Pollution Control Administration publ. no. AP-62. Washington, D. C.: Government Printing Office.

_____. 1970b. Air Quality Criteria for Hydrocarbons. National Air Pollution Control Administration publ. no. AP-64. Washington, D. C.: Government Printing Office.

_____. 1970c. Air Quality Criteria for Photochemical Oxidants. National Air Pollution Control Administration publ. no. AP-63. Washington, D. C.: Government Printing Office.

_____. 1969a. Air Quality Criteria for Particulate Matter. National Air Pollution Control Administration publ. no. AP-49. Washington, D. C.: Government Printing Office.

_____. 1969b. Air Quality Criteria for Sulfur Oxides. National Air Pollution Control publ. no. AP-50. Washington, D. C.: Government Printing Office.

_____. 1969c. Toward a Social Report. Washington, D. C.: Government Printing Office.

_____. 1969d. Vital Statistics of the United States: 1967. Washington, D. C.: Government Printing Office.

U.S. Environmental Protection Agency. 1976. Radiological Quality of the Environment. Office of Radiation Programs, EPA 520/1-76-010. Springfield, Virginia: National Technical Information Service.

_____. 1974. Briefing Notes—A Status Report on Sulfur Oxides. Research Triangle Park, North Carolina: National Environmental Research Center.

U. S. , Environmental Protection Agency. 1973. Alternate Futures and Environmental Quality. Office of Research and Development, Washington Environmental Research Center. Washington, D. C. : Superintendent of Documents.

_____. 1971. Air Quality Criteria for Nitrogen Oxides. Air Pollution Control Office publ. no. AP-84. Washington, D. C. : Government Printing Office.

U. S. , Federal Energy Administration. 1976. National Energy Outlook. Washington, D. C. : Federal Energy Administration.

U. S. , Nuclear Regulatory Commission. 1975. Reactor Safety Study: An Assessment of Accident Risks in U. S. Commercial Nuclear Power Plants. WASH 1400, NUREG-75/014. Washington, D. C. : Government Printing Office.

United States vs. Reserve Mining Company. 1976. 7 ELR 20051, 8th Civ. , October 28.

Vanston, J. H. 1977. "Alternate Scenario Planning. " (Technology forecast.) Social Change 10 (2): 159-80.

Waddington, Conrad H. 1977. Tools for Thought. New York: Basis Books.

Wald, Neal. 1975. "Radiation Injury. " In Textbook of Medicine, edited by P. B. Beeson and W. McDormott, pp. 67-72. Philadelphia: Saunders.

Warkov, Seymour, ed. 1978. Energy Policy in the United States. New York: Praeger.

Warren, Donald I. and David L. Clifford. 1975. Local Neighborhood Social Structure and Response to the Energy Crisis of 1973-74. Ann Arbor: University of Michigan, Institute of Labor and Industrial Relations.

Weinberg, Alvin M. 1972. "Social Institutions and Nuclear Energy. " Science (July 7): 33.

____. 1967. "Social Problems and National Socio-Technical Institutes." In Applied Science and Technological Progress, National Academy of Sciences for the U. S. Congress, House Committee on Science and Astronautics, pp. 415-34. Washington, D. C. : Government Printing Office, June.

____. 1966. "Can Technology Replace Social Engineering?" University of Chicago Magazine 59 (October): 6-10.

Weiss, Carol H. 1977. "Research for Policy's Sake: The Enlightenment Function of Social Research." Policy Analysis 3 (Fall): 531-45.

Weizenbaum, Joseph. 1976. Computer Power and Human Reason. San Francisco: W. H. Freeman.

Wilbanks, Thomas J. Forthcoming. "Social Science Research to Support Energy Policymaking." Oak Ridge, Tenn. : Oak Ridge National Laboratory.

____. 1979. "Effective Social Science Research for Energy Policy." Paper presented at the annual meeting of the American Association for the Advancement of Science, Houston, January.

____. 1977. "The Role of Social Science Research in Meeting Energy Needs." Oak Ridge, Tenn. : Oak Ridge National Laboratory, October.

Wilensky, Harold L. 1967. Organizational Intelligence. New York: Basis Books.

Williams, John S. , Jr. , William Kruvant, and Dorothy Newman. 1976. Metropolitan Impacts of Alternative Energy Futures. Washington, D. C. : Metro-Study Corporation.

Winner, Langdon. 1977a. Autonomous Technology. Cambridge: Massachusetts Institute of Technology Press.

____. 1977b. "On Criticizing Technology." In Technology and Man's Future, edited by Albert H. Teich, pp. 354-375. New York: St. Martin's Press.

____. 1975. "Complexity and the Limits of Human Understanding." In Organized Social Complexity, edited by Todd LaPorte, pp. 40-76. Princeton: Princeton University Press.

Wolf, Charles P. 1977. "Social Impact Assessment: The State of the Art Updated." Paper presented at the Symposium for Social Impact Assessment Group, St. Louis, January 17-18.

Yale University. 1976. "Mapping Project on Energy and Social Sciences." Proposal to the U.S. Energy Research and Development Administration. New Haven: Yale University, June 1.

INDEX

ABOUT THE EDITOR AND CONTRIBUTORS

JOEL DARMSTADTER is a senior fellow at the Center for Energy Policy Research at Resources for the Future in Washington, D. C. Previously, he was an economist with the National Planning Association. Darmstadter is the author or coauthor of a number of books on energy, including How Industrial Societies Use Energy (1977) and Energy in America's Future (1979). He is a frequent consultant to government agencies.

KAREN M. GENTEMANN is a research associate with the Institute for Research in Social Science at the University of North Carolina at Chapel Hill. Before coming to UNC, she was special assistant to the provost at the University of Pittsburgh. Prior to that she was a researcher with an experimental educational program, the Experiment in Higher Education, at Southern Illinois University. A former community organizer, Dr. Gentemann remains interested in applied aspects of the social sciences. Her primary research interests are in the areas of energy attitude and behavior change, domestic violence, and the cultural context of education.

ROGER P. HANSEN is a lawyer and energy development consultant with D'Appolonia Consulting Engineers, Inc. of Denver, Colorado. Previously, he directed a national-level "Coal Technology Assessment" for the U. S. Environmental Protection Agency at Research Triangle Park, North Carolina. He is the founder and was the executive director of the Rocky Mountain Center on Environment, an environmental service center for eight Rocky Mountain states, headquartered in Denver. Hansen is an adjunct professor of environmental law at the University of Denver College of Law.

JOHN W. HATCH is an associate professor of health education at the University of North Carolina at Chapel Hill. He is the project director of several health-related projects, including an Agency for International Development health development training project in the Cameroon, West Africa, and a collective self-help project in North Carolina black churches. Hatch has been an environmental management consultant to rural health centers in the southern U. S. and was formerly the director of Community Health Action at the Tufts Delta Health Center in Mississippi. His work has been published extensively, and he consults widely on rural health care and consumer involvement.

EDWARD L. HELMINSKI is the deputy director of the White House Management Task Force on Energy Shortages. He was formerly the staff director of the Committee on National Resources and Environmental Management and the director of the Energy and Natural Resources Program at the National Governor's Association in Washington, D.C. Helminski has also served as director of the Office of Science and Technology, National Conference on State Legislatures (NCSL), and as committee staff director to the NCSL Committee on Science and Technology. He has written for numerous publications on states' roles in energy management and development and on state science and technology capacity-building efforts. He is a former assistant professor of physics at Tuskeegee Institute.

ELIZABETH MARTIN is on the staff of the National Academy of Sciences, working with a panel of the Committee on National Statistics on the problems of measuring subjective phenomena in surveys. She was formerly director of the Social Science Data Library, associate director of the Louis Harris Data Center of the Institute for Research in Social Science, and assistant professor of sociology at the University of North Carolina. Her principal research interests concern altruism and its social effects, public opinion, and survey methods.

MARVIN E. OLSEN is a professor of sociology at Washington State University. He is also a visiting scientist at the Social Change Study Center of the Battelle Human Affairs Research Centers in Seattle. He has directed numerous research projects dealing with the social factors involved in energy conservation and development programs. Olsen has written extensively on energy conservation, including Social Aspects of Energy Conservation (with Jill Goodnight, 1977) and "Policies for Promoting Consumer Energy Conservation: An American-European Perspective" (with Bernward Joerges, unpublished paper available from International Institute for Environment and Society, Berlin, West Germany).

DAVID W. ORR is codirector of the Meadow Creek Project, Inc., Fox, Arkansas. He has authored articles on energy and environmental policy for the Journal of Politics, the International Studies Quarterly, Polity, Dissent, Human Ecology, The Western Political Quarterly, and other journals. Orr is also a coeditor of and contributor to the Global Predicament: Ecological Perspectives on World Order (Chapel Hill: University of North Carolina Press, 1979).

CARL M. SHY is a professor in the Department of Epidemiology at the University of North Carolina at Chapel Hill. He previously directed the Institute for Environmental Studies at that university. He chairs the Health Effects Resource Group of the Committee on Nuclear and Alternative Energy Systems at the National Academy of Sciences and is a consultant to numerous national and international agencies concerned with health and environment.

ANNE D. STUBBS is program manager of the Environmental Resources and Development unit of the Council of State Governments (CSG), Lexington, Kentucky. She directs a staff that is undertaking analysis of state environmental, natural resources, and energy policies and programs. She was formerly policy assistant for Environmental Affairs, Office of the Governor, Rhode Island, where she provided policy liaison with state agencies, regional organizations, and public interest groups. Stubbs has also served the CSG as special assistant for Housing and Community Development, where she was principal researcher and author of several publications dealing with community development, energy conservation, and growth management.

TONY L. WHITEHEAD is an assistant professor of social anthropology at the University of North Carolina at Chapel Hill. He has had local, regional, and international experience with community organization studies, including projects in poor communities in the West Indies, the Middle East, and the urban and rural U. S. Whitehead is currently directing a study to investigate the relationship between southern food habits and elevated blood pressure. He has been published in the areas of family planning, low income survival strategies, and the use of cultural theories in applied contexts.

THOMAS J. WILBANKS is a senior planner with the Energy Division of Oak Ridge National Laboratory, where, among other duties, he serves as a catalyst for discussions on the role of social science research in meeting energy needs. A geographer by training, he was executive director of the Urban Transportation Institute at Syracuse

University, research director of the Syracuse-Yugoslav Project on Environmental Policy and Planning, chair of the Department of Geography at the University of Oklahoma, and research fellow in the Science and Public Policy Program at the University of Oklahoma. Wilbanks has authored or coauthored numerous professional publications, most of which are related to energy policy, locational decision making, regional development, or environmental management. He has served as a staff contributor to several Office of Technology Assessment documents and as a consultant to various government agencies. In 1978-79, he headed an interdisciplinary team providing impact assessments as part of the formulation of National Energy Plan II.